PRAISE FOR **GRAY**

"I can resist everything except a really clever contemporary take on The Picture of Dorian Gray.*"*

— David Baddiel

Best-Selling British Comedian and Author of
The Parent Agency and *The Secret Purpose*

"A contemporary retelling that holds nothing back. GRAY is savagely funny, horrifically thrilling and brutally human. A classic story that clearly needs to be told now, putting the present moment in its crosshairs."

-Jordan Blum

Creator & Showrunner, Marvel's *M.O.D.O.K.*

"Gray claims to be 'inspired by Oscar Wilde's The Picture of Dorian Gray' *— but don't be fooled, David and Koumaki have created something wholly original, daring, and entertaining here. It's GRAY — both the book and its titular hero — that will leave readers inspired."*

-Vivek J. Tiwary

Author of Eisner Award-Winning *The Fifth Beatle*

GRAY

INSPIRED BY OSCAR WILDE'S *THE PICTURE OF DORIAN GRAY*

Arvind Ethan David

CREATED/WRITTEN BY

Arvind Ethan David

PENCILS BY

Eugenia Koumaki

INKS BY

Diana Greenhalgh

COLORS BY

Joana Lafuente

DESIGN/LETTERS BY

Robbie Robbins

EDITED BY

Brittany Chapman, Lisa Deng & Diana Greenhalgh

COVER BY

Aron Weisenfeld

"By the Light of the Silvery Moon"
Written by Gus Edwards

*CONTENT WARNING: THIS BOOK CONTAINS MATERIAL
RELATED TO SEXUAL VIOLENCE THAT MAY BE
DISTURBING OR UPSETTING FOR SOME READERS.*

ISBN: 978-1-951038-32-8 • 25 24 23 22 21   1 2 3 4 5

www.CloverPress.us   twitter: @Clover_Press   facebook: /CloverPressUS   instagram: @Clover_Press

Clover Press: Matt Ruzicka, President/CFO • Robbie Robbins, Vice President/Art Director • Hank Kanalz, Publisher • Ted Adams, Factotum
Tim Bell, Shipping • Christian Ruzicka, Shipping Assistant
Clover Press Founders: Ted Adams, Elaine LaRosa, Nate Murray, Robbie Robbins

Dedications

To Maya Khemlani David, Sheila Devi David, Janine
N'jie David & Odetta Elsie N'jie David—the most
dangerous women in my life. And to Oscar.
—*Arvind*

To Reg & Joyce Greenhalgh, who filled
my childhood with creativity and adventure.
It's always tea time somewhere.
—*Diana*

To all my loved ones, thank you for the
support through some crazy times.
To Brian, Mika, and to my family.
—*Eugenia*

Chapter 1

"I was a woman who stood in symbolic relations to the art and culture of my age. I had realized this for myself at the very dawn of my womanhood, and had forced my age to realise it afterwards."

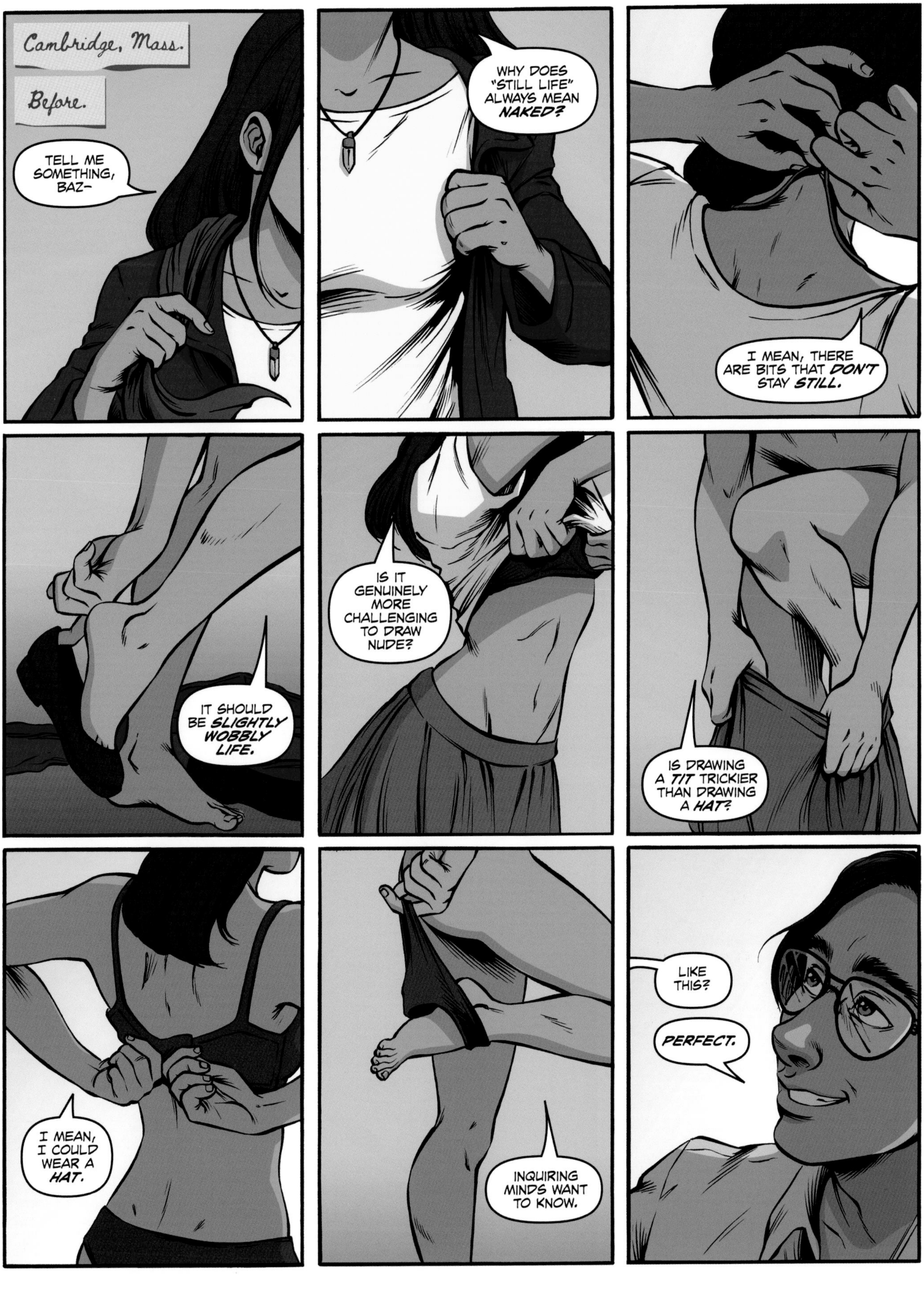

Cambridge, Mass.
Before.
TELL ME SOMETHING, BAZ-
WHY DOES "STILL LIFE" ALWAYS MEAN *NAKED?*
I MEAN, THERE ARE BITS THAT *DON'T* STAY *STILL.*
IT SHOULD BE *SLIGHTLY WOBBLY LIFE.*
IS IT GENUINELY MORE CHALLENGING TO DRAW NUDE?
IS DRAWING A *TIT* TRICKIER THAN DRAWING A *HAT?*
I MEAN, I COULD WEAR A *HAT.*
INQUIRING MINDS WANT TO KNOW.
LIKE THIS?
PERFECT.

I HEAR *PLAYBOY* IS DOING A "WOMEN OF THE IVY LEAGUE". OFFERING GOOD MONEY. I WAS GOING TO—

PRURIENT NONSENSE.

AND THIS IS DIFFERENT... BECAUSE?

IT'S DIFFERENT FOR *EVERY* REASON.

FIRSTLY, THIS ISN'T *PHOTOGRAPHY*. NO *POINT AND CLICK*, HERE. WHAT I AM DOING TAKES SKILL, TRAINING, DEXTERITY AND MOST OF ALL, *IMAGINATION*—I'M NOT *COPYING* YOU, I'M *CREATING* SOMETHING NEW.

ARE YOU MAKING A *MORAL* DISTINCTION OR AN *ARTISTIC* ONE?

THERE ARE NO MORAL DISTINCTIONS WHEN IT COMES TO ART.

HAH!

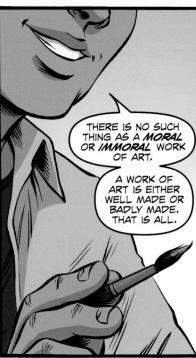

THERE IS NO SUCH THING AS A *MORAL* OR *IMMORAL* WORK OF ART.

A WORK OF ART IS EITHER WELL MADE OR BADLY MADE. THAT IS ALL.

THAT'S *GOOD*.

YOU THINK OF THAT YOURSELF?

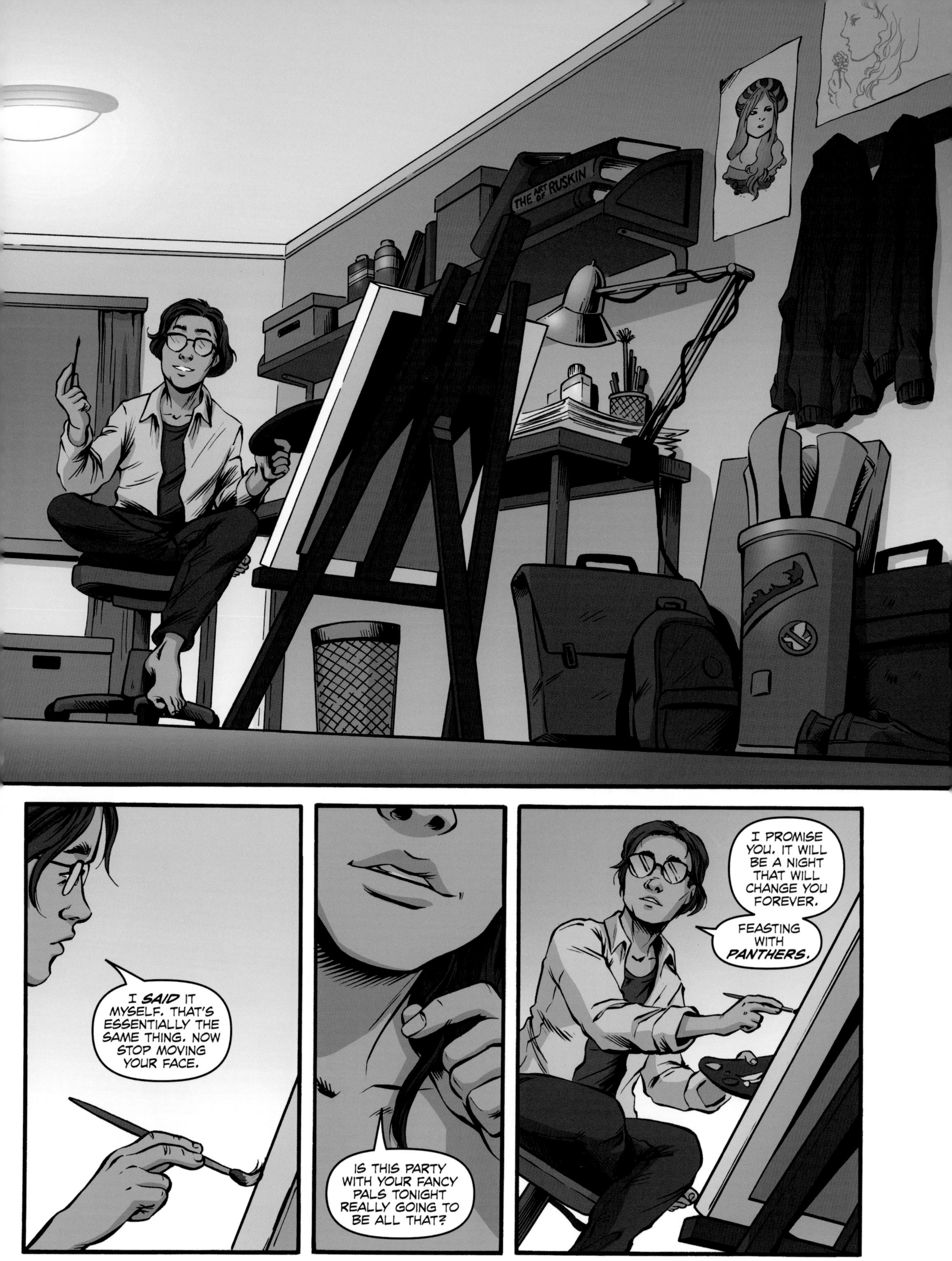
THE ART OF RUSKIN
I SAID IT MYSELF. THAT'S ESSENTIALLY THE SAME THING. NOW STOP MOVING YOUR FACE.
IS THIS PARTY WITH YOUR FANCY PALS TONIGHT REALLY GOING TO BE ALL THAT?
I PROMISE YOU. IT WILL BE A NIGHT THAT WILL CHANGE YOU FOREVER.
FEASTING WITH PANTHERS.

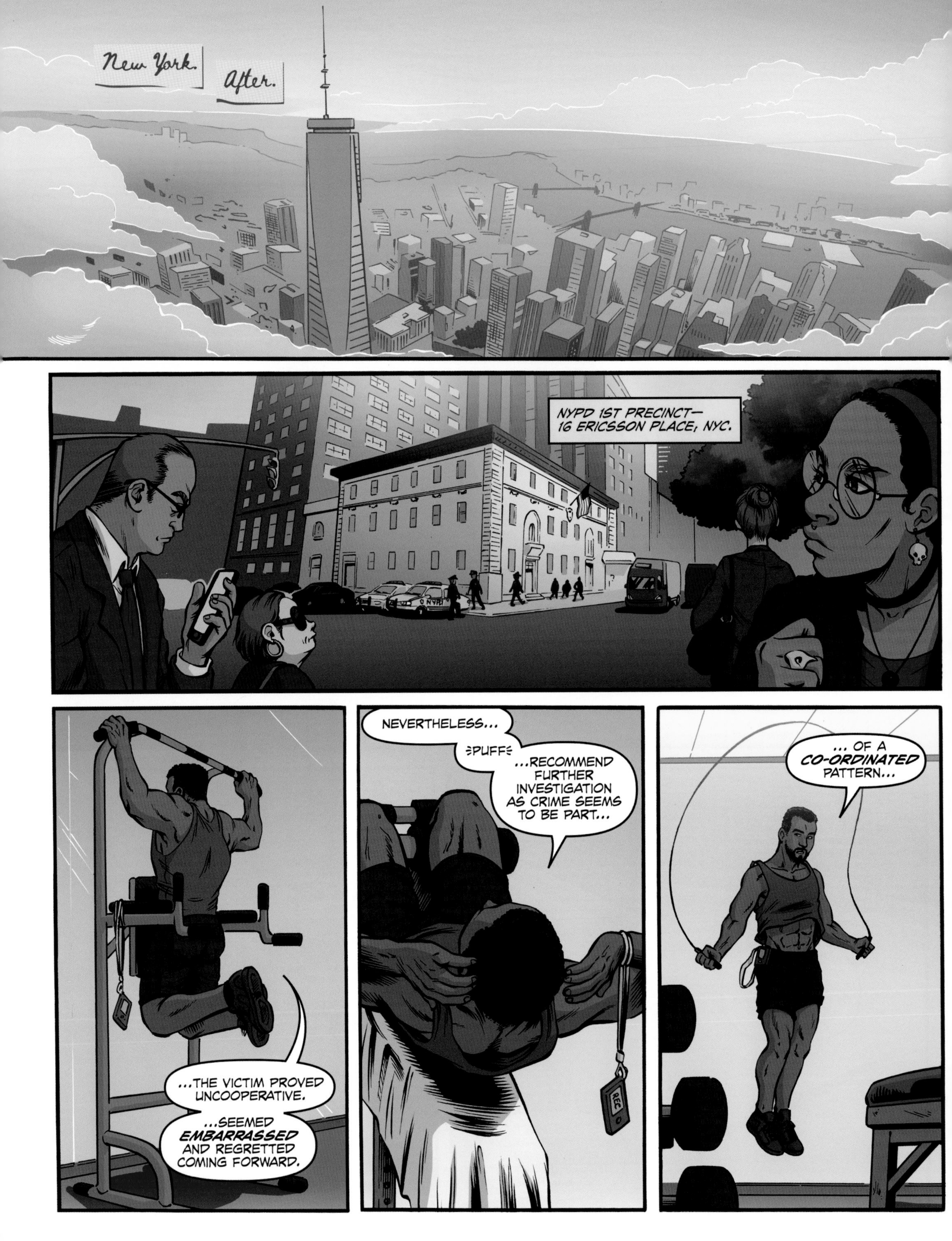

New York.
After.
NYPD 1ST PRECINCT—
16 ERICSSON PLACE; NYC.
...THE VICTIM PROVED UNCOOPERATIVE.
...SEEMED EMBARRASSED AND REGRETTED COMING FORWARD.
NEVERTHELESS...
PUFF
...RECOMMEND FURTHER INVESTIGATION AS CRIME SEEMS TO BE PART...
... OF A CO-ORDINATED PATTERN...

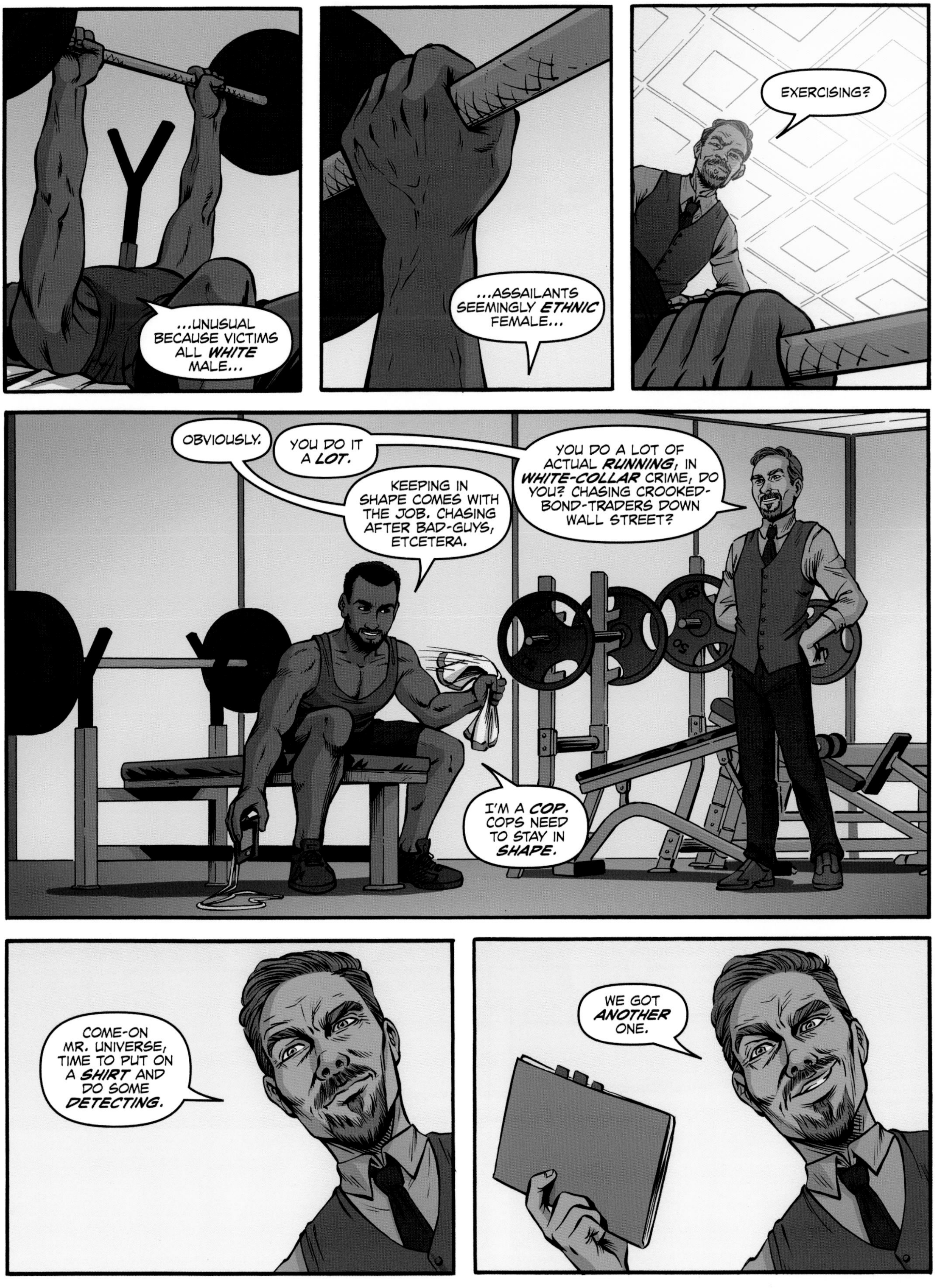
...UNUSUAL BECAUSE VICTIMS ALL WHITE MALE...
...ASSAILANTS SEEMINGLY ETHNIC FEMALE...
EXERCISING?
OBVIOUSLY.
YOU DO IT A LOT.
KEEPING IN SHAPE COMES WITH THE JOB. CHASING AFTER BAD-GUYS, ETCETERA.
YOU DO A LOT OF ACTUAL RUNNING, IN WHITE-COLLAR CRIME, DO YOU? CHASING CROOKED-BOND-TRADERS DOWN WALL STREET?
I'M A COP. COPS NEED TO STAY IN SHAPE.
COME-ON MR. UNIVERSE, TIME TO PUT ON A SHIRT AND DO SOME DETECTING.
WE GOT ANOTHER ONE.

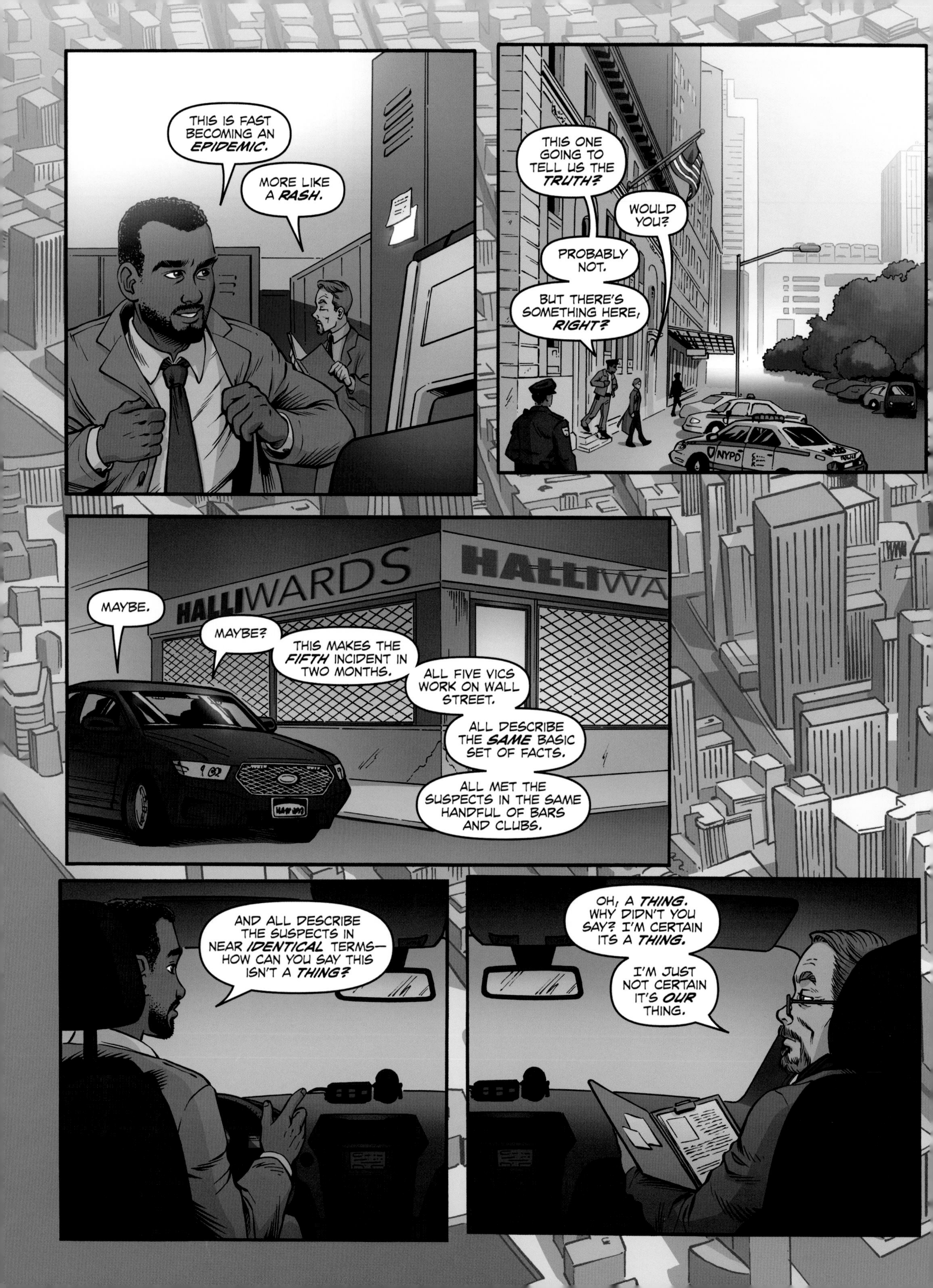
THIS IS FAST BECOMING AN *EPIDEMIC*.
MORE LIKE A *RASH*.
THIS ONE GOING TO TELL US THE *TRUTH?*
WOULD YOU?
PROBABLY NOT.
BUT THERE'S SOMETHING HERE, *RIGHT?*
NYPD
HALLIWARDS
HALLIWA
MAYBE.
MAYBE?
THIS MAKES THE *FIFTH* INCIDENT IN TWO MONTHS.
ALL FIVE VICS WORK ON WALL STREET.
ALL DESCRIBE THE *SAME* BASIC SET OF FACTS.
ALL MET THE SUSPECTS IN THE SAME HANDFUL OF BARS AND CLUBS.
AND ALL DESCRIBE THE SUSPECTS IN NEAR *IDENTICAL* TERMS— HOW CAN YOU SAY THIS ISN'T A *THING?*
OH, A *THING*. WHY DIDN'T YOU SAY? I'M CERTAIN ITS A *THING*.
I'M JUST NOT CERTAIN IT'S *OUR* THING.

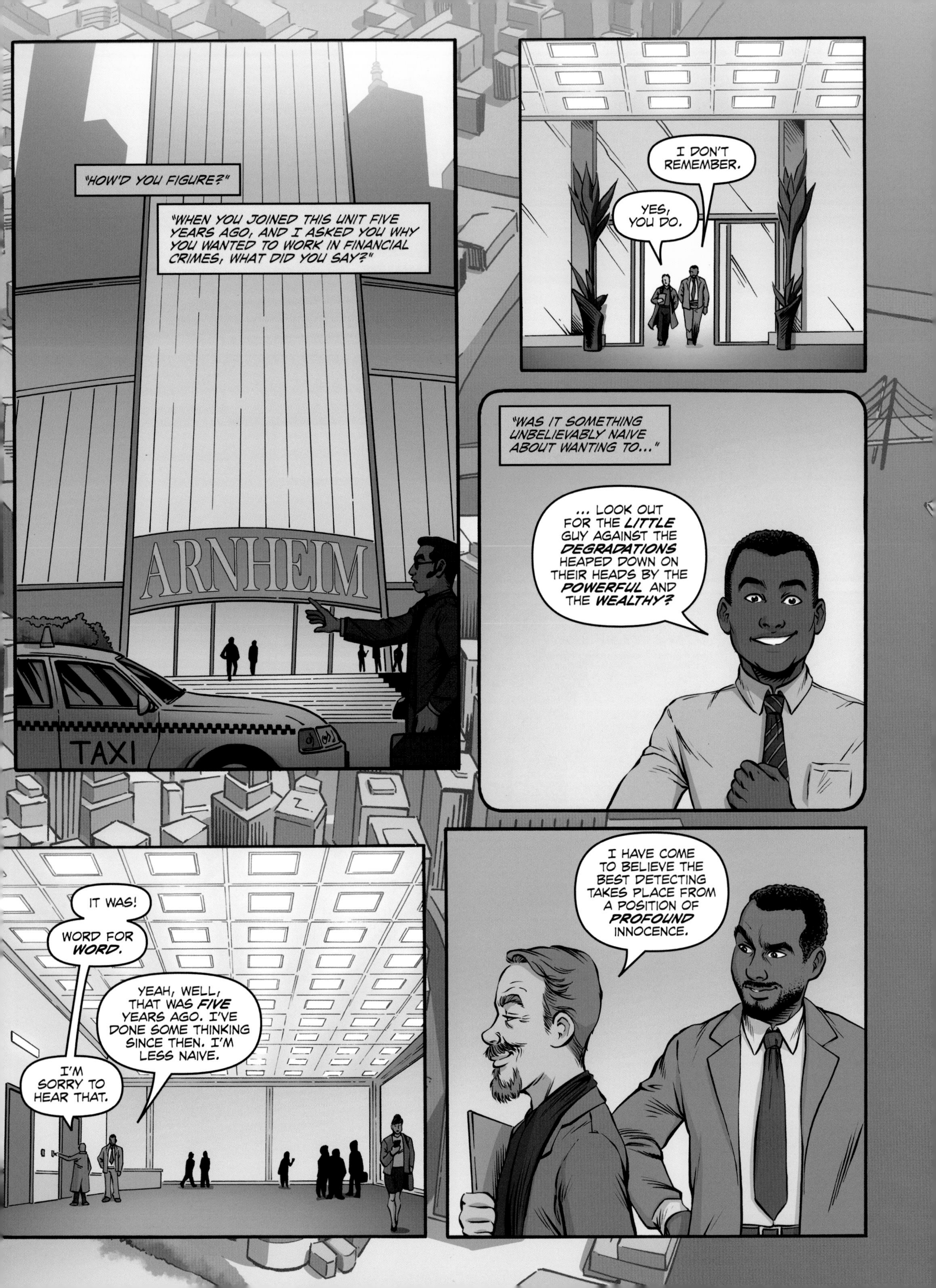
"HOW'D YOU FIGURE?"
"WHEN YOU JOINED THIS UNIT FIVE YEARS AGO, AND I ASKED YOU WHY YOU WANTED TO WORK IN FINANCIAL CRIMES, WHAT DID YOU SAY?"
ARNHEIM
TAXI
I DON'T REMEMBER.
YES, YOU DO.
"WAS IT SOMETHING UNBELIEVABLY NAIVE ABOUT WANTING TO..."
... LOOK OUT FOR THE *LITTLE* GUY AGAINST THE ***DEGRADATIONS*** HEAPED DOWN ON THEIR HEADS BY THE ***POWERFUL*** AND THE ***WEALTHY?***
IT WAS!
WORD FOR ***WORD.***
YEAH, WELL, THAT WAS *FIVE* YEARS AGO. I'VE DONE SOME THINKING SINCE THEN. I'M LESS NAIVE.
I'M SORRY TO HEAR THAT.
I HAVE COME TO BELIEVE THE BEST DETECTING TAKES PLACE FROM A POSITION OF ***PROFOUND*** INNOCENCE.

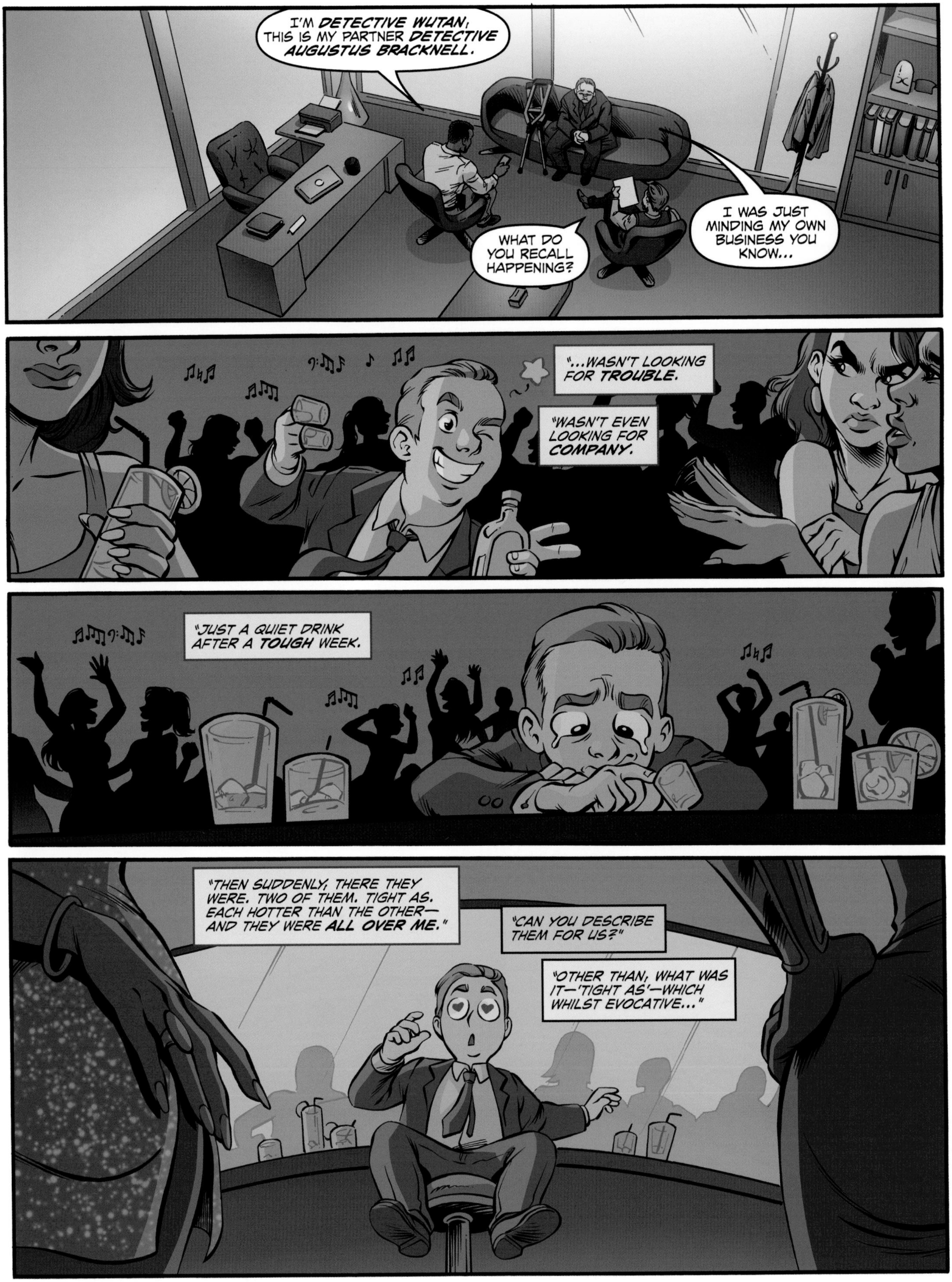

I'M DETECTIVE WUTAN; THIS IS MY PARTNER DETECTIVE AUGUSTUS BRACKNELL.
WHAT DO YOU RECALL HAPPENING?
I WAS JUST MINDING MY OWN BUSINESS YOU KNOW...
"...WASN'T LOOKING FOR TROUBLE.
"WASN'T EVEN LOOKING FOR COMPANY.
"JUST A QUIET DRINK AFTER A TOUGH WEEK.
"THEN SUDDENLY, THERE THEY WERE. TWO OF THEM. TIGHT AS. EACH HOTTER THAN THE OTHER—AND THEY WERE ALL OVER ME."
"CAN YOU DESCRIBE THEM FOR US?"
"OTHER THAN, WHAT WAS IT—'TIGHT AS'—WHICH WHILST EVOCATIVE..."

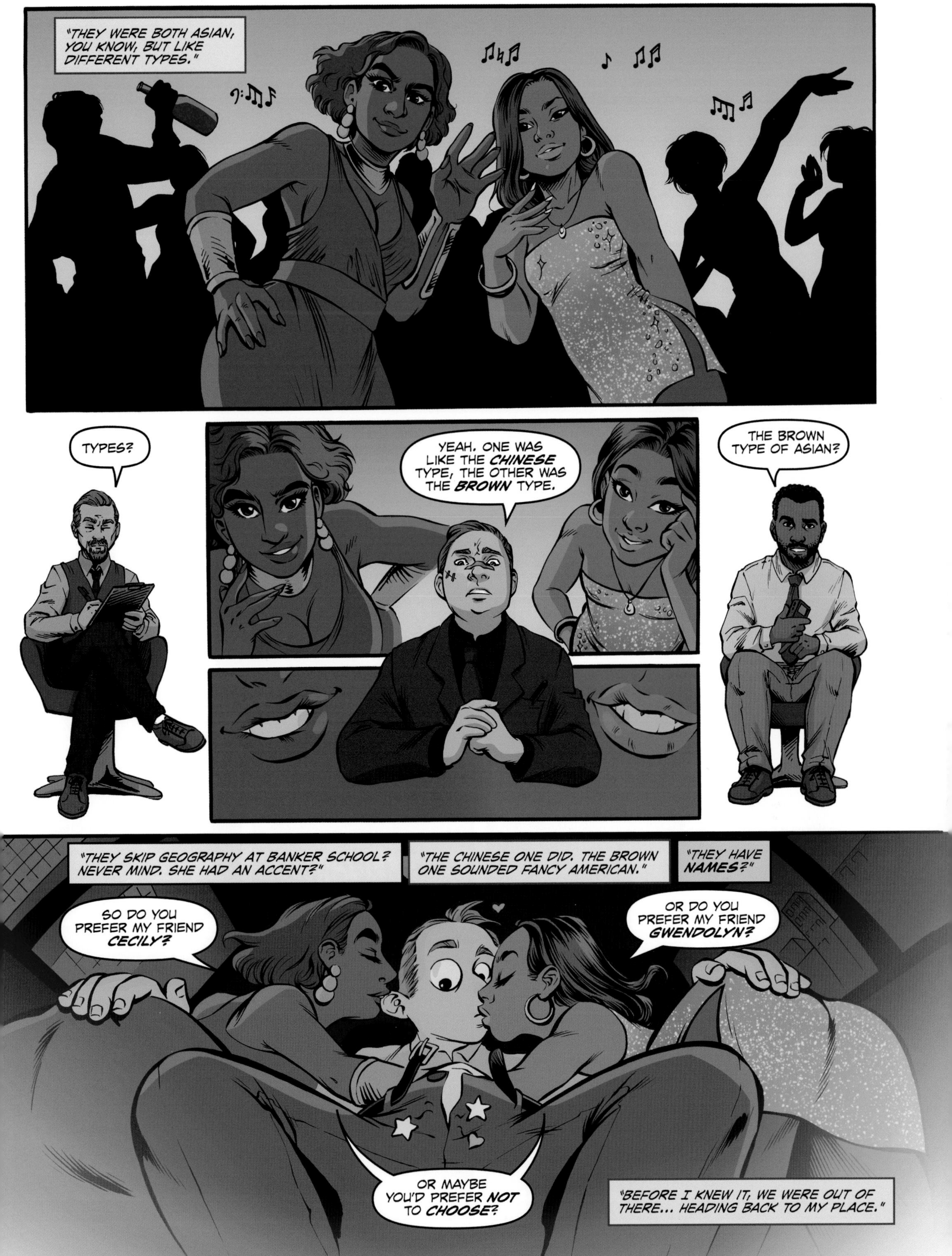
"THEY WERE BOTH ASIAN, YOU KNOW, BUT LIKE DIFFERENT TYPES."
TYPES?
YEAH. ONE WAS LIKE THE CHINESE TYPE, THE OTHER WAS THE BROWN TYPE.
THE BROWN TYPE OF ASIAN?
"THEY SKIP GEOGRAPHY AT BANKER SCHOOL? NEVER MIND. SHE HAD AN ACCENT?"
"THE CHINESE ONE DID. THE BROWN ONE SOUNDED FANCY AMERICAN."
"THEY HAVE NAMES?"
SO DO YOU PREFER MY FRIEND CECILY?
OR DO YOU PREFER MY FRIEND GWENDOLYN?
OR MAYBE YOU'D PREFER NOT TO CHOOSE?
"BEFORE I KNEW IT, WE WERE OUT OF THERE... HEADING BACK TO MY PLACE."

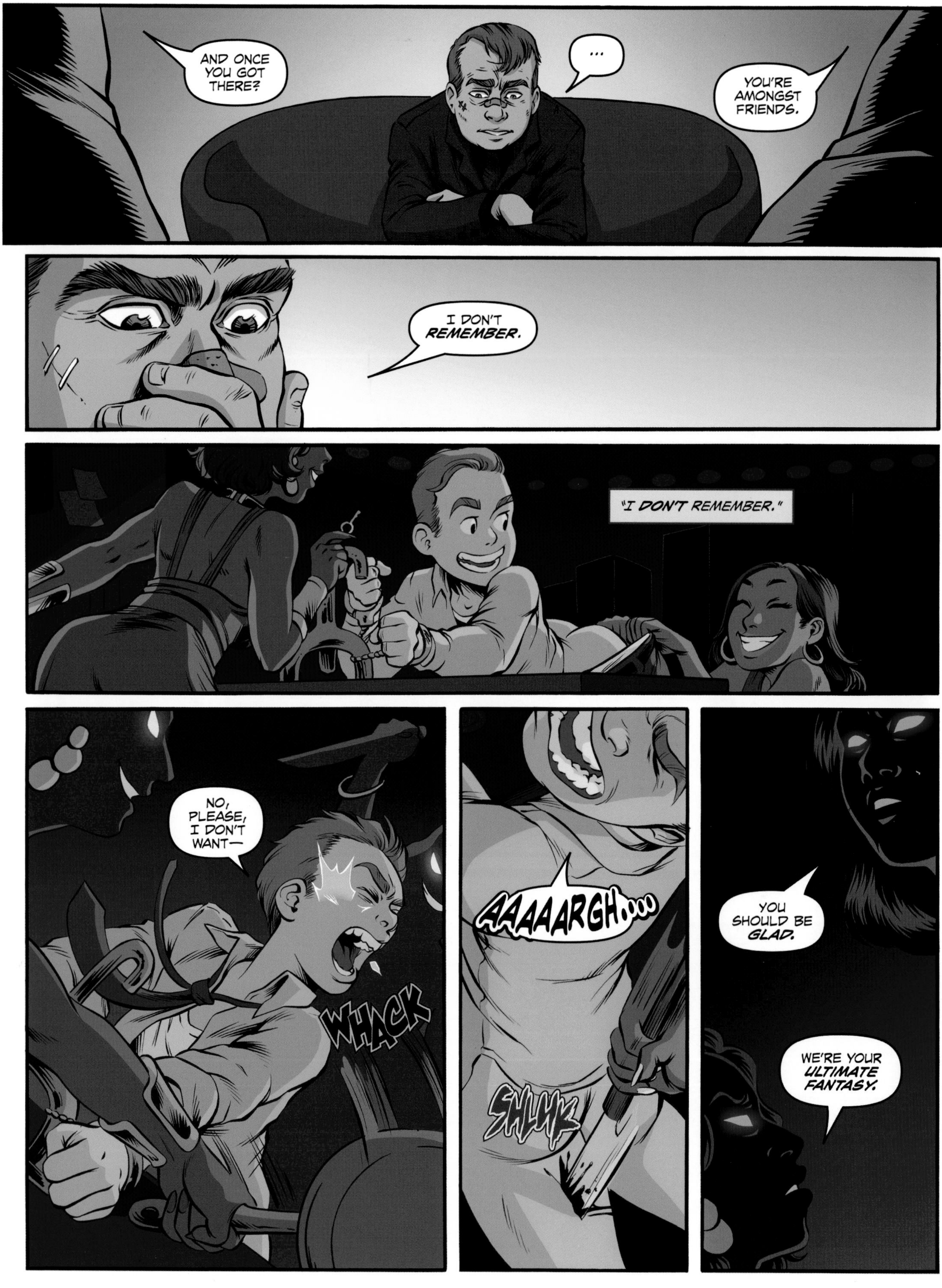
AND ONCE YOU GOT THERE?
...
YOU'RE AMONGST FRIENDS.
I DON'T REMEMBER.
"I DON'T REMEMBER."
NO, PLEASE, I DON'T WANT—
WHACK
AAAAARGH....
SHLUK
YOU SHOULD BE GLAD.
WE'RE YOUR ULTIMATE FANTASY.

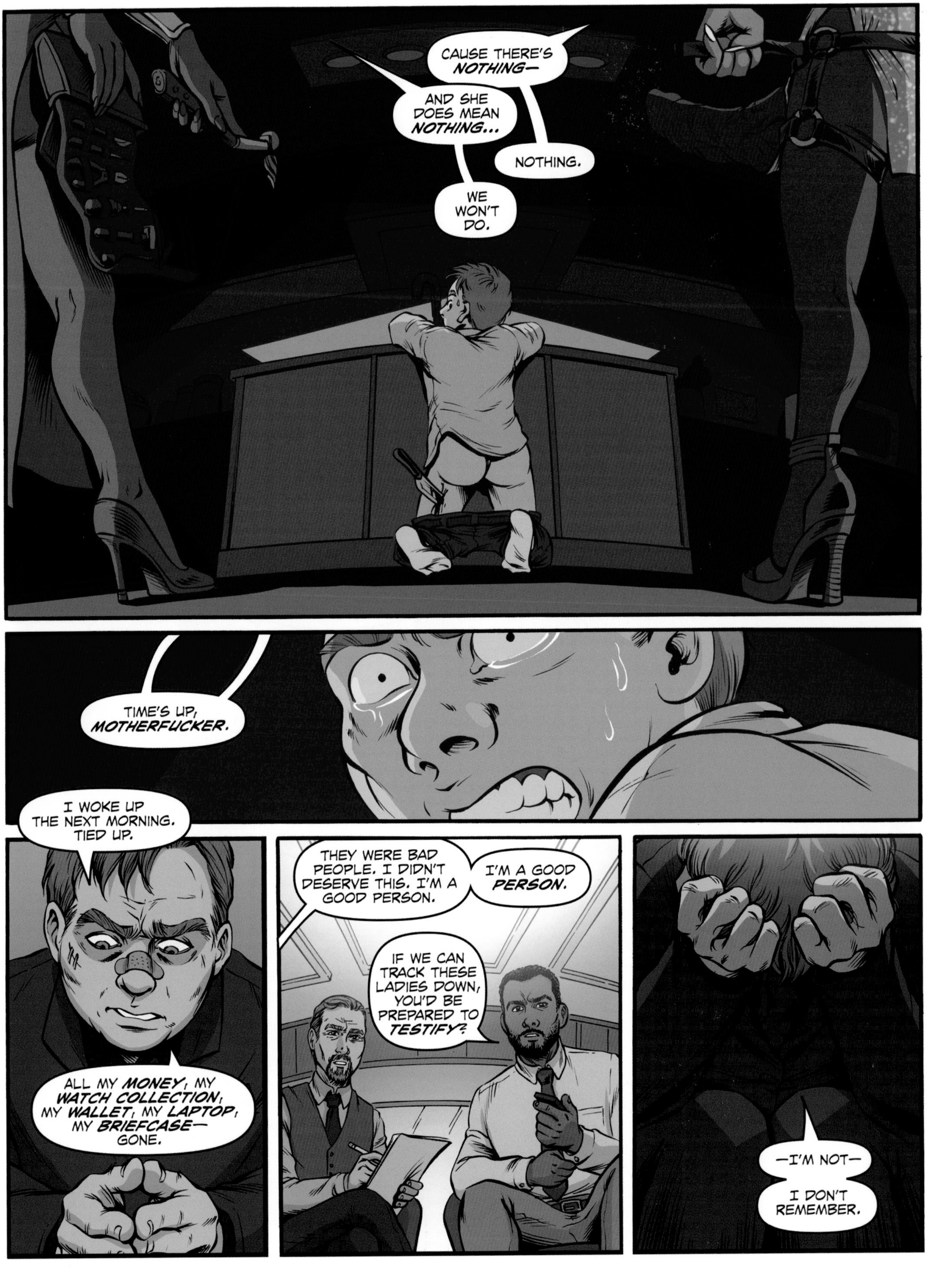
CAUSE THERE'S NOTHING—
AND SHE DOES MEAN NOTHING...
NOTHING.
WE WON'T DO.
TIME'S UP, MOTHERFUCKER.
I WOKE UP THE NEXT MORNING. TIED UP.
ALL MY MONEY, MY WATCH COLLECTION, MY WALLET, MY LAPTOP, MY BRIEFCASE— GONE.
THEY WERE BAD PEOPLE. I DIDN'T DESERVE THIS. I'M A GOOD PERSON.
I'M A GOOD PERSON.
IF WE CAN TRACK THESE LADIES DOWN, YOU'D BE PREPARED TO TESTIFY?
—I'M NOT—
I DON'T REMEMBER.

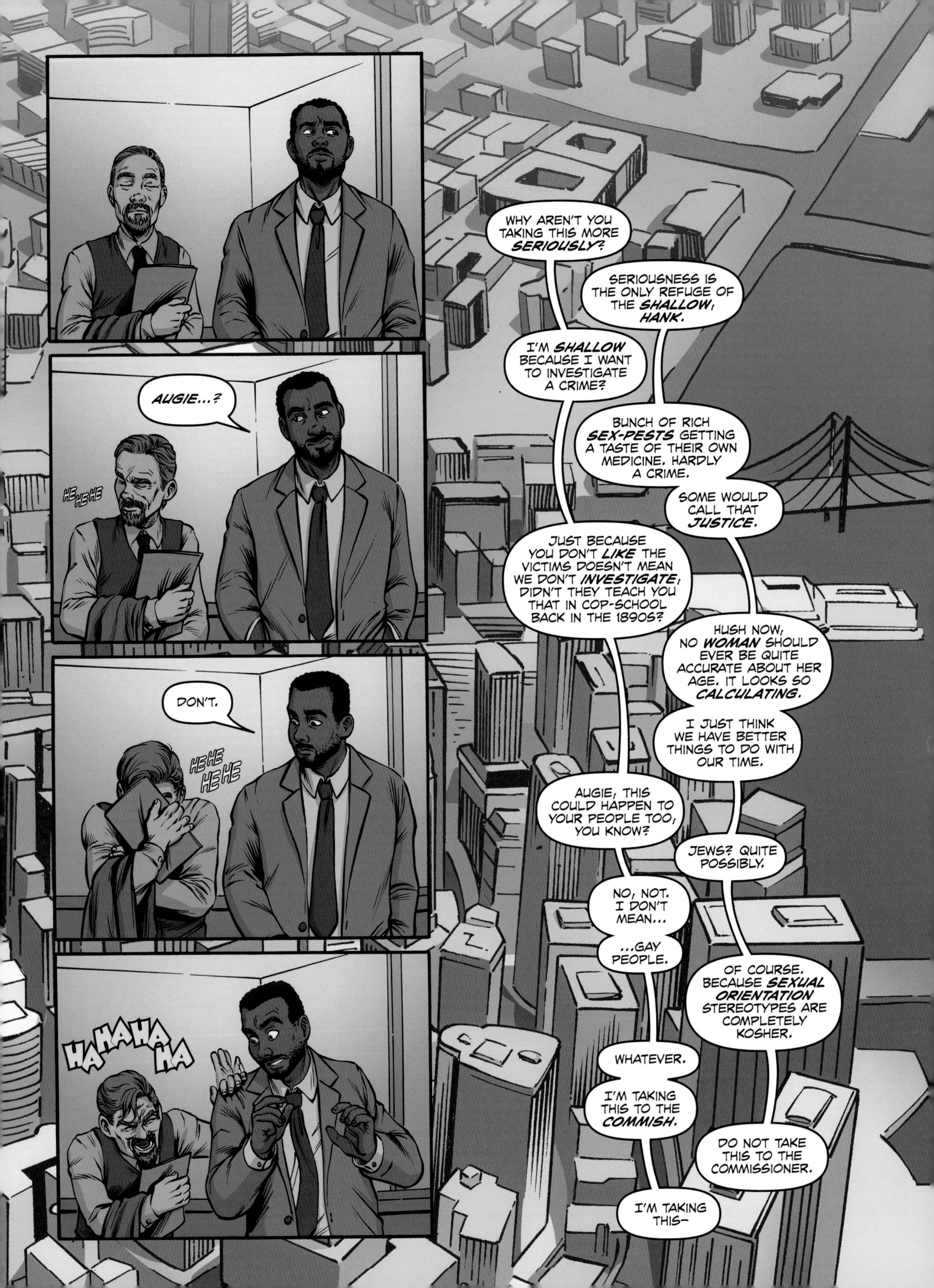
WHY AREN'T YOU TAKING THIS MORE SERIOUSLY?
SERIOUSNESS IS THE ONLY REFUGE OF THE SHALLOW, HANK.
I'M SHALLOW BECAUSE I WANT TO INVESTIGATE A CRIME?
BUNCH OF RICH SEX-PESTS GETTING A TASTE OF THEIR OWN MEDICINE. HARDLY A CRIME.
SOME WOULD CALL THAT JUSTICE.
AUGIE...?
HE HE HE
JUST BECAUSE YOU DON'T LIKE THE VICTIMS DOESN'T MEAN WE DON'T INVESTIGATE, DIDN'T THEY TEACH YOU THAT IN COP-SCHOOL BACK IN THE 1890S?
HUSH NOW, NO WOMAN SHOULD EVER BE QUITE ACCURATE ABOUT HER AGE. IT LOOKS SO CALCULATING.
I JUST THINK WE HAVE BETTER THINGS TO DO WITH OUR TIME.
DON'T.
HEHE HEHE
AUGIE, THIS COULD HAPPEN TO YOUR PEOPLE TOO, YOU KNOW?
JEWS? QUITE POSSIBLY.
NO, NOT. I DON'T MEAN...
...GAY PEOPLE.
OF COURSE. BECAUSE SEXUAL ORIENTATION STEREOTYPES ARE COMPLETELY KOSHER.
HAHAHAHA
WHATEVER.
I'M TAKING THIS TO THE COMMISH.
DO NOT TAKE THIS TO THE COMMISSIONER.
I'M TAKING THIS-

HMMMM.

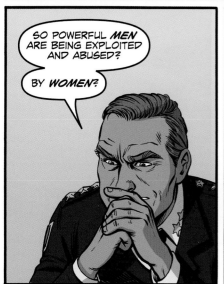

SO POWERFUL *MEN* ARE BEING EXPLOITED AND ABUSED?

BY *WOMEN?*

THAT GOES AGAINST THE *NATURAL ORDER* OF THINGS.

I *LIKE* IT.

COMMISSIONER *GORING*, THIS MAY BE PART OF A—

I DID WARN THE LAD.

SHAME WE HAVE TO STOP IT, BUT WE DO.

DETECTIVE WUTAN, HOW DO YOU FEEL ABOUT, HOW SHALL I PUT THIS, BEING THE *HONEY* IN OUR *TRAP?*

?

HA HA HA

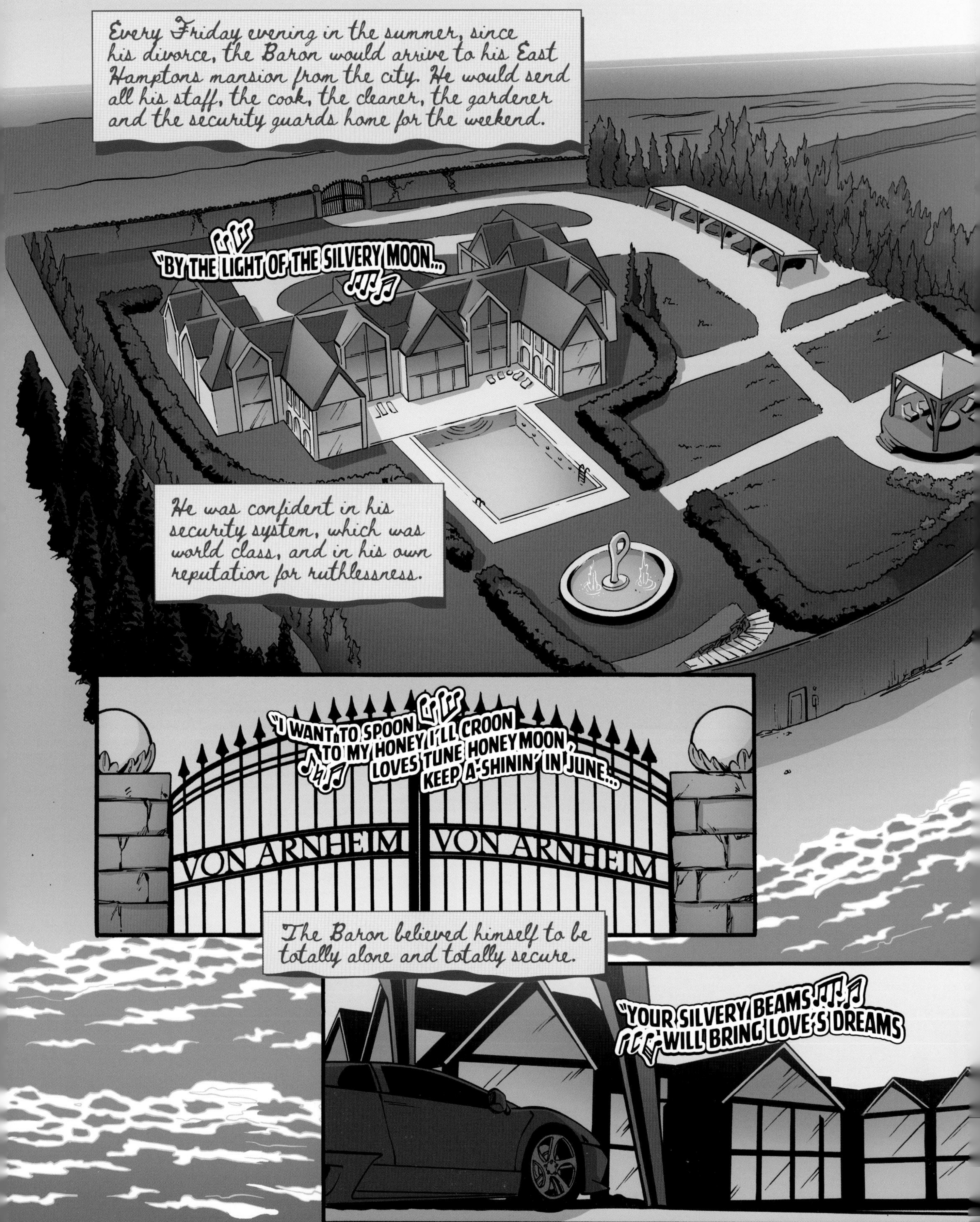
Every Friday evening in the summer, since his divorce, the Baron would arrive to his East Hamptons mansion from the city. He would send all his staff, the cook, the cleaner, the gardener and the security guards home for the weekend.
"BY THE LIGHT OF THE SILVERY MOON...
He was confident in his security system, which was world class, and in his own reputation for ruthlessness.
"I WANT TO SPOON TO MY HONEY I'LL CROON LOVES TUNE HONEYMOON, KEEP A-SHININ' IN JUNE...
VON ARNHEIM
VON ARNHEIM
The Baron believed himself to be totally alone and totally secure.
"YOUR SILVERY BEAMS WILL BRING LOVE'S DREAMS

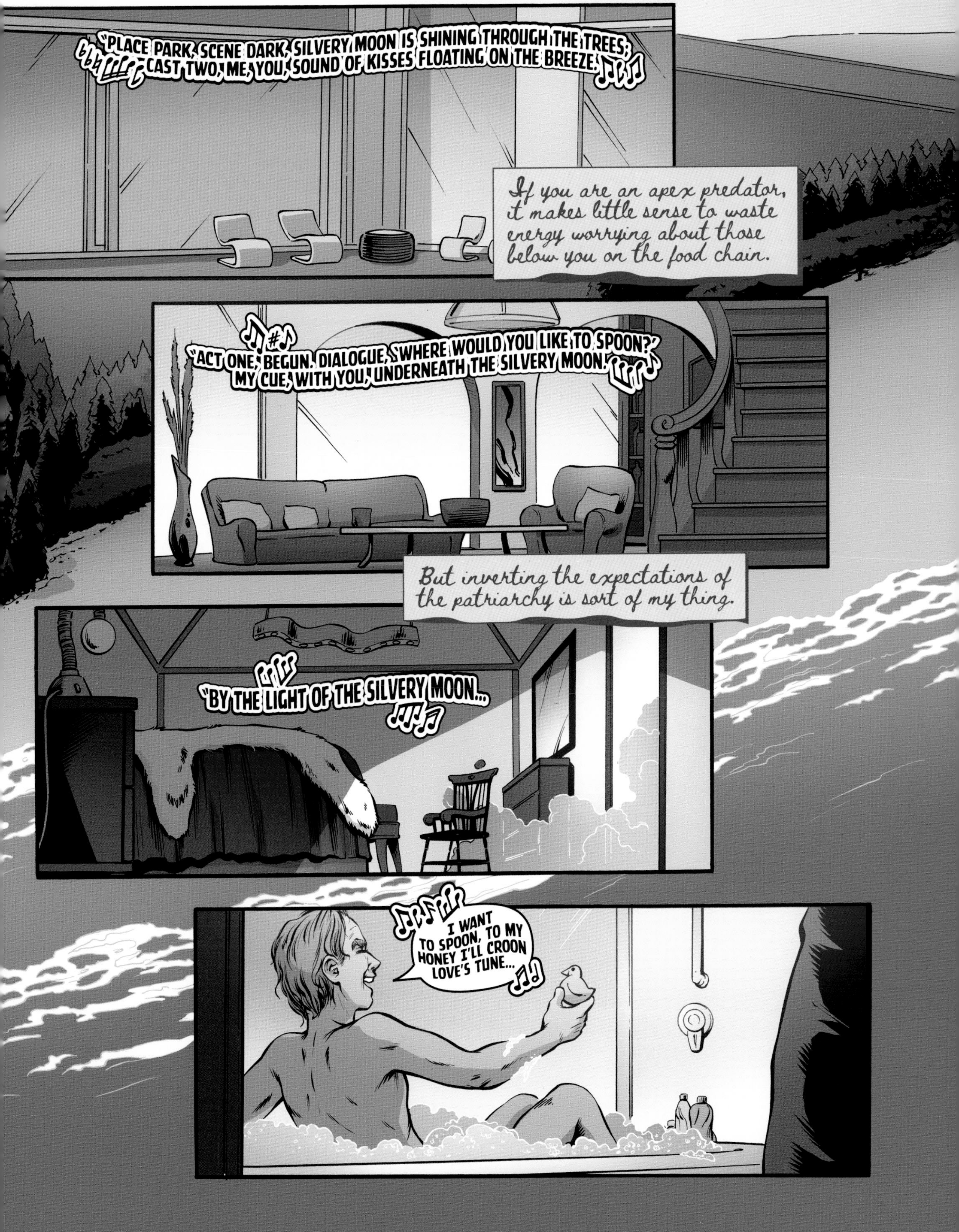
"PLACE PARK, SCENE DARK, SILVERY MOON IS SHINING THROUGH THE TREES;
CAST TWO, ME, YOU, SOUND OF KISSES FLOATING ON THE BREEZE.
If you are an apex predator, it makes little sense to waste energy worrying about those below you on the food chain.
"ACT ONE, BEGUN. DIALOGUE, WHERE WOULD YOU LIKE TO SPOON?
MY CUE, WITH YOU, UNDERNEATH THE SILVERY MOON.
But inverting the expectations of the patriarchy is sort of my thing.
"BY THE LIGHT OF THE SILVERY MOON...
I WANT TO SPOON, TO MY HONEY I'LL CROON LOVE'S TUNE...

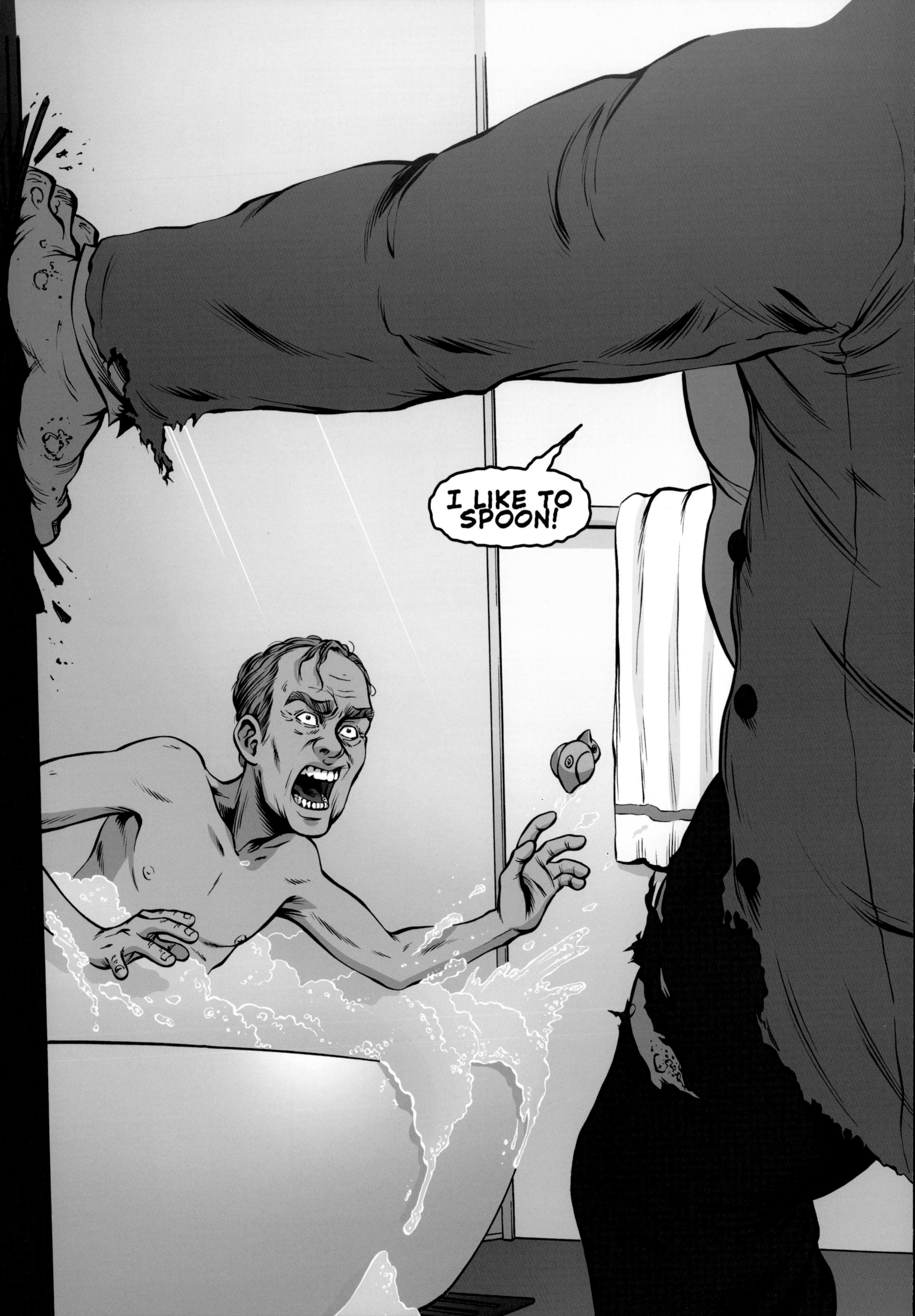
I LIKE TO SPOON!

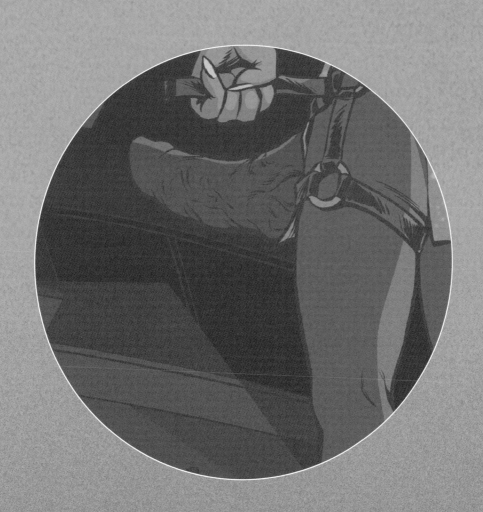

Chapter 2

"There is purification in punishment.
Not 'Forgive us our sins,' but 'Smite
us for our iniquities,' should be the
prayer of a man to a most just God."

AS CLUES GO, THIS ONE'S REALLY CUTE.
SQUEAK SQUEAK
AS CLUES GO, I THINK YOU MAY BE MISSING THE BIG ONE.

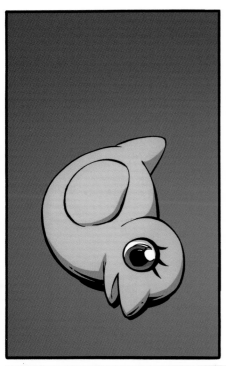

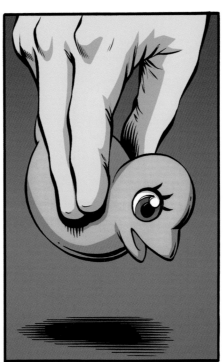

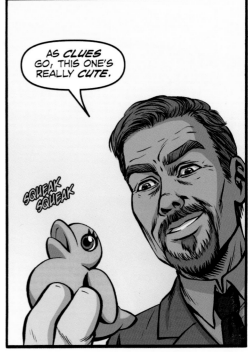

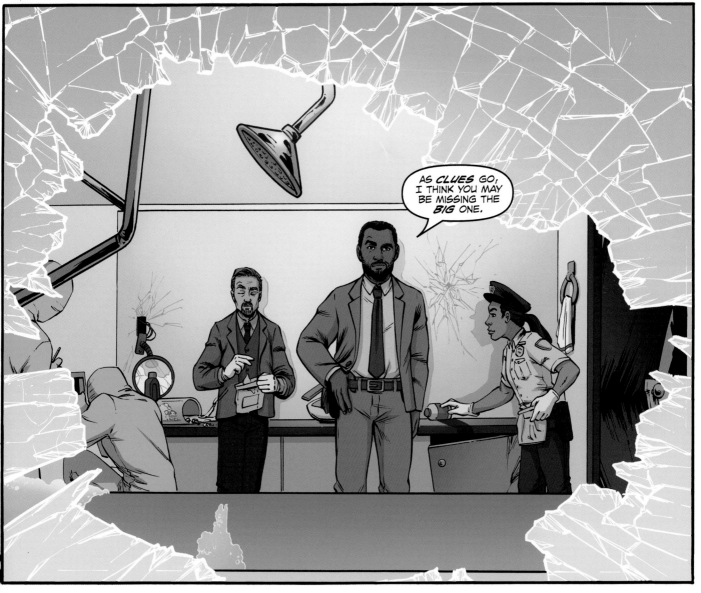

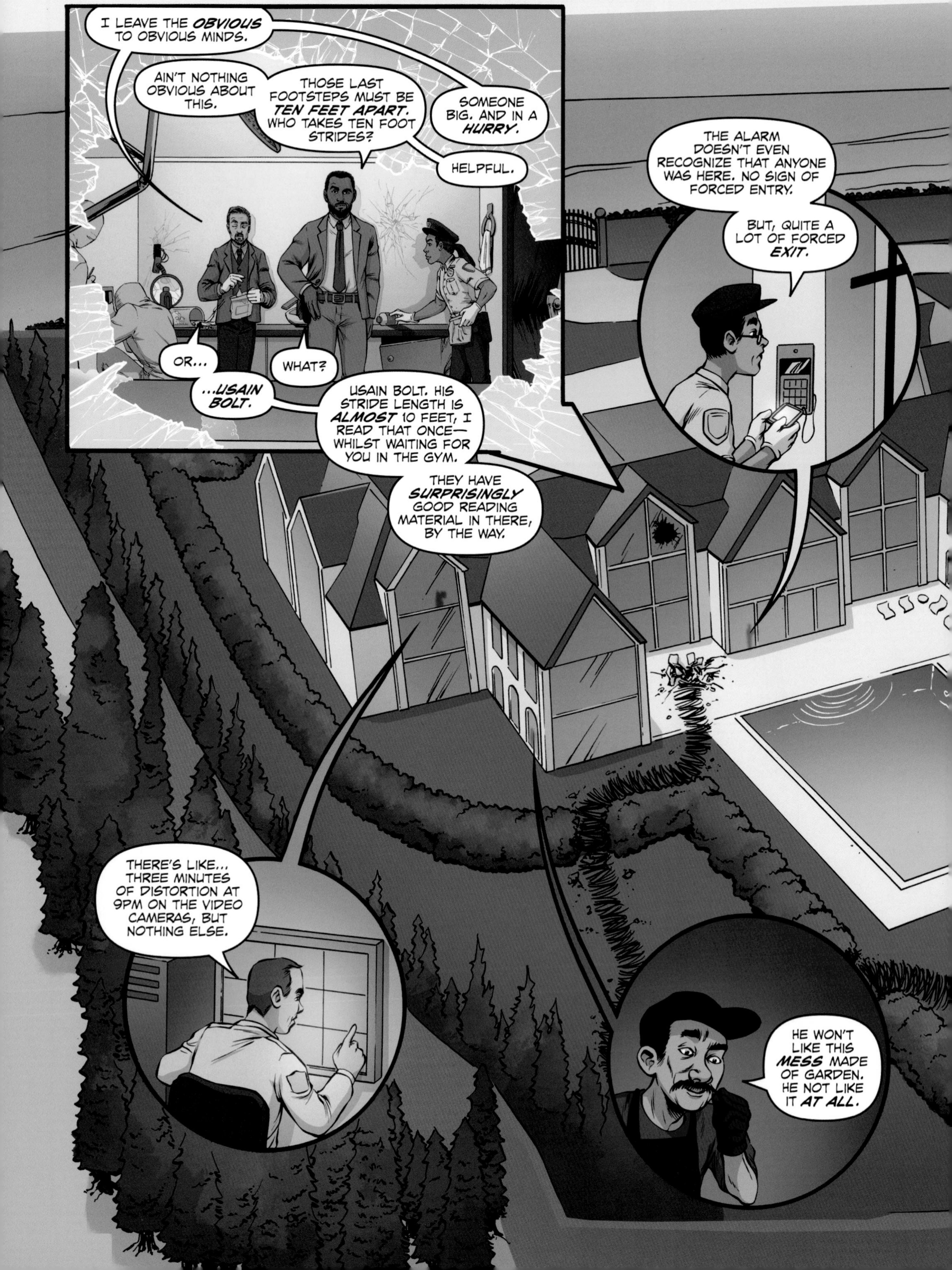

I LEAVE THE OBVIOUS TO OBVIOUS MINDS.
AIN'T NOTHING OBVIOUS ABOUT THIS.
THOSE LAST FOOTSTEPS MUST BE TEN FEET APART. WHO TAKES TEN FOOT STRIDES?
SOMEONE BIG. AND IN A HURRY.
HELPFUL.
OR...
WHAT?
...USAIN BOLT.
USAIN BOLT. HIS STRIDE LENGTH IS ALMOST 10 FEET, I READ THAT ONCE— WHILST WAITING FOR YOU IN THE GYM.
THEY HAVE SURPRISINGLY GOOD READING MATERIAL IN THERE, BY THE WAY.
THE ALARM DOESN'T EVEN RECOGNIZE THAT ANYONE WAS HERE. NO SIGN OF FORCED ENTRY.
BUT, QUITE A LOT OF FORCED EXIT.
THERE'S LIKE... THREE MINUTES OF DISTORTION AT 9PM ON THE VIDEO CAMERAS, BUT NOTHING ELSE.
HE WON'T LIKE THIS MESS MADE OF GARDEN. HE NOT LIKE IT AT ALL.

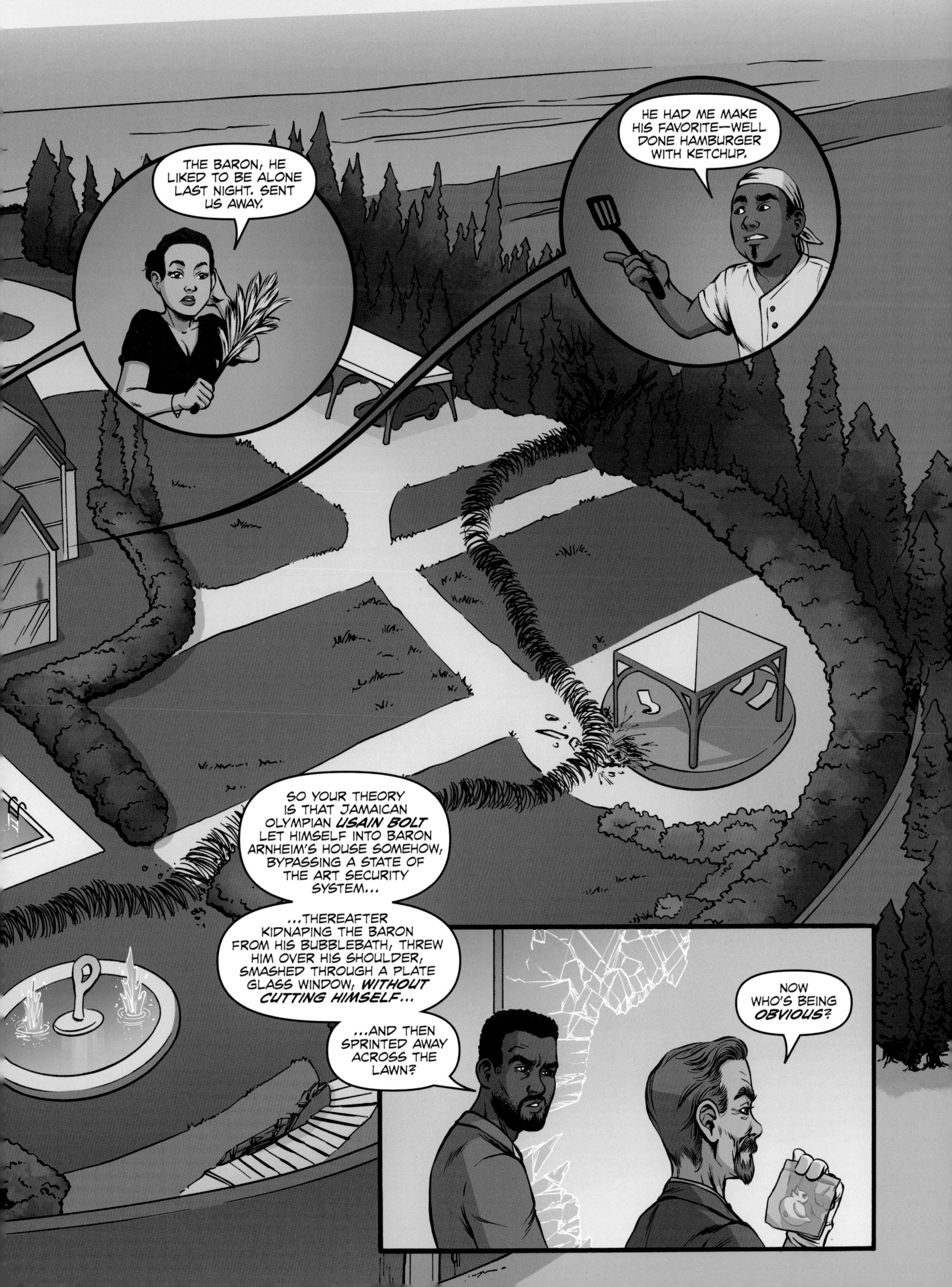
THE BARON, HE LIKED TO BE ALONE LAST NIGHT. SENT US AWAY.
HE HAD ME MAKE HIS FAVORITE—WELL DONE HAMBURGER WITH KETCHUP.
SO YOUR THEORY IS THAT JAMAICAN OLYMPIAN USAIN BOLT LET HIMSELF INTO BARON ARNHEIM'S HOUSE SOMEHOW, BYPASSING A STATE OF THE ART SECURITY SYSTEM...
...THEREAFTER KIDNAPING THE BARON FROM HIS BUBBLEBATH, THREW HIM OVER HIS SHOULDER, SMASHED THROUGH A PLATE GLASS WINDOW, WITHOUT CUTTING HIMSELF...
...AND THEN SPRINTED AWAY ACROSS THE LAWN?
NOW WHO'S BEING OBVIOUS?

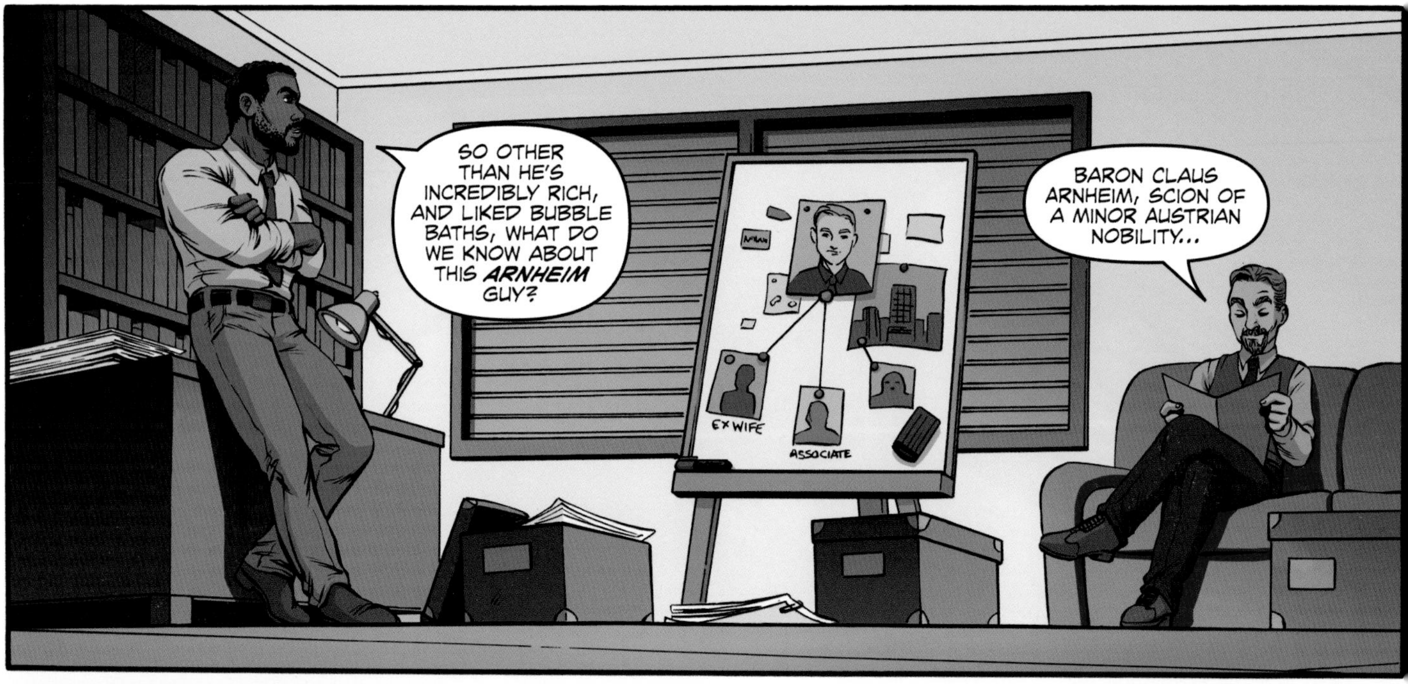

SO OTHER THAN HE'S INCREDIBLY RICH, AND LIKED BUBBLE BATHS, WHAT DO WE KNOW ABOUT THIS ***ARNHEIM*** GUY?
EX WIFE
ASSOCIATE
BARON CLAUS ARNHEIM, SCION OF A MINOR AUSTRIAN NOBILITY...

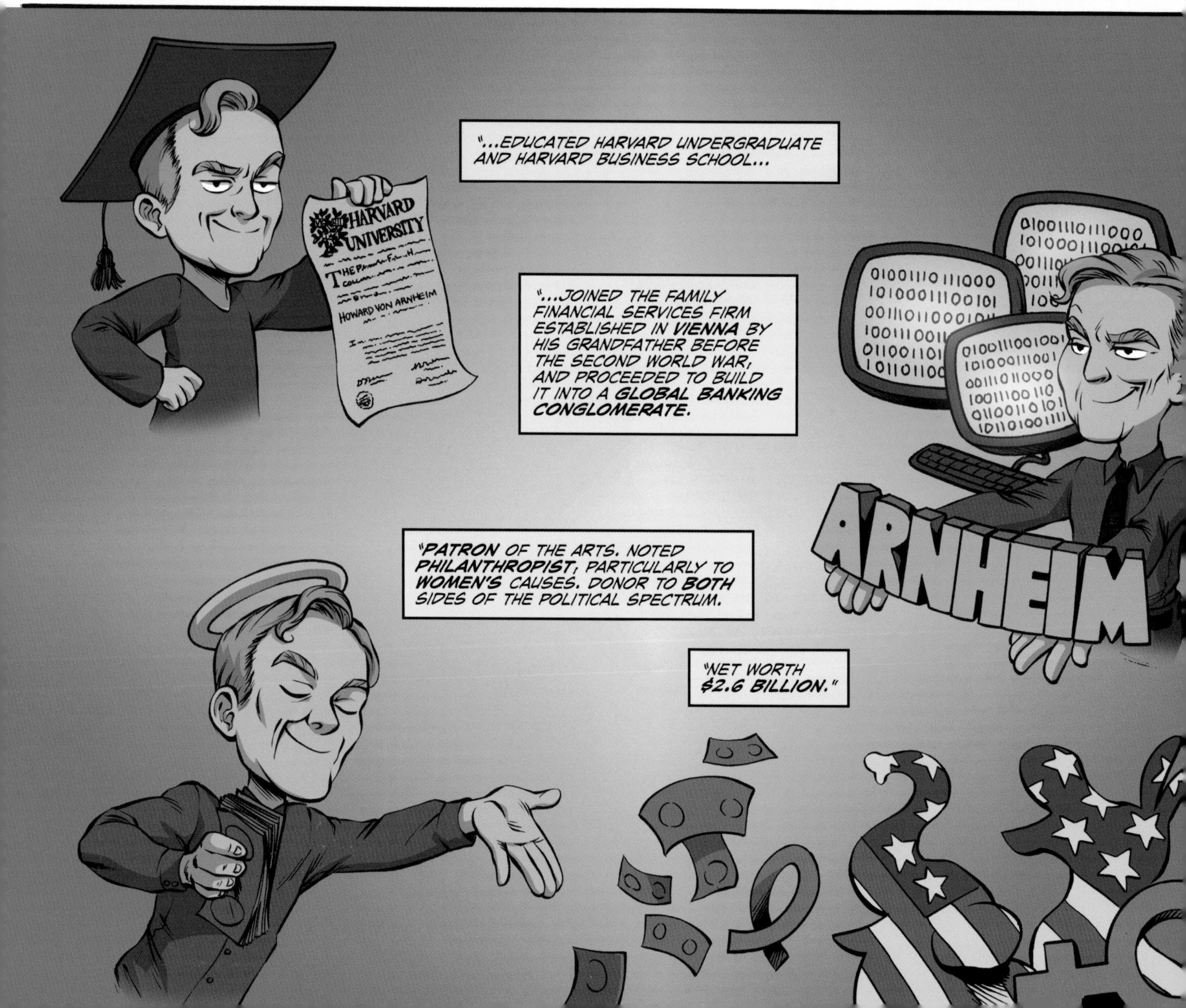

"...EDUCATED HARVARD UNDERGRADUATE AND HARVARD BUSINESS SCHOOL...
HARVARD UNIVERSITY
HOWARD VON ARNHEIM
"...JOINED THE FAMILY FINANCIAL SERVICES FIRM ESTABLISHED IN **VIENNA** BY HIS GRANDFATHER BEFORE THE SECOND WORLD WAR, AND PROCEEDED TO BUILD IT INTO A **GLOBAL BANKING CONGLOMERATE.**
ARNHEIM
"**PATRON** OF THE ARTS. NOTED **PHILANTHROPIST**, PARTICULARLY TO **WOMEN'S** CAUSES. DONOR TO **BOTH** SIDES OF THE POLITICAL SPECTRUM.
"NET WORTH **$2.6 BILLION.**"

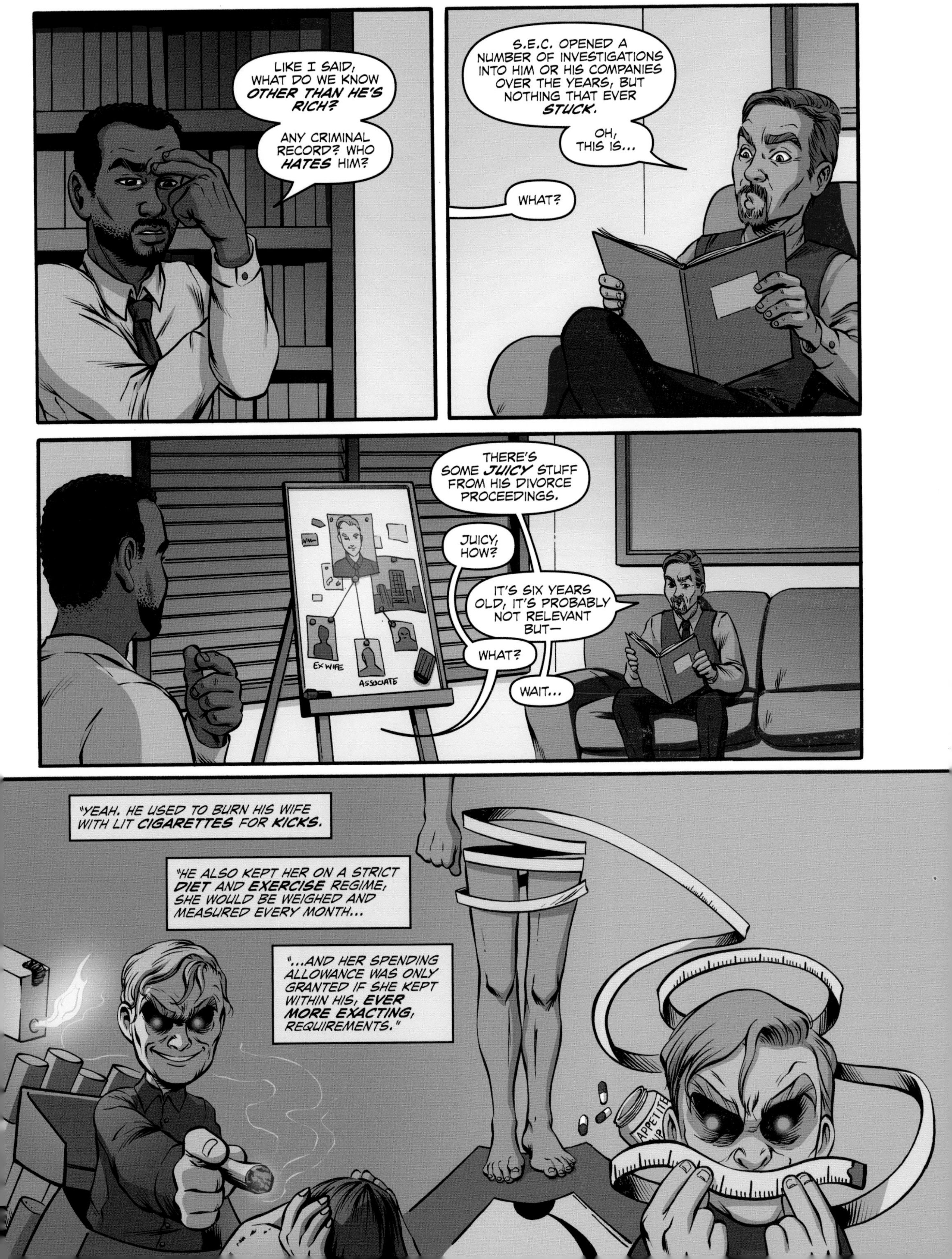

LIKE I SAID, WHAT DO WE KNOW OTHER THAN HE'S RICH?
ANY CRIMINAL RECORD? WHO HATES HIM?
S.E.C. OPENED A NUMBER OF INVESTIGATIONS INTO HIM OR HIS COMPANIES OVER THE YEARS, BUT NOTHING THAT EVER STUCK.
OH, THIS IS...
WHAT?
THERE'S SOME JUICY STUFF FROM HIS DIVORCE PROCEEDINGS.
JUICY, HOW?
IT'S SIX YEARS OLD, IT'S PROBABLY NOT RELEVANT BUT—
WHAT?
WAIT...
EX WIFE
ASSOCIATE
"YEAH. HE USED TO BURN HIS WIFE WITH LIT CIGARETTES FOR KICKS.
"HE ALSO KEPT HER ON A STRICT DIET AND EXERCISE REGIME, SHE WOULD BE WEIGHED AND MEASURED EVERY MONTH...
"...AND HER SPENDING ALLOWANCE WAS ONLY GRANTED IF SHE KEPT WITHIN HIS, EVER MORE EXACTING, REQUIREMENTS."

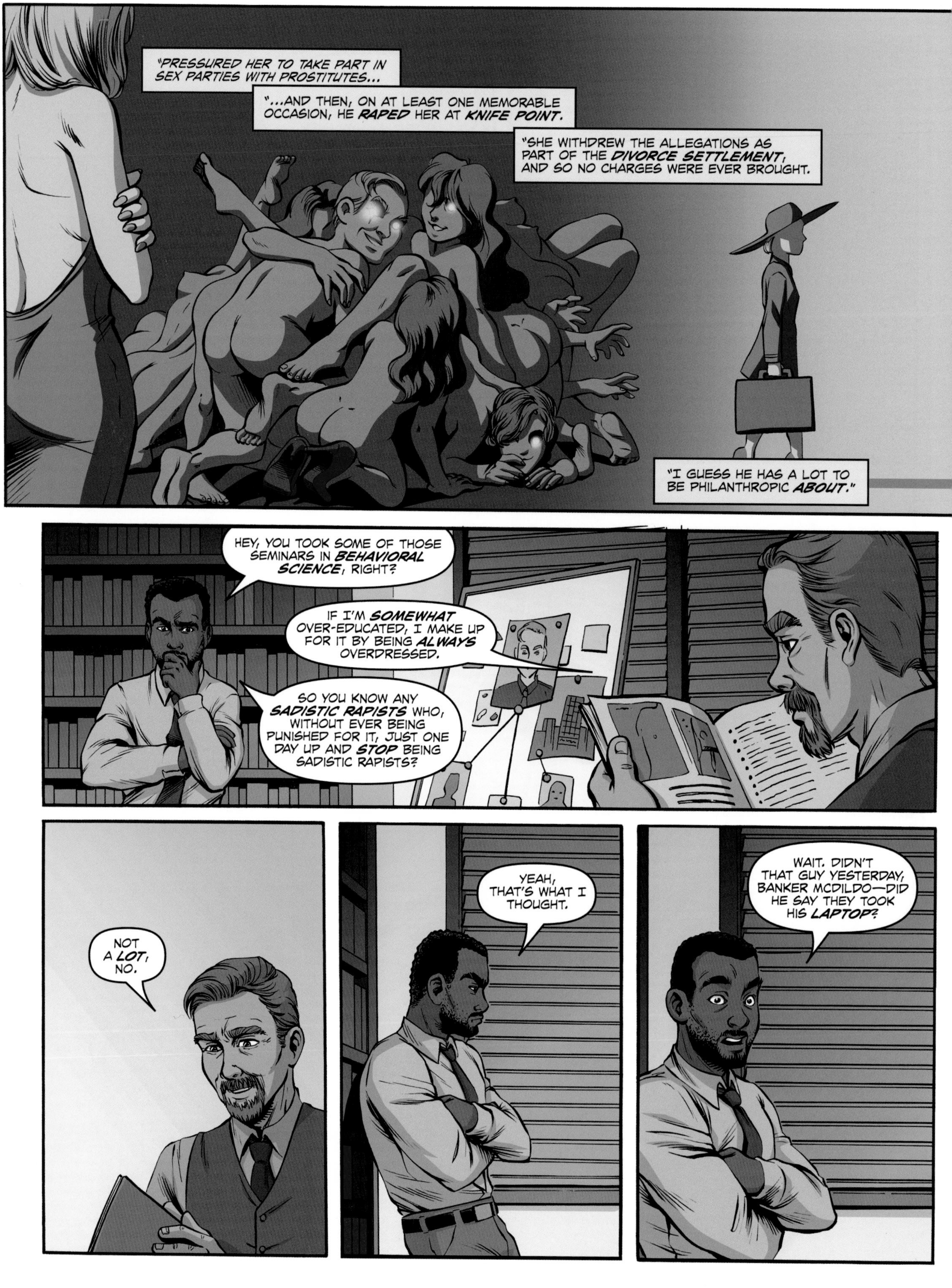
"PRESSURED HER TO TAKE PART IN SEX PARTIES WITH PROSTITUTES...
"...AND THEN, ON AT LEAST ONE MEMORABLE OCCASION, HE RAPED HER AT KNIFE POINT.
"SHE WITHDREW THE ALLEGATIONS AS PART OF THE DIVORCE SETTLEMENT, AND SO NO CHARGES WERE EVER BROUGHT.
"I GUESS HE HAS A LOT TO BE PHILANTHROPIC ABOUT."
HEY, YOU TOOK SOME OF THOSE SEMINARS IN BEHAVIORAL SCIENCE, RIGHT?
IF I'M SOMEWHAT OVER-EDUCATED, I MAKE UP FOR IT BY BEING ALWAYS OVERDRESSED.
SO YOU KNOW ANY SADISTIC RAPISTS WHO, WITHOUT EVER BEING PUNISHED FOR IT, JUST ONE DAY UP AND STOP BEING SADISTIC RAPISTS?
NOT A LOT, NO.
YEAH, THAT'S WHAT I THOUGHT.
WAIT. DIDN'T THAT GUY YESTERDAY, BANKER MCDILDO—DID HE SAY THEY TOOK HIS LAPTOP?

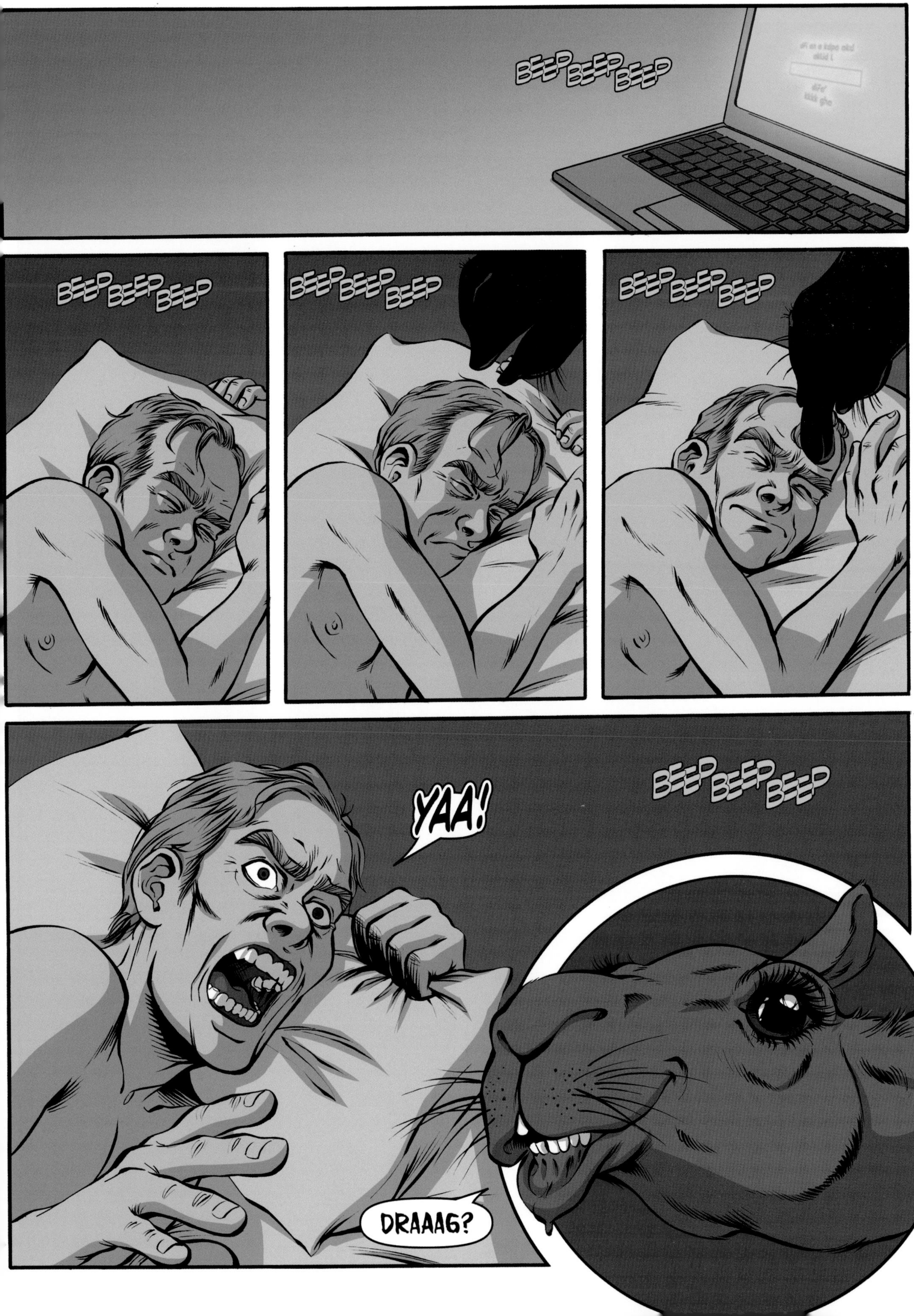
BEEP BEEP BEEP
BEEP BEEP BEEP
BEEP BEEP BEEP
BEEP BEEP BEEP
YAA!
BEEP BEEP BEEP
DRAAAG?

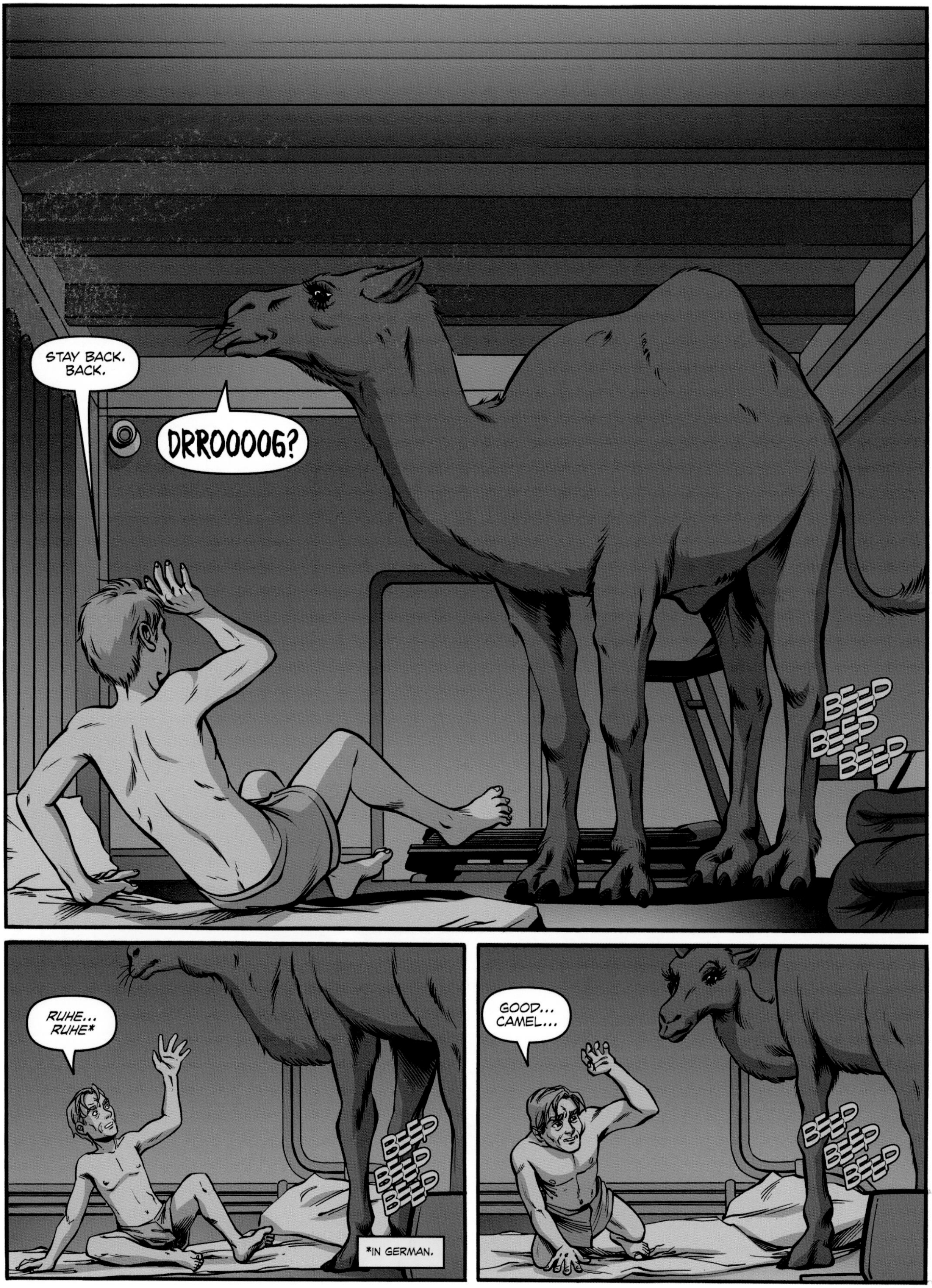
STAY BACK.
BACK.
DRROOOOG?
BEEP BEEP BEEP
RUHE...
RUHE*
BEEP BEEP BEEP
*IN GERMAN.
GOOD...
CAMEL...
BEEP BEEP BEEP

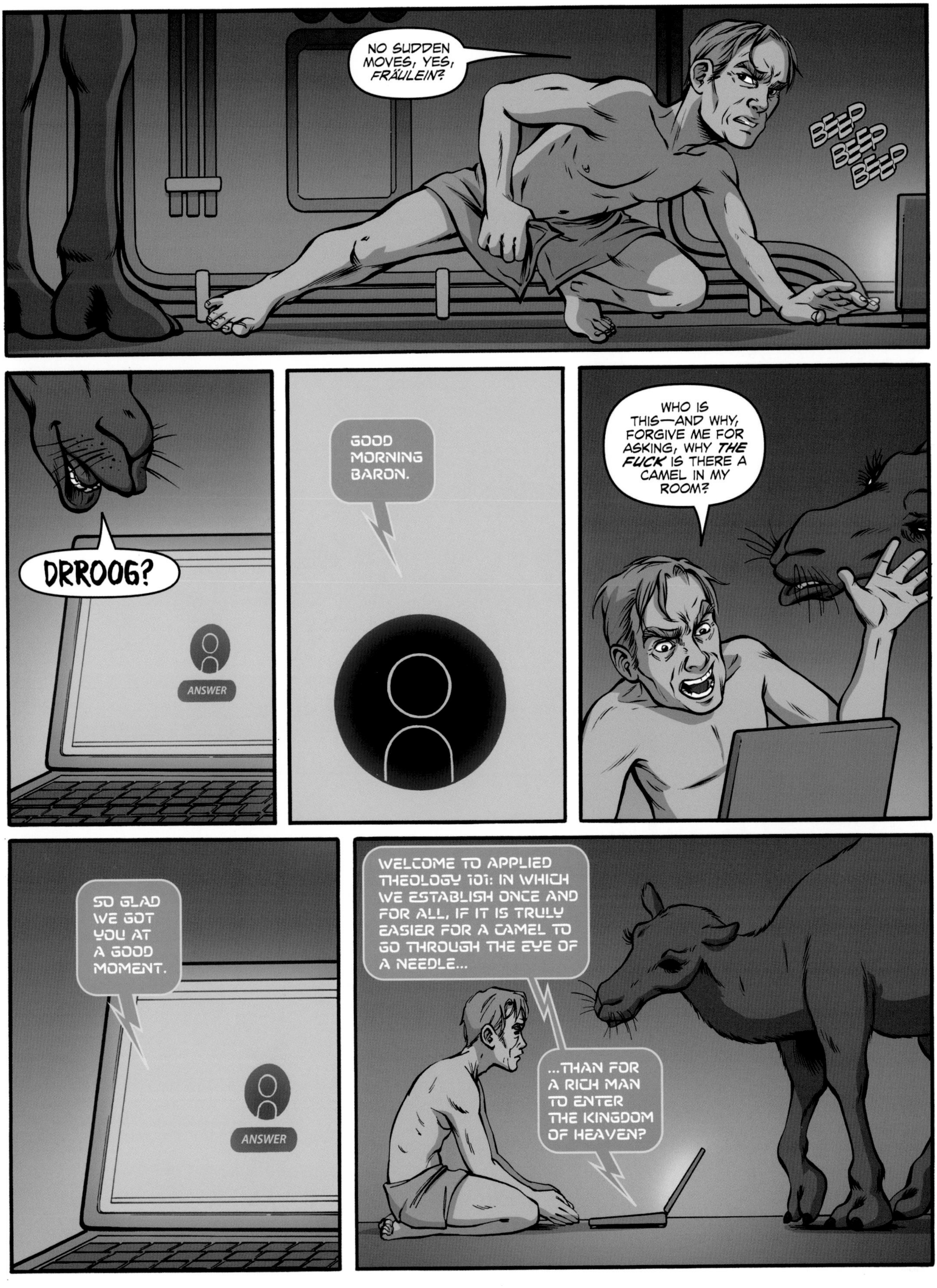
NO SUDDEN MOVES, YES, FRÄULEIN?
BEEP BEEP BEEP
DRROOG?
ANSWER
GOOD MORNING BARON.
WHO IS THIS—AND WHY, FORGIVE ME FOR ASKING, WHY THE FUCK IS THERE A CAMEL IN MY ROOM?
SO GLAD WE GOT YOU AT A GOOD MOMENT.
ANSWER
WELCOME TO APPLIED THEOLOGY 101: IN WHICH WE ESTABLISH ONCE AND FOR ALL, IF IT IS TRULY EASIER FOR A CAMEL TO GO THROUGH THE EYE OF A NEEDLE...
...THAN FOR A RICH MAN TO ENTER THE KINGDOM OF HEAVEN?

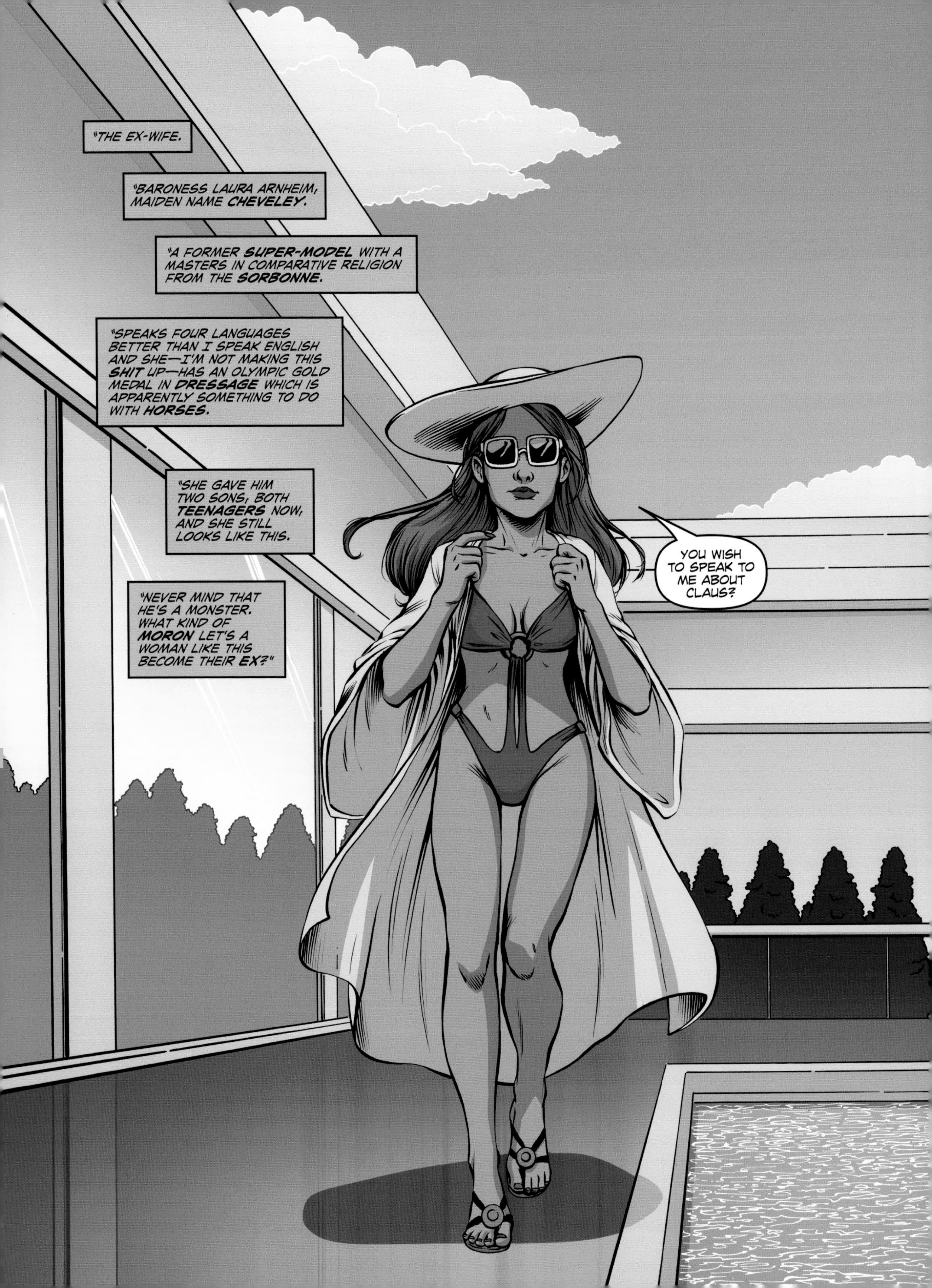
"THE EX-WIFE.
"BARONESS LAURA ARNHEIM, MAIDEN NAME CHEVELEY.
"A FORMER SUPER-MODEL WITH A MASTERS IN COMPARATIVE RELIGION FROM THE SORBONNE.
"SPEAKS FOUR LANGUAGES BETTER THAN I SPEAK ENGLISH AND SHE—I'M NOT MAKING THIS SHIT UP—HAS AN OLYMPIC GOLD MEDAL IN DRESSAGE WHICH IS APPARENTLY SOMETHING TO DO WITH HORSES.
"SHE GAVE HIM TWO SONS, BOTH TEENAGERS NOW, AND SHE STILL LOOKS LIKE THIS.
"NEVER MIND THAT HE'S A MONSTER. WHAT KIND OF MORON LET'S A WOMAN LIKE THIS BECOME THEIR EX?"
YOU WISH TO SPEAK TO ME ABOUT CLAUS?

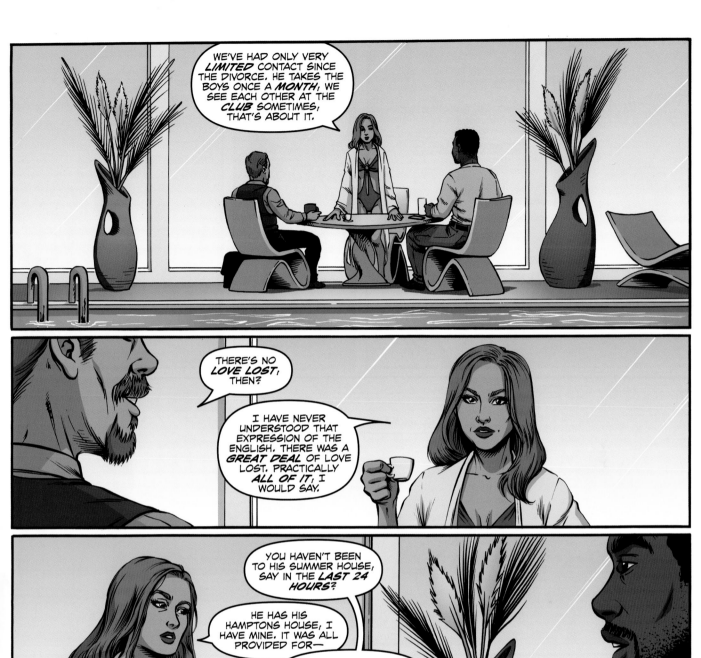

WE'VE HAD ONLY VERY *LIMITED* CONTACT SINCE THE DIVORCE. HE TAKES THE BOYS ONCE A *MONTH*, WE SEE EACH OTHER AT THE *CLUB* SOMETIMES, THAT'S ABOUT IT.

THERE'S NO *LOVE LOST*, THEN?

I HAVE NEVER UNDERSTOOD THAT EXPRESSION OF THE ENGLISH. THERE WAS A *GREAT DEAL* OF LOVE LOST. PRACTICALLY *ALL OF IT*, I WOULD SAY.

YOU HAVEN'T BEEN TO HIS SUMMER HOUSE, SAY IN THE *LAST 24 HOURS*?

HE HAS HIS HAMPTONS HOUSE, I HAVE MINE. IT WAS ALL PROVIDED FOR—

YES, BUT HERE'S THE THING, YOU SEE—WHOEVER... THIS INTRUDER WAS LAST NIGHT... THEY HAD A CODE FOR THE SECURITY SYSTEM.

YOUR CODE.

THIS MAKES NO SENSE. MY CODES HAVEN'T WORKED FOR *YEARS*. EVEN WHEN WE WERE TOGETHER, HE HAD THEM CHANGED EVERY MONTH.

CLAUS WAS VERY *PASSIONATE* ABOUT *PRIVACY*.

NO, I LIED. YOUR CODE WASN'T USED, AND IT WOULDN'T HAVE WORKED IF IT HAD BEEN.

SORRY, JUST NEEDED TO TAKE THE SHOT.

*SALE COUP!**

*DIRTY TRICK!

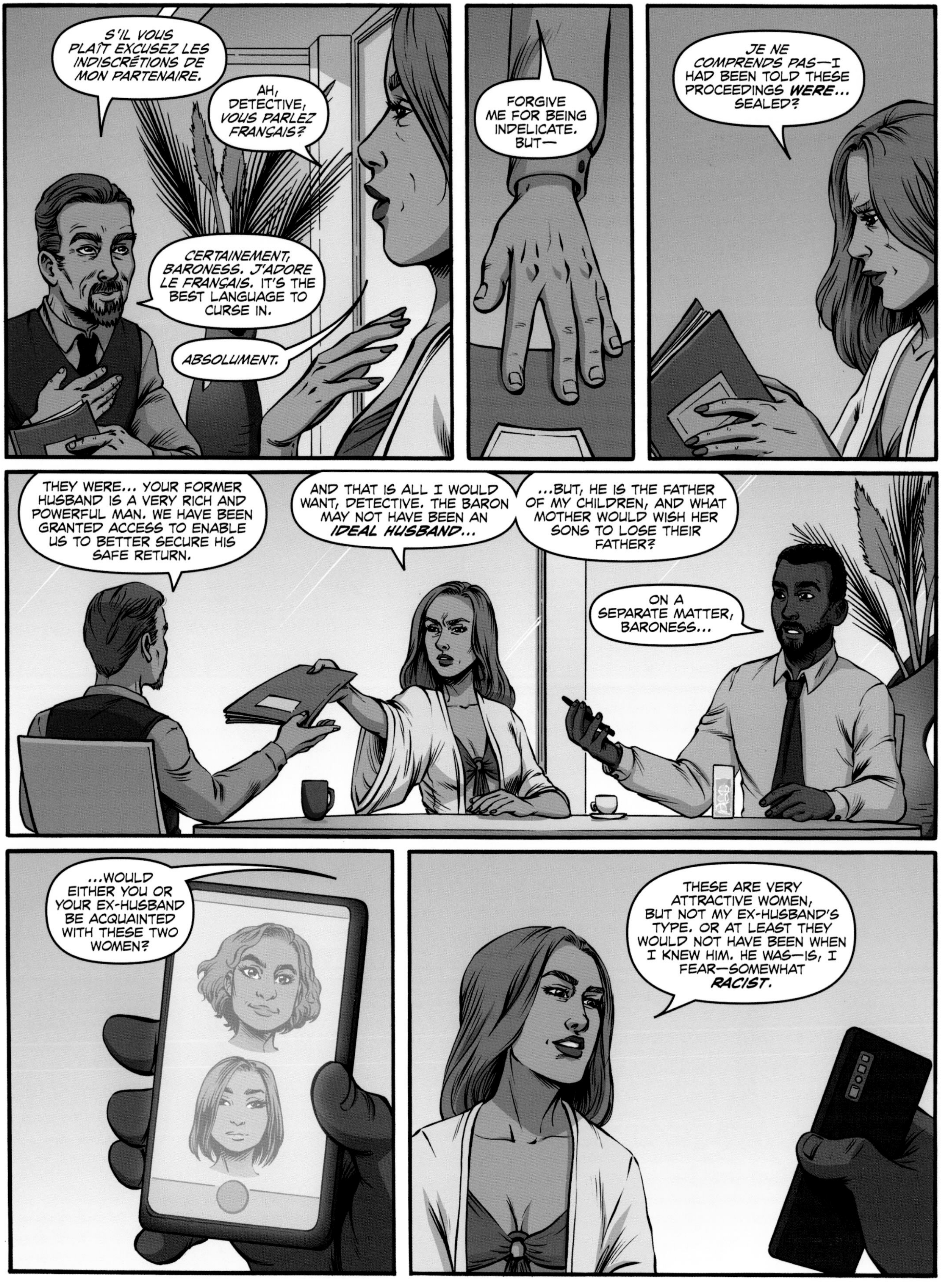
S'IL VOUS PLAÎT EXCUSEZ LES INDISCRÉTIONS DE MON PARTENAIRE.
AH, DETECTIVE, VOUS PARLEZ FRANÇAIS?
CERTAINEMENT, BARONESS. J'ADORE LE FRANÇAIS. IT'S THE BEST LANGUAGE TO CURSE IN.
ABSOLUMENT.
FORGIVE ME FOR BEING INDELICATE. BUT—
JE NE COMPRENDS PAS—I HAD BEEN TOLD THESE PROCEEDINGS WERE... SEALED?
THEY WERE... YOUR FORMER HUSBAND IS A VERY RICH AND POWERFUL MAN. WE HAVE BEEN GRANTED ACCESS TO ENABLE US TO BETTER SECURE HIS SAFE RETURN.
AND THAT IS ALL I WOULD WANT, DETECTIVE. THE BARON MAY NOT HAVE BEEN AN IDEAL HUSBAND...
...BUT, HE IS THE FATHER OF MY CHILDREN, AND WHAT MOTHER WOULD WISH HER SONS TO LOSE THEIR FATHER?
ON A SEPARATE MATTER, BARONESS...
...WOULD EITHER YOU OR YOUR EX-HUSBAND BE ACQUAINTED WITH THESE TWO WOMEN?
THESE ARE VERY ATTRACTIVE WOMEN, BUT NOT MY EX-HUSBAND'S TYPE. OR AT LEAST THEY WOULD NOT HAVE BEEN WHEN I KNEW HIM. HE WAS—IS, I FEAR—SOMEWHAT RACIST.

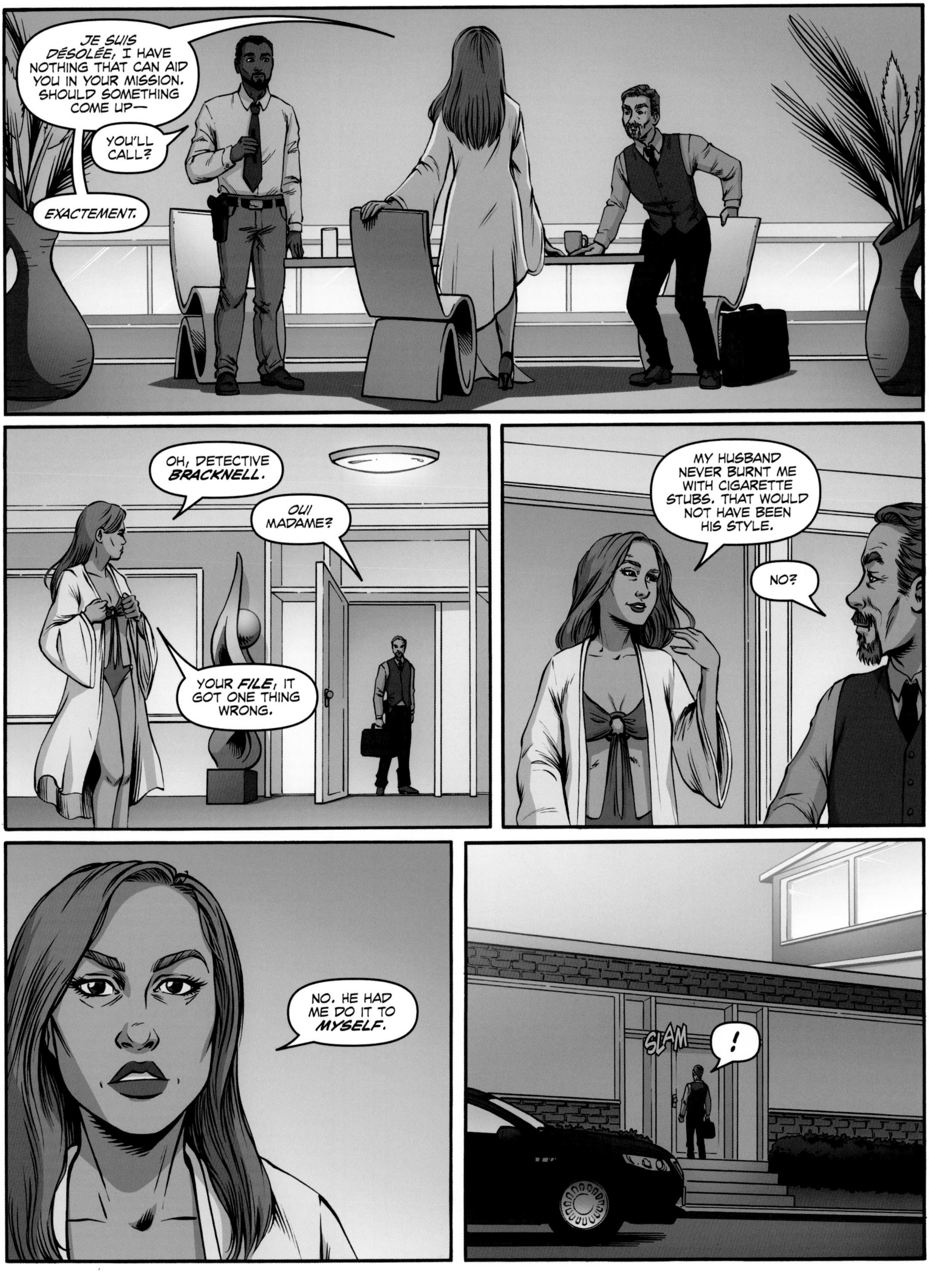
JE SUIS DÉSOLÉE, I HAVE NOTHING THAT CAN AID YOU IN YOUR MISSION. SHOULD SOMETHING COME UP—
YOU'LL CALL?
EXACTEMENT.
OH, DETECTIVE BRACKNELL.
OUI MADAME?
YOUR FILE, IT GOT ONE THING WRONG.
MY HUSBAND NEVER BURNT ME WITH CIGARETTE STUBS. THAT WOULD NOT HAVE BEEN HIS STYLE.
NO?
NO. HE HAD ME DO IT TO MYSELF.
SLAM
!

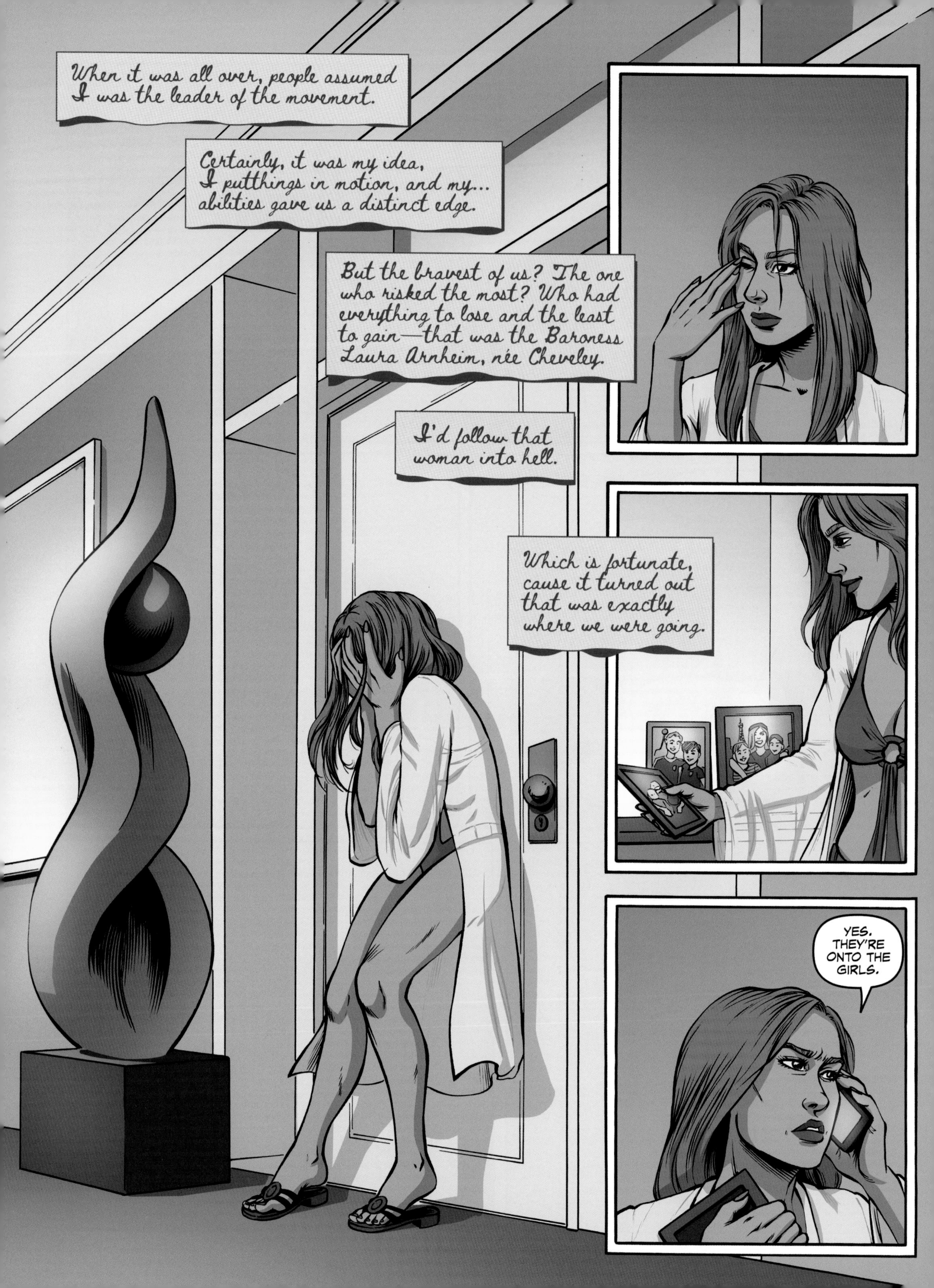
When it was all over, people assumed I was the leader of the movement.
Certainly, it was my idea. I putthings in motion, and my... abilities gave us a distinct edge.
But the bravest of us? The one who risked the most? Who had everything to lose and the least to gain—that was the Baroness Laura Arnheim, née Cheveley.
I'd follow that woman into hell.
Which is fortunate, cause it turned out that was exactly where we were going.
YES. THEY'RE ONTO THE GIRLS.

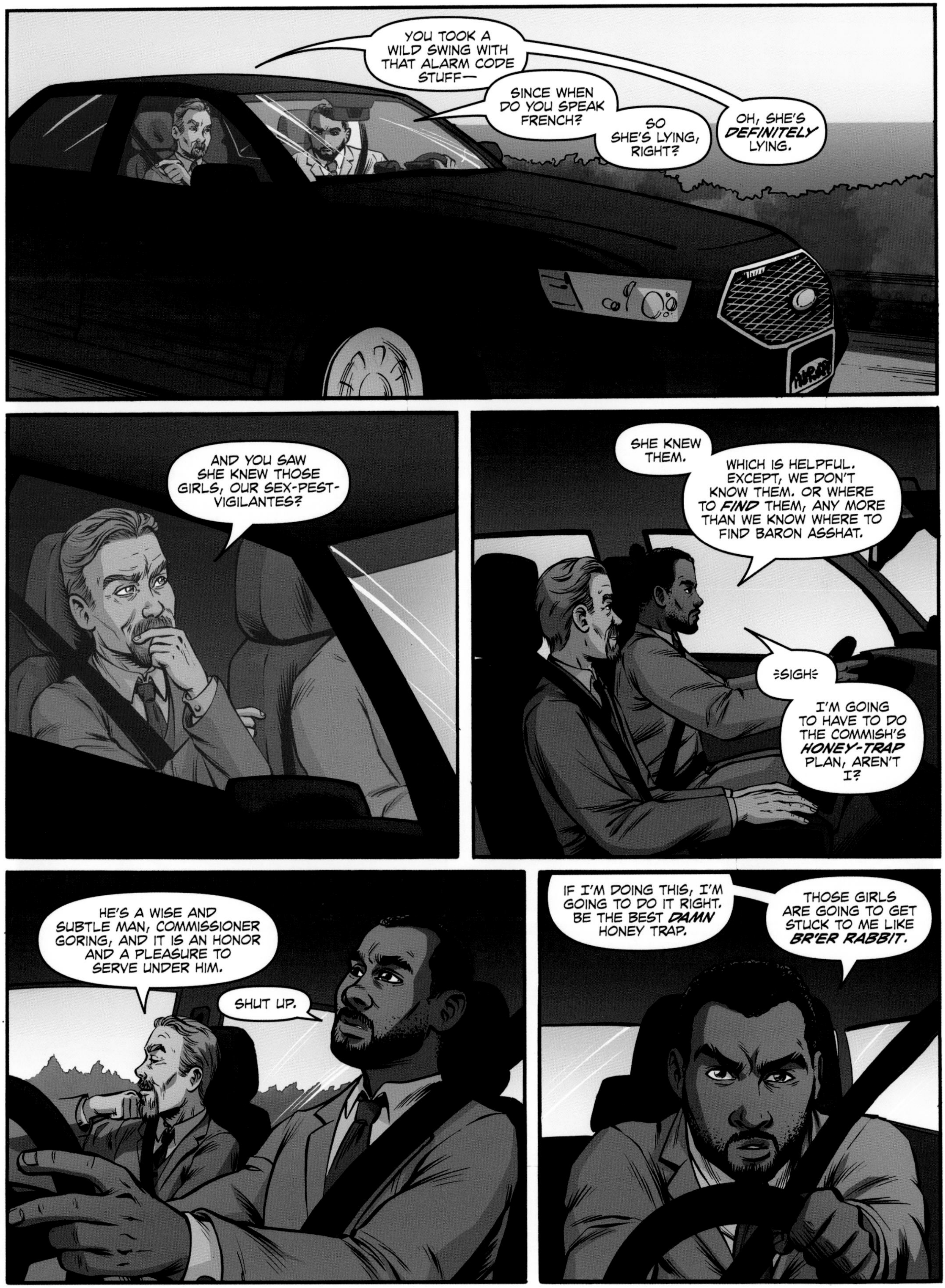
YOU TOOK A WILD SWING WITH THAT ALARM CODE STUFF—
SINCE WHEN DO YOU SPEAK FRENCH?
SO SHE'S LYING, RIGHT?
OH, SHE'S *DEFINITELY* LYING.
AND YOU SAW SHE KNEW THOSE GIRLS, OUR SEX-PEST-VIGILANTES?
SHE KNEW THEM.
WHICH IS HELPFUL. EXCEPT, WE DON'T KNOW THEM. OR WHERE TO *FIND* THEM, ANY MORE THAN WE KNOW WHERE TO FIND BARON ASSHAT.
=SIGH=
I'M GOING TO HAVE TO DO THE COMMISH'S *HONEY-TRAP* PLAN, AREN'T I?
HE'S A WISE AND SUBTLE MAN, COMMISSIONER GORING, AND IT IS AN HONOR AND A PLEASURE TO SERVE UNDER HIM.
SHUT UP.
IF I'M DOING THIS, I'M GOING TO DO IT RIGHT. BE THE BEST *DAMN* HONEY TRAP.
THOSE GIRLS ARE GOING TO GET STUCK TO ME LIKE *BR'ER RABBIT*.

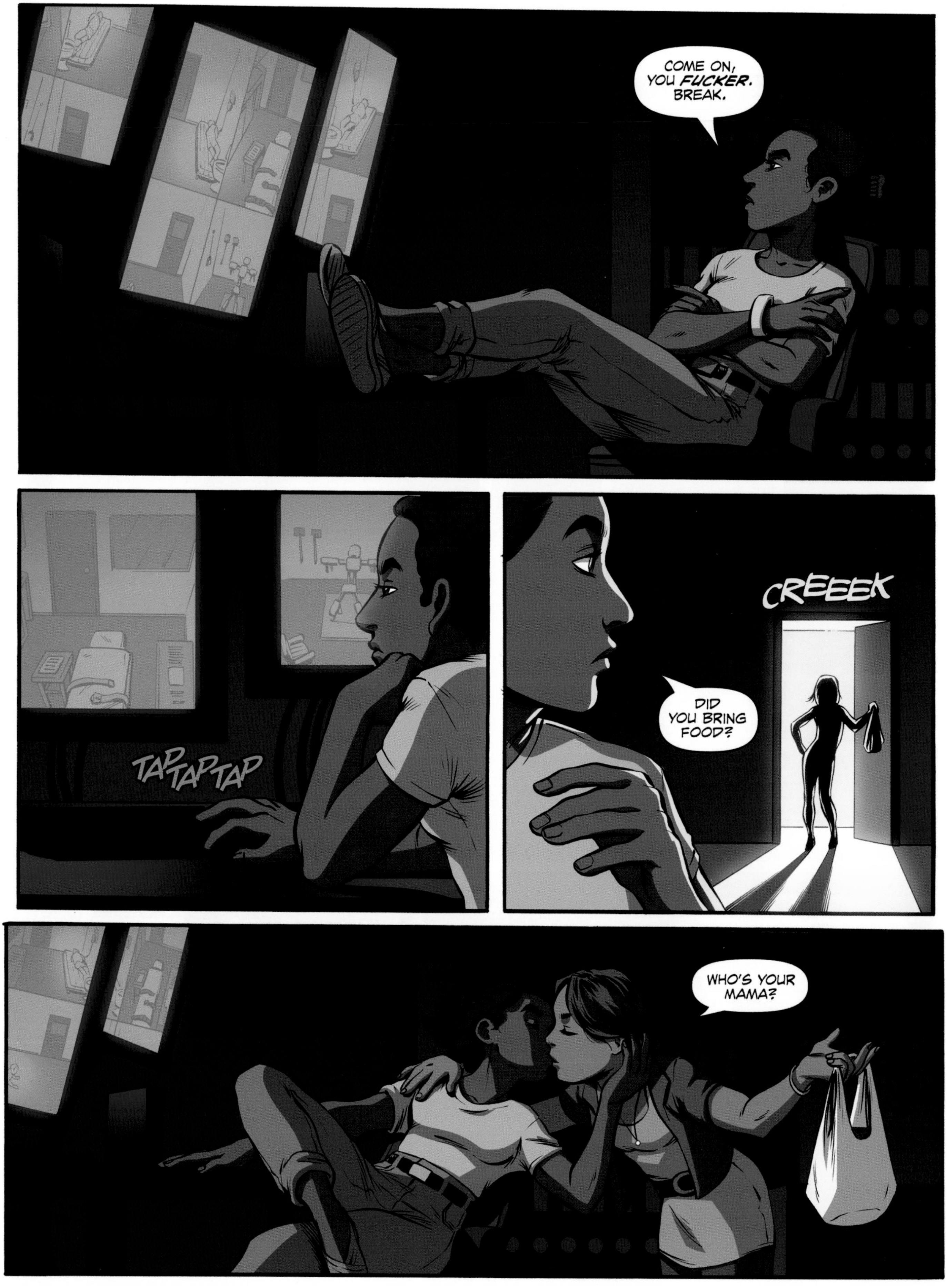
COME ON, YOU *FUCKER*. BREAK.
TAPTAPTAP
CREEEK
DID YOU BRING FOOD?
WHO'S YOUR MAMA?

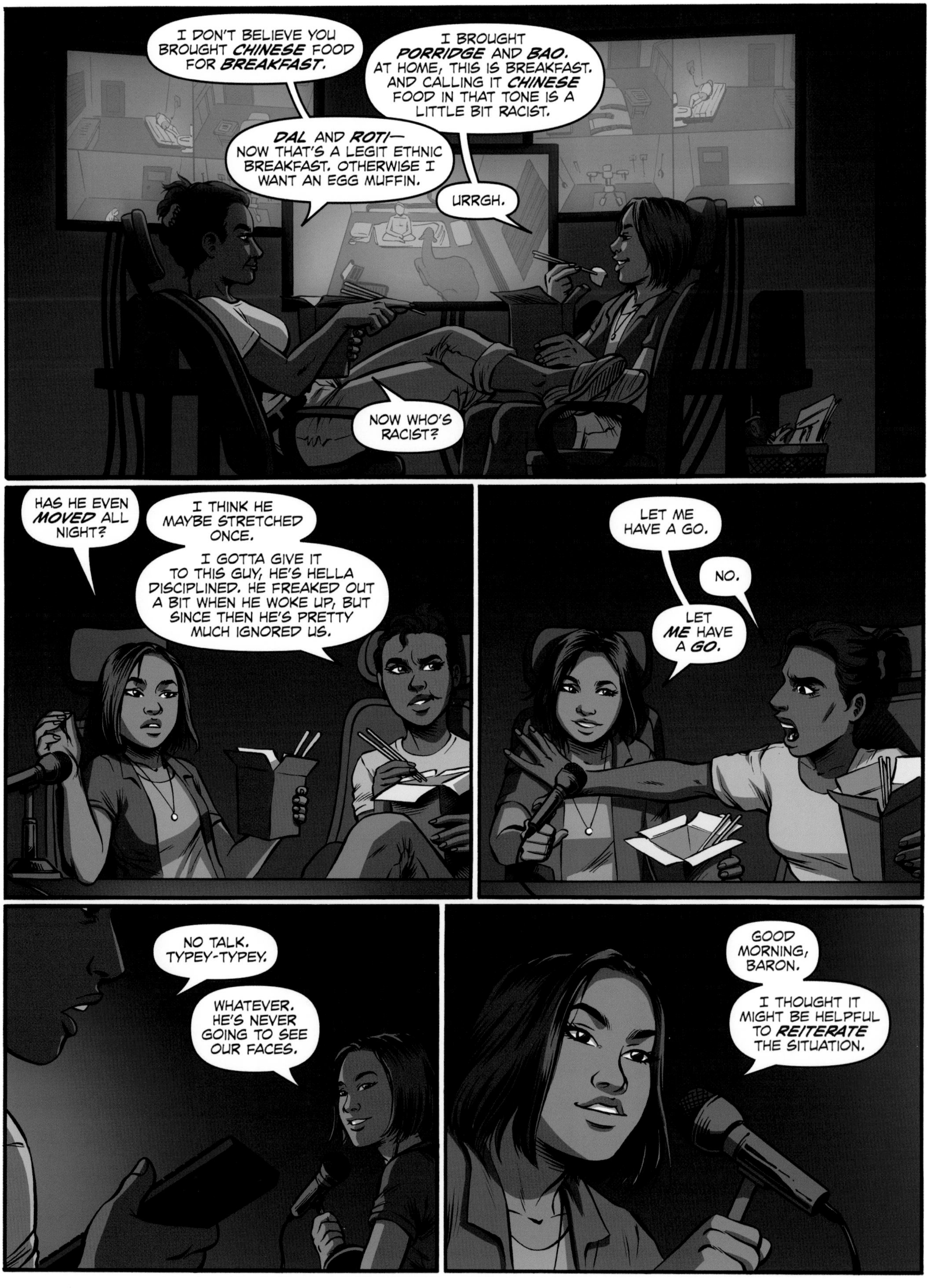
I DON'T BELIEVE YOU BROUGHT CHINESE FOOD FOR BREAKFAST.
I BROUGHT PORRIDGE AND BAO. AT HOME, THIS IS BREAKFAST. AND CALLING IT CHINESE FOOD IN THAT TONE IS A LITTLE BIT RACIST.
DAL AND ROTI— NOW THAT'S A LEGIT ETHNIC BREAKFAST. OTHERWISE I WANT AN EGG MUFFIN.
URRGH.
NOW WHO'S RACIST?
HAS HE EVEN MOVED ALL NIGHT?
I THINK HE MAYBE STRETCHED ONCE.
I GOTTA GIVE IT TO THIS GUY; HE'S HELLA DISCIPLINED. HE FREAKED OUT A BIT WHEN HE WOKE UP, BUT SINCE THEN HE'S PRETTY MUCH IGNORED US.
LET ME HAVE A GO.
NO.
LET ME HAVE A GO.
NO TALK. TYPEY-TYPEY.
WHATEVER. HE'S NEVER GOING TO SEE OUR FACES.
GOOD MORNING, BARON.
I THOUGHT IT MIGHT BE HELPFUL TO REITERATE THE SITUATION.

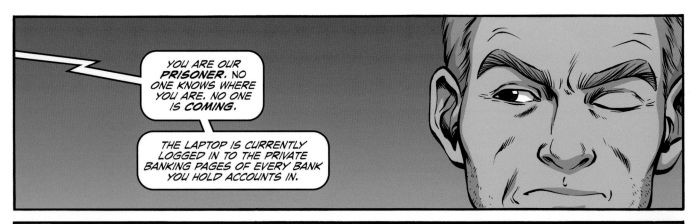

YOU ARE OUR *PRISONER*. NO ONE KNOWS WHERE YOU ARE. NO ONE IS *COMING*.

THE LAPTOP IS CURRENTLY LOGGED IN TO THE PRIVATE BANKING PAGES OF EVERY BANK YOU HOLD ACCOUNTS IN.

YOUR LIQUID OR SEMI-LIQUID ASSETS ARE CURRENTLY VALUED AT $900M. THAT'S *SOMEWHAT* SHORT OF THE $2.6 BILLION THAT YOU'VE CLAIMED AS YOUR NET-WORTH IN THE PRESS, BUT IT WILL DO FOR *STARTERS*.

SO HERE'S THE *DEAL*. TRANSFER THAT MONEY IN *$10M* CHUNKS TO OUR ACCOUNTS, AND FOR EACH TRANSFER YOU GET SOMETHING YOU WANT.

EARL GREY TEA? SMOKED KIPPERS? LIBERAL TEARS? THE SOUL OF THE OPPRESSED MASSES?

YOU DON'T PAY, NO FOOD, NO WATER, NO SOFT-TOILET PAPER, JUST YOU AND LARRY THE CAMEL, FOR AS LONG AS IT TAKES.

CLEAR, YOUR BARON-NESS? ANYTHING YOU'D LIKE FURTHER *EXPLAINED*?

NO, THAT'S PERFECTLY CLEAR. THANK YOU FOR REITERATING.

I JUST HAVE ONE QUESTION?

WHAT?

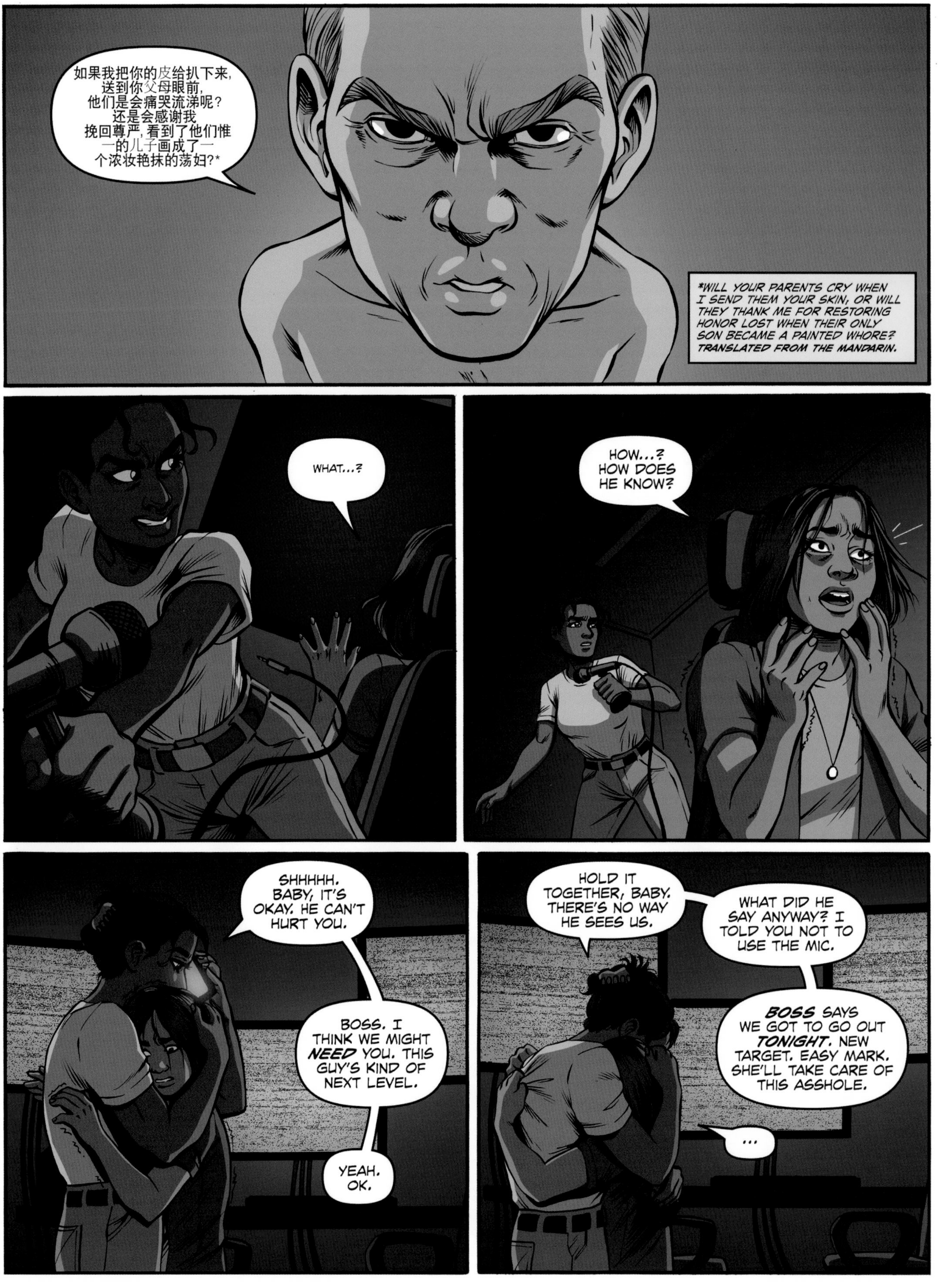
如果我把你的皮给扒下来, 送到你父母眼前, 他们是会痛哭流涕呢? 还是会感谢我 挽回尊严,看到了他们惟 一的儿子画成了一 个浓妆艳抹的荡妇?*
*WILL YOUR PARENTS CRY WHEN I SEND THEM YOUR SKIN, OR WILL THEY THANK ME FOR RESTORING HONOR LOST WHEN THEIR ONLY SON BECAME A PAINTED WHORE? TRANSLATED FROM THE MANDARIN.
WHAT...?
HOW...? HOW DOES HE KNOW?
SHHHHH. BABY, IT'S OKAY. HE CAN'T HURT YOU.
BOSS. I THINK WE MIGHT NEED YOU. THIS GUY'S KIND OF NEXT LEVEL.
YEAH. OK.
HOLD IT TOGETHER, BABY. THERE'S NO WAY HE SEES US.
WHAT DID HE SAY ANYWAY? I TOLD YOU NOT TO USE THE MIC.
BOSS SAYS WE GOT TO GO OUT TONIGHT. NEW TARGET. EASY MARK. SHE'LL TAKE CARE OF THIS ASSHOLE.
...

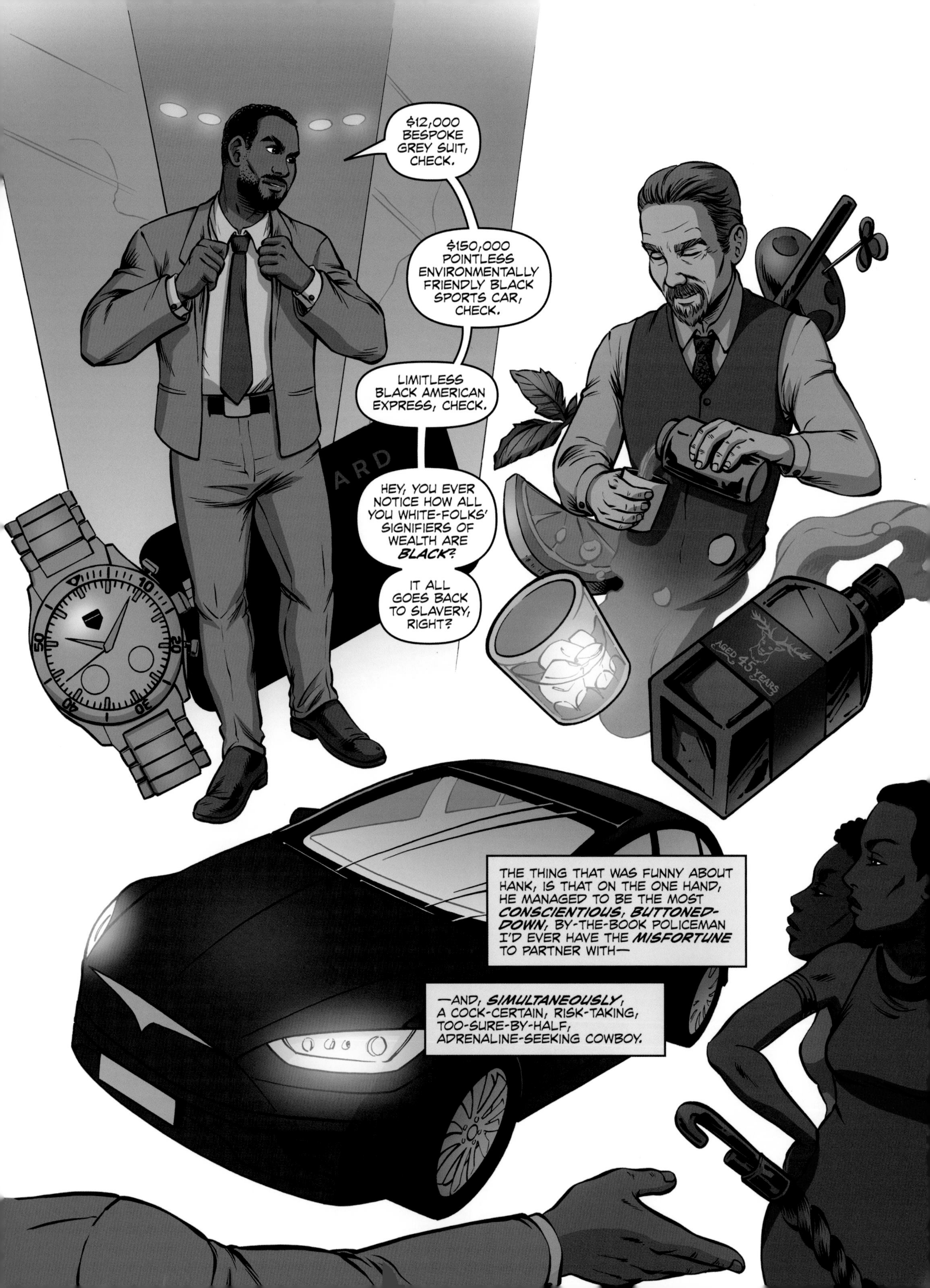
$12,000 BESPOKE GREY SUIT, CHECK.
$150,000 POINTLESS ENVIRONMENTALLY FRIENDLY BLACK SPORTS CAR, CHECK.
LIMITLESS BLACK AMERICAN EXPRESS, CHECK.
ARD
HEY, YOU EVER NOTICE HOW ALL YOU WHITE-FOLKS' SIGNIFIERS OF WEALTH ARE *BLACK*?
IT ALL GOES BACK TO SLAVERY, RIGHT?
AGED 45 YEARS
THE THING THAT WAS FUNNY ABOUT HANK, IS THAT ON THE ONE HAND, HE MANAGED TO BE THE MOST *CONSCIENTIOUS, BUTTONED-DOWN*, BY-THE-BOOK POLICEMAN I'D EVER HAVE THE *MISFORTUNE* TO PARTNER WITH—
—AND, *SIMULTANEOUSLY*, A COCK-CERTAIN, RISK-TAKING, TOO-SURE-BY-HALF, ADRENALINE-SEEKING COWBOY.

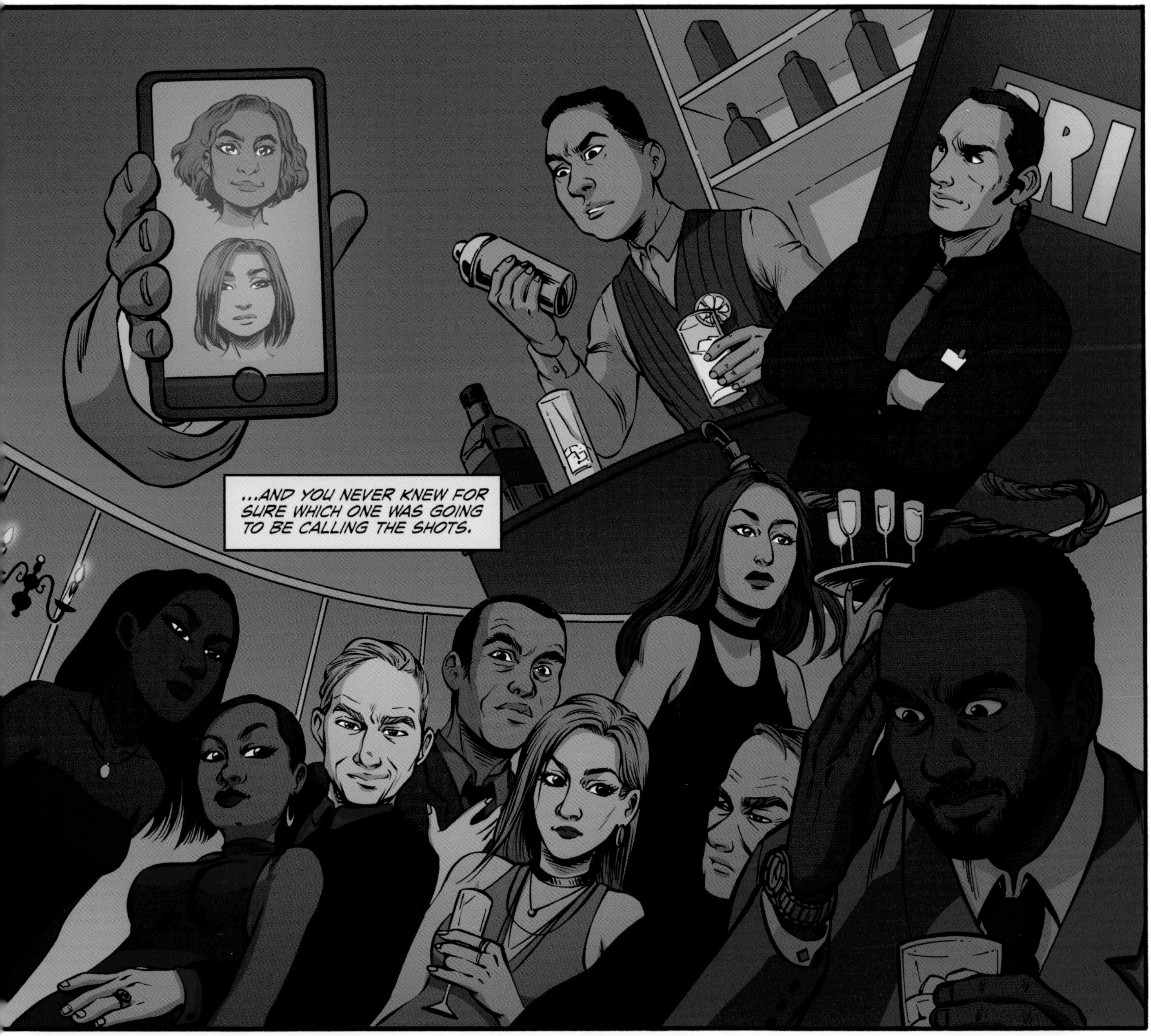
...AND YOU NEVER KNEW FOR SURE WHICH ONE WAS GOING TO BE CALLING THE SHOTS.

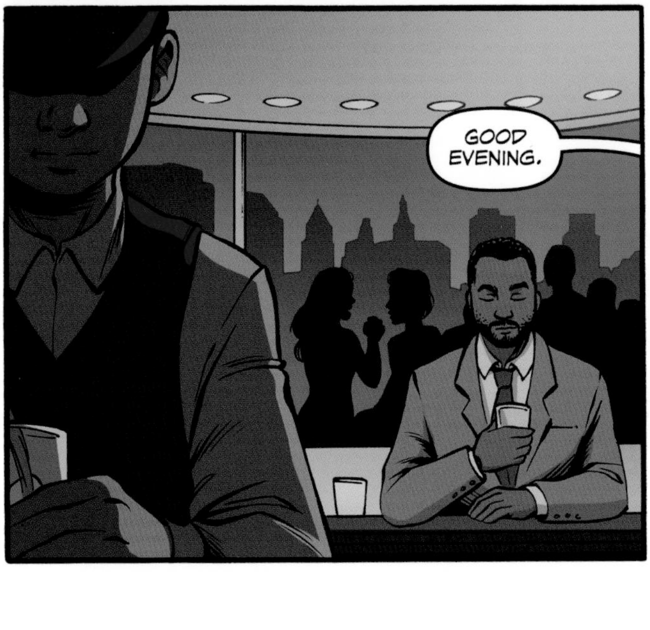
GOOD EVENING.

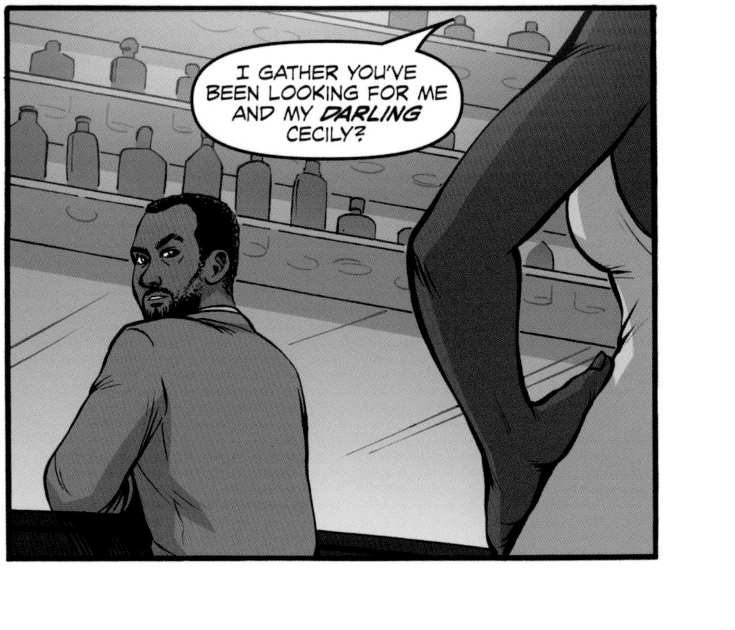
I GATHER YOU'VE BEEN LOOKING FOR ME AND MY *DARLING* CECILY?

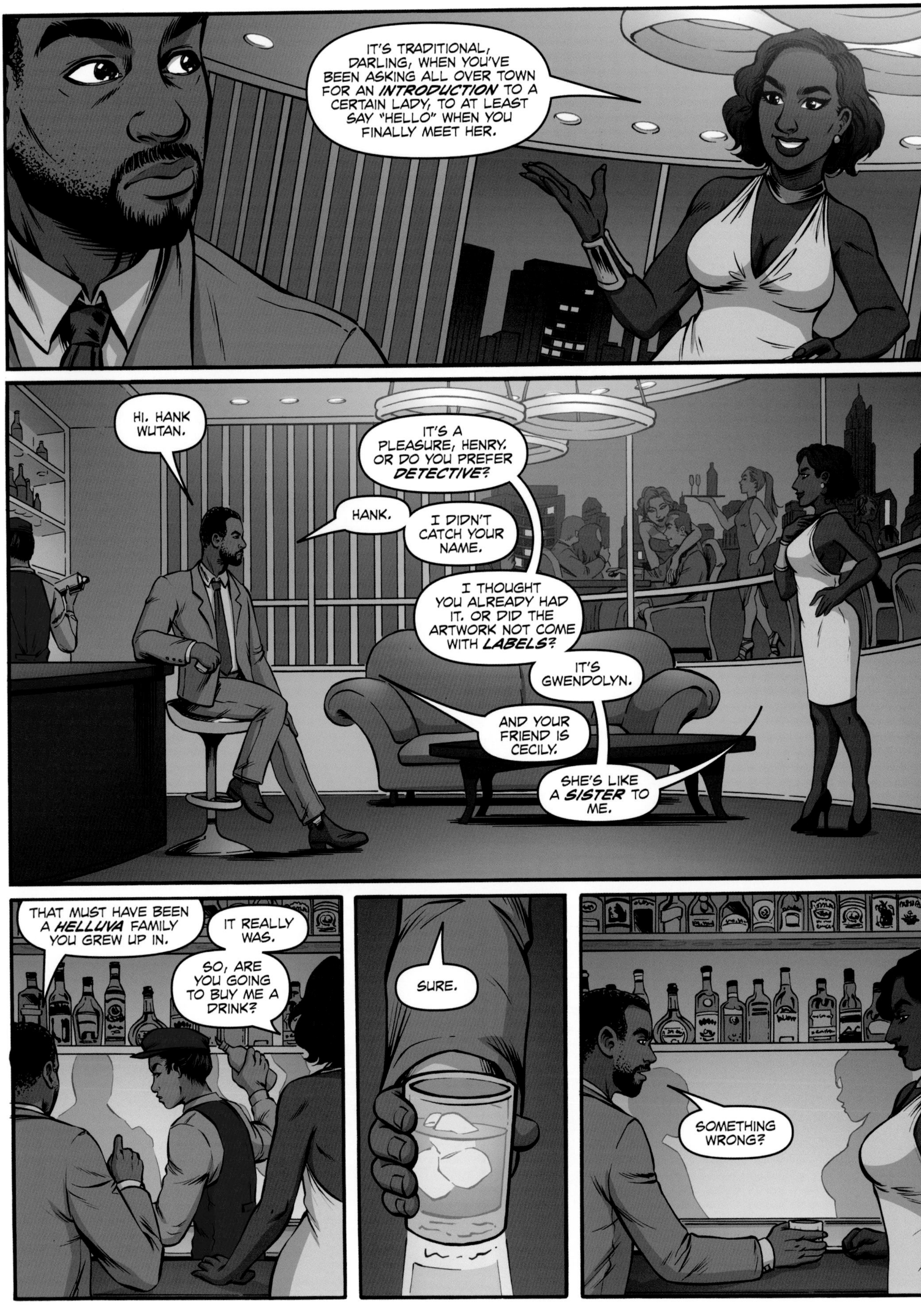
IT'S TRADITIONAL, DARLING, WHEN YOU'VE BEEN ASKING ALL OVER TOWN FOR AN *INTRODUCTION* TO A CERTAIN LADY, TO AT LEAST SAY "HELLO" WHEN YOU FINALLY MEET HER.
HI. HANK WUTAN.
IT'S A PLEASURE, HENRY. OR DO YOU PREFER *DETECTIVE*?
HANK.
I DIDN'T CATCH YOUR NAME.
I THOUGHT YOU ALREADY HAD IT. OR DID THE ARTWORK NOT COME WITH *LABELS*?
IT'S GWENDOLYN.
AND YOUR FRIEND IS CECILY.
SHE'S LIKE A *SISTER* TO ME.
THAT MUST HAVE BEEN A *HELLUVA* FAMILY YOU GREW UP IN.
IT REALLY WAS.
SO, ARE YOU GOING TO BUY ME A DRINK?
SURE.
SOMETHING WRONG?

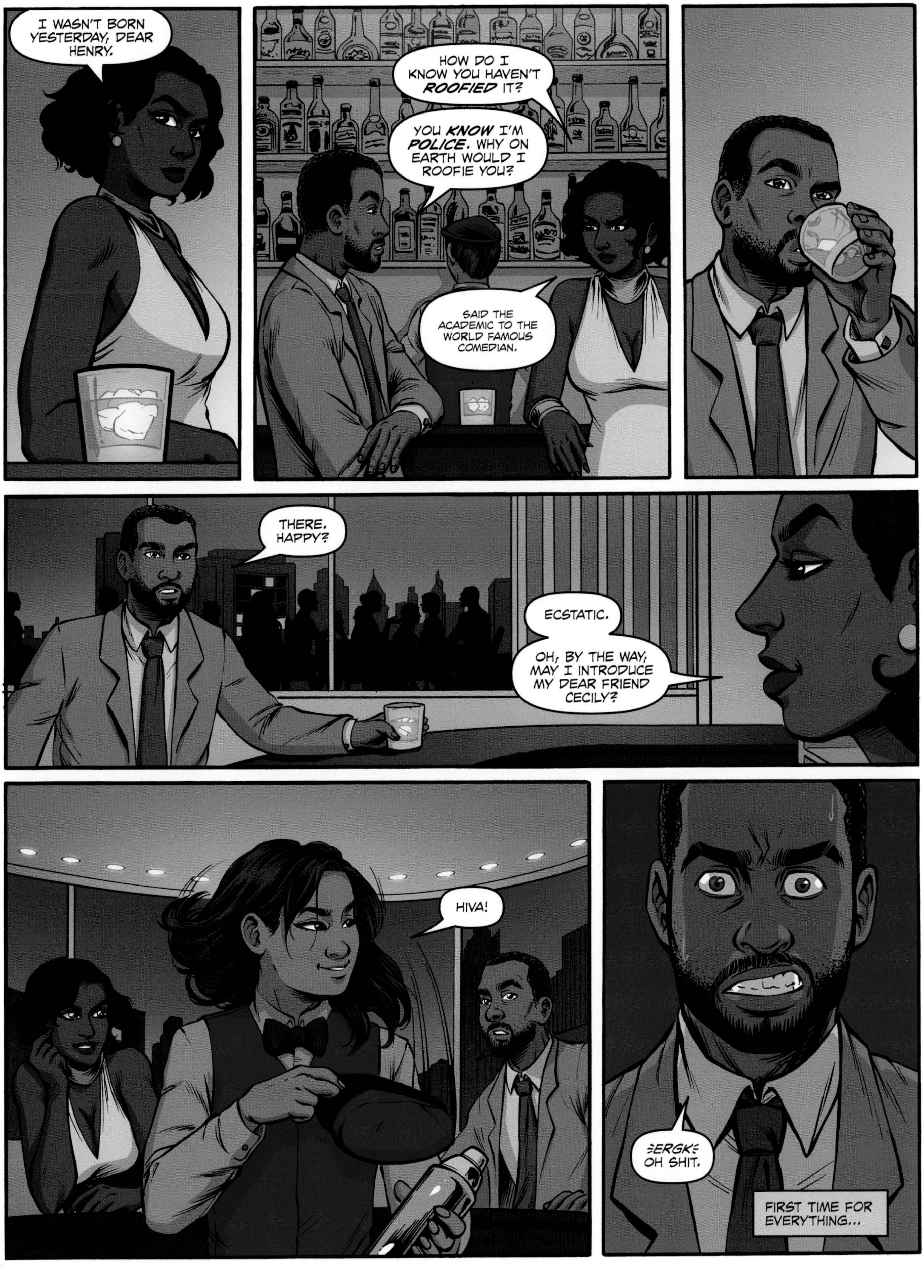
I WASN'T BORN YESTERDAY, DEAR HENRY.
HOW DO I KNOW YOU HAVEN'T ROOFIED IT?
YOU KNOW I'M POLICE. WHY ON EARTH WOULD I ROOFIE YOU?
SAID THE ACADEMIC TO THE WORLD FAMOUS COMEDIAN.
THERE. HAPPY?
ECSTATIC.
OH, BY THE WAY, MAY I INTRODUCE MY DEAR FRIEND CECILY?
HIYA!
ERGK OH SHIT.
FIRST TIME FOR EVERYTHING...

...AND THIS WAS MY FIRST TIME GETTING ROOFIED.
IF YOUR PLAN IS *TORTURE*, YOU'RE GOING TO FIND I HAVE A PRETTY HIGH PAIN THRESHOLD.
OH DETECTIVE, HOW *MELODRAMATIC*.
WHY ON EARTH WOULD I TORTURE YOU? WHAT COULD YOU POSSIBLY KNOW THAT I DON'T?
YOU'RE LOOKING FOR *ME*, REMEMBER?

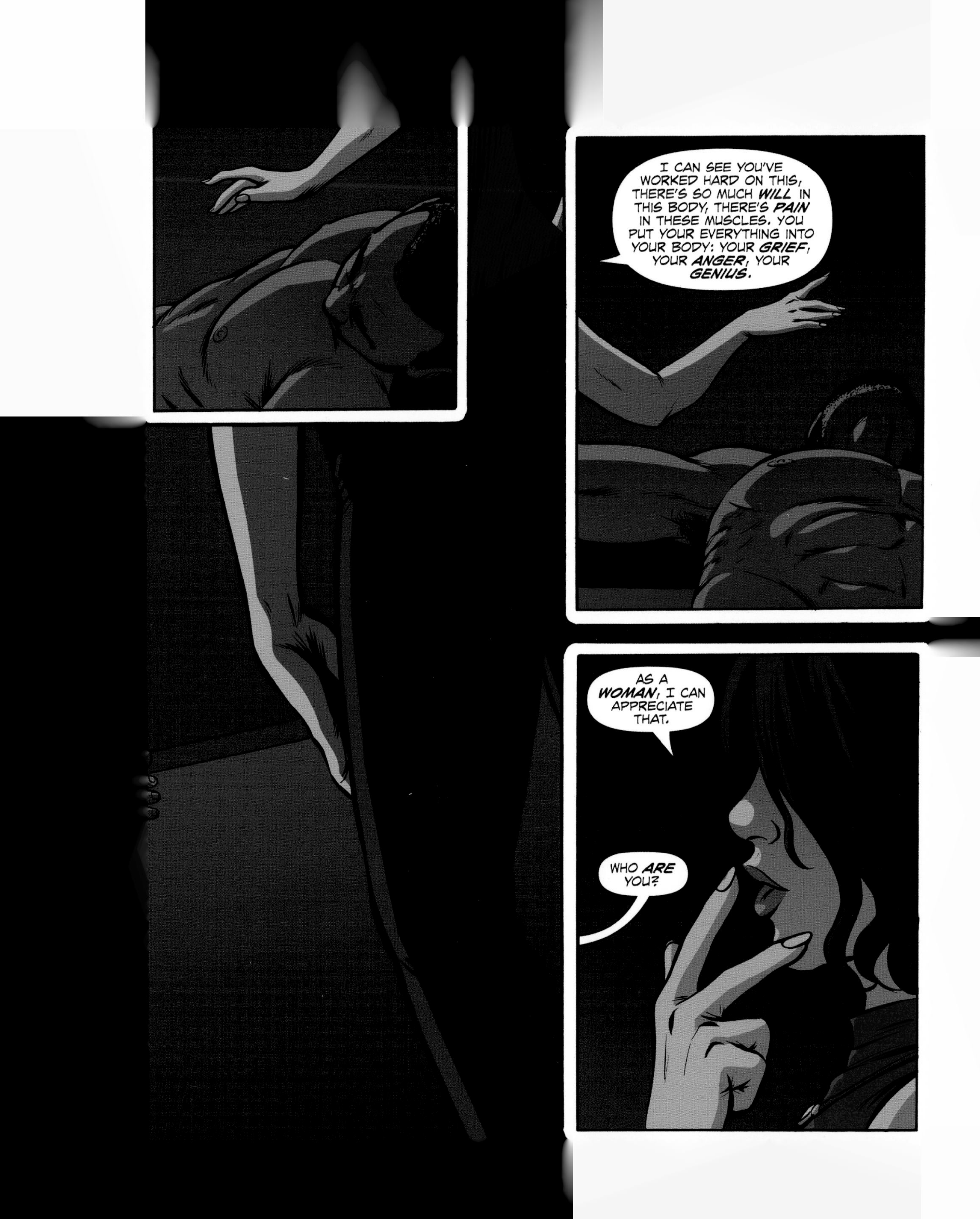
I CAN SEE YOU'VE WORKED HARD ON THIS, THERE'S SO MUCH WILL IN THIS BODY, THERE'S PAIN IN THESE MUSCLES. YOU PUT YOUR EVERYTHING INTO YOUR BODY: YOUR GRIEF, YOUR ANGER, YOUR GENIUS.
AS A WOMAN, I CAN APPRECIATE THAT.
WHO ARE YOU?

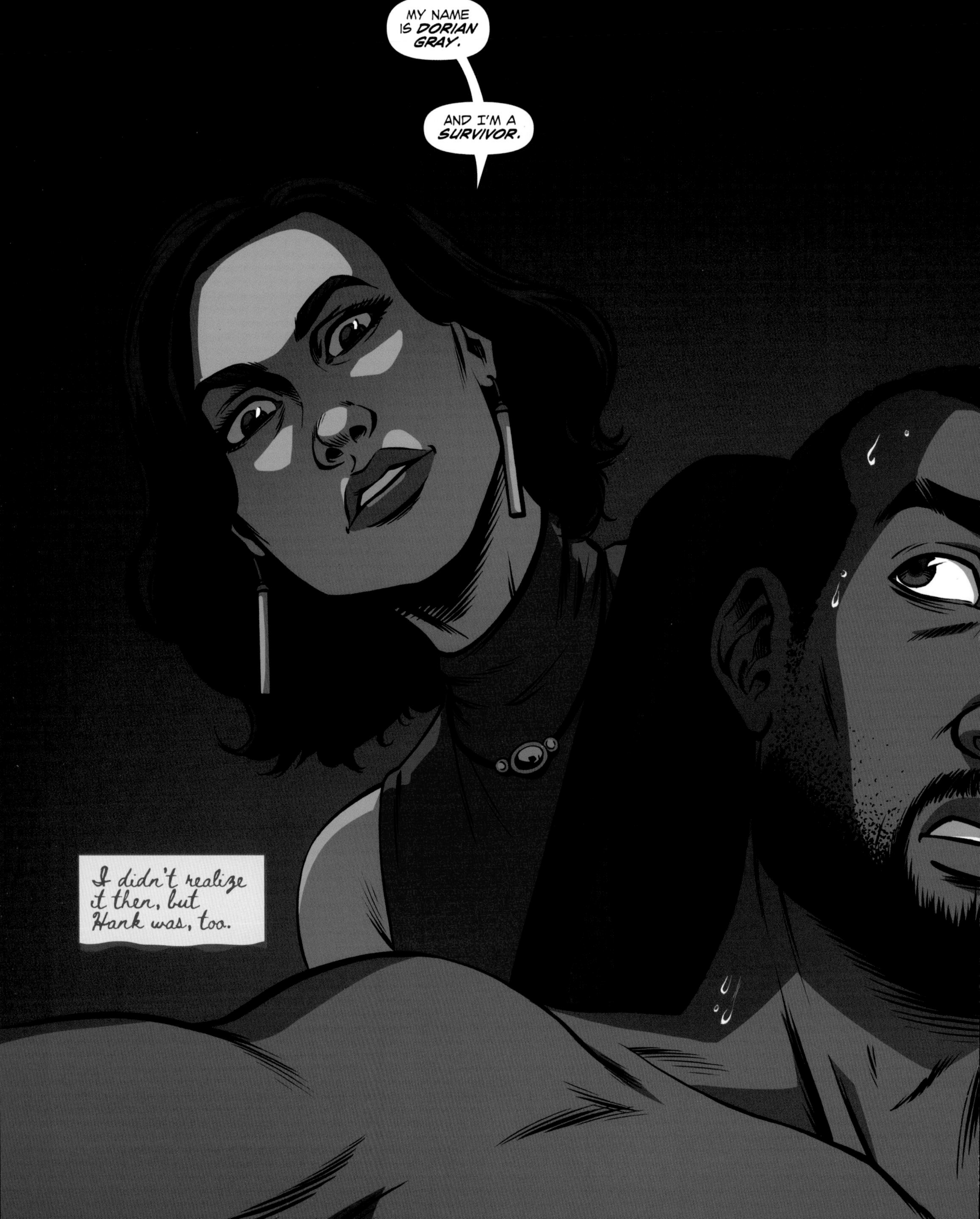
MY NAME IS DORIAN GRAY.
AND I'M A SURVIVOR.
I didn't realize it then, but Hank was, too.

Chapter 3

"All women become like their mothers. That is their tragedy. No man does, and that is his."

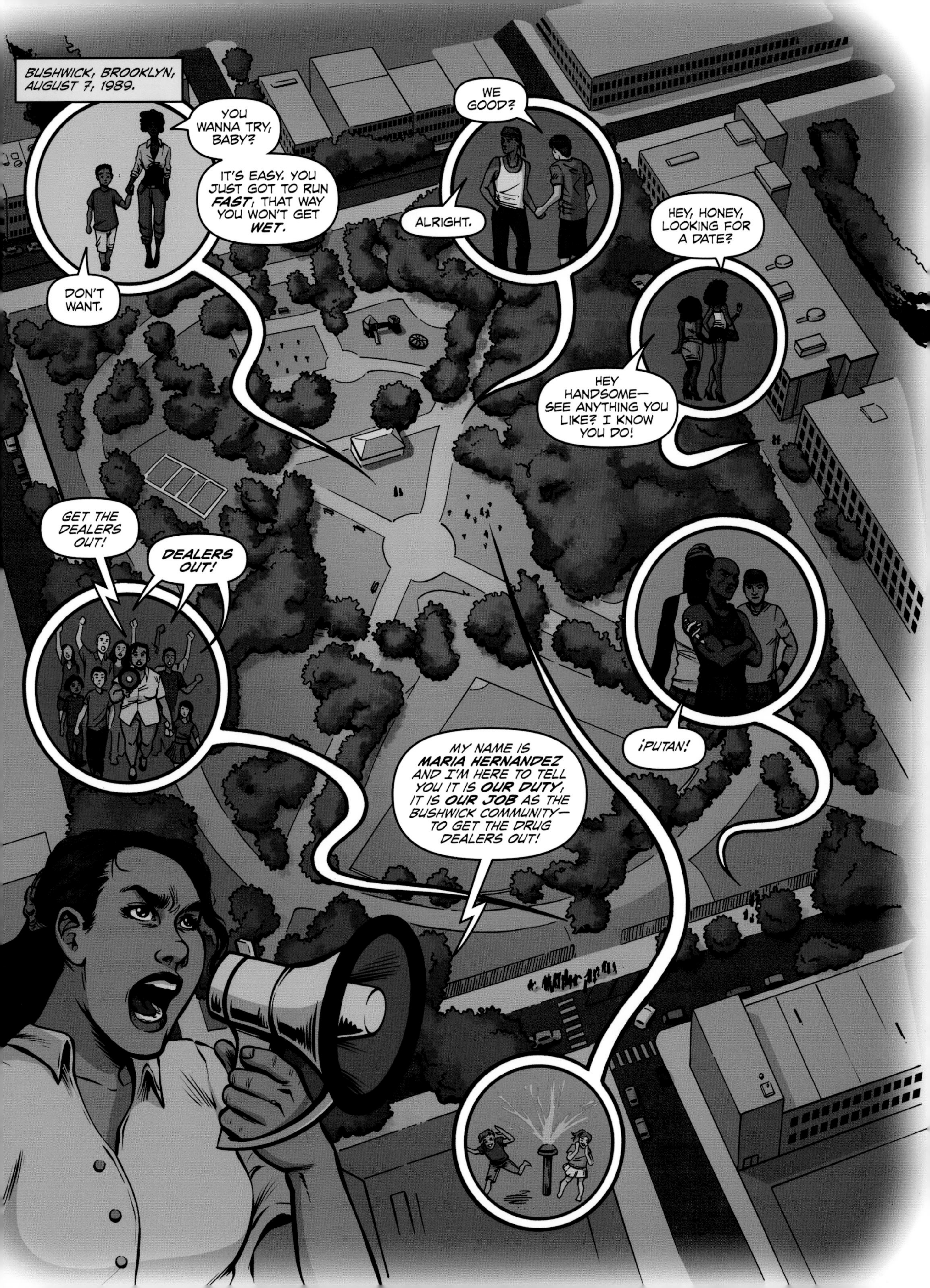
BUSHWICK, BROOKLYN, AUGUST 7, 1989.
YOU WANNA TRY, BABY?
IT'S EASY. YOU JUST GOT TO RUN FAST, THAT WAY YOU WON'T GET WET.
DON'T WANT.
WE GOOD?
ALRIGHT.
HEY, HONEY, LOOKING FOR A DATE?
HEY HANDSOME— SEE ANYTHING YOU LIKE? I KNOW YOU DO!
GET THE DEALERS OUT!
DEALERS OUT!
¡PUTAN!
MY NAME IS MARIA HERNANDEZ AND I'M HERE TO TELL YOU IT IS OUR DUTY, IT IS OUR JOB AS THE BUSHWICK COMMUNITY— TO GET THE DRUG DEALERS OUT!

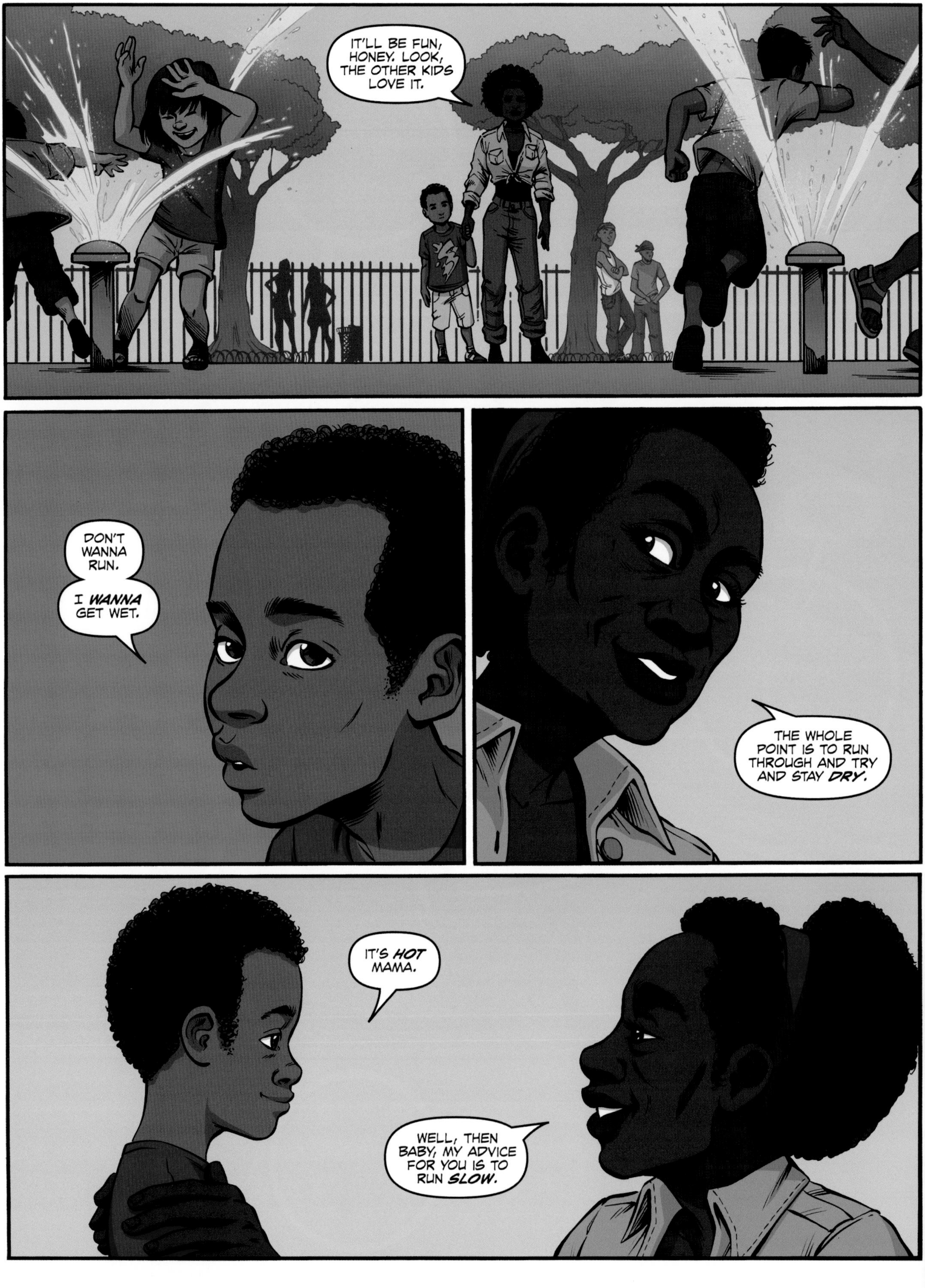
IT'LL BE FUN, HONEY. LOOK, THE OTHER KIDS LOVE IT.
DON'T WANNA RUN.
I *WANNA* GET WET.
THE WHOLE POINT IS TO RUN THROUGH AND TRY AND STAY *DRY*.
IT'S *HOT* MAMA.
WELL, THEN BABY, MY ADVICE FOR YOU IS TO RUN *SLOW*.

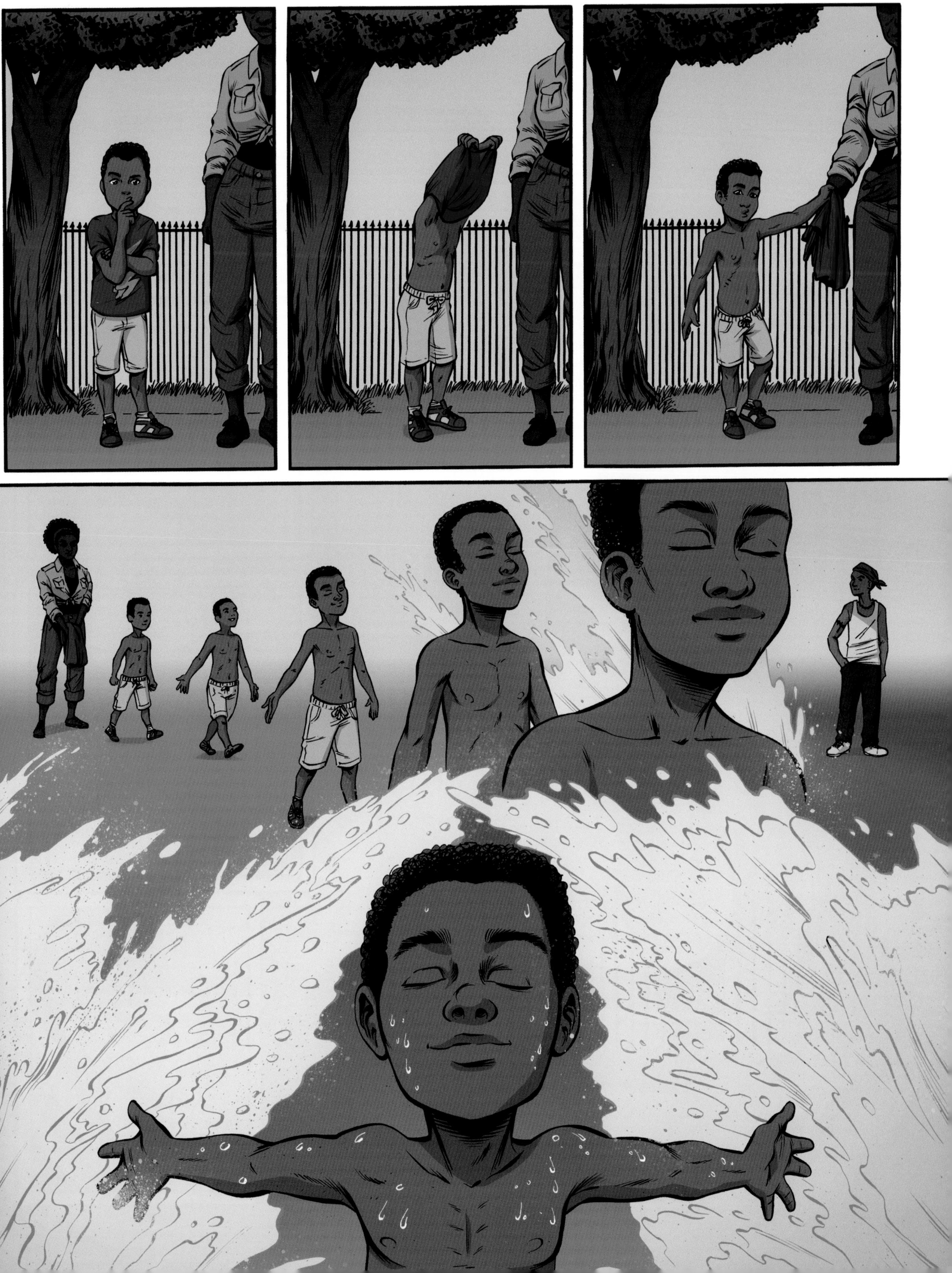

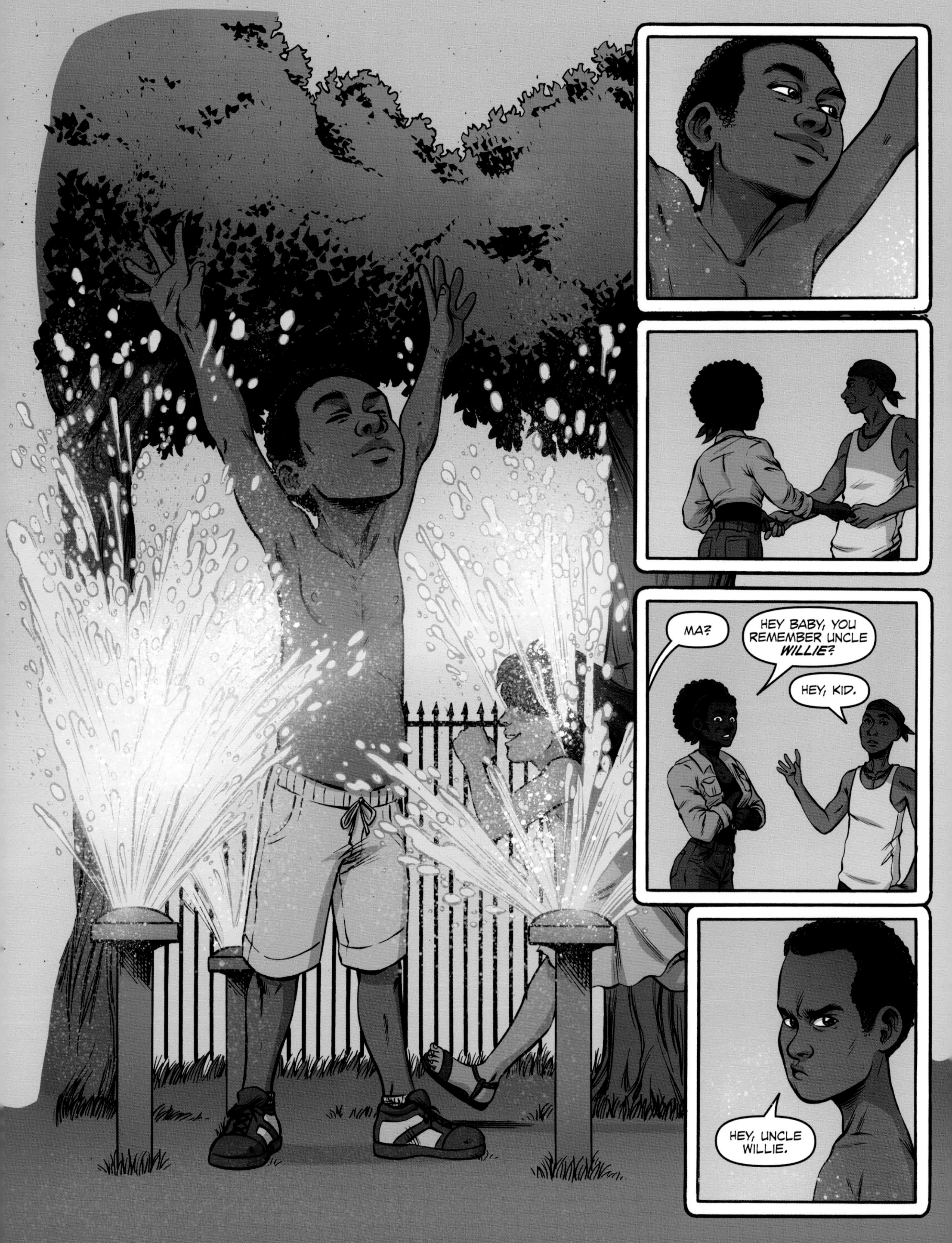
MA?
HEY BABY, YOU REMEMBER UNCLE WILLIE?
HEY, KID.
HEY, UNCLE WILLIE.

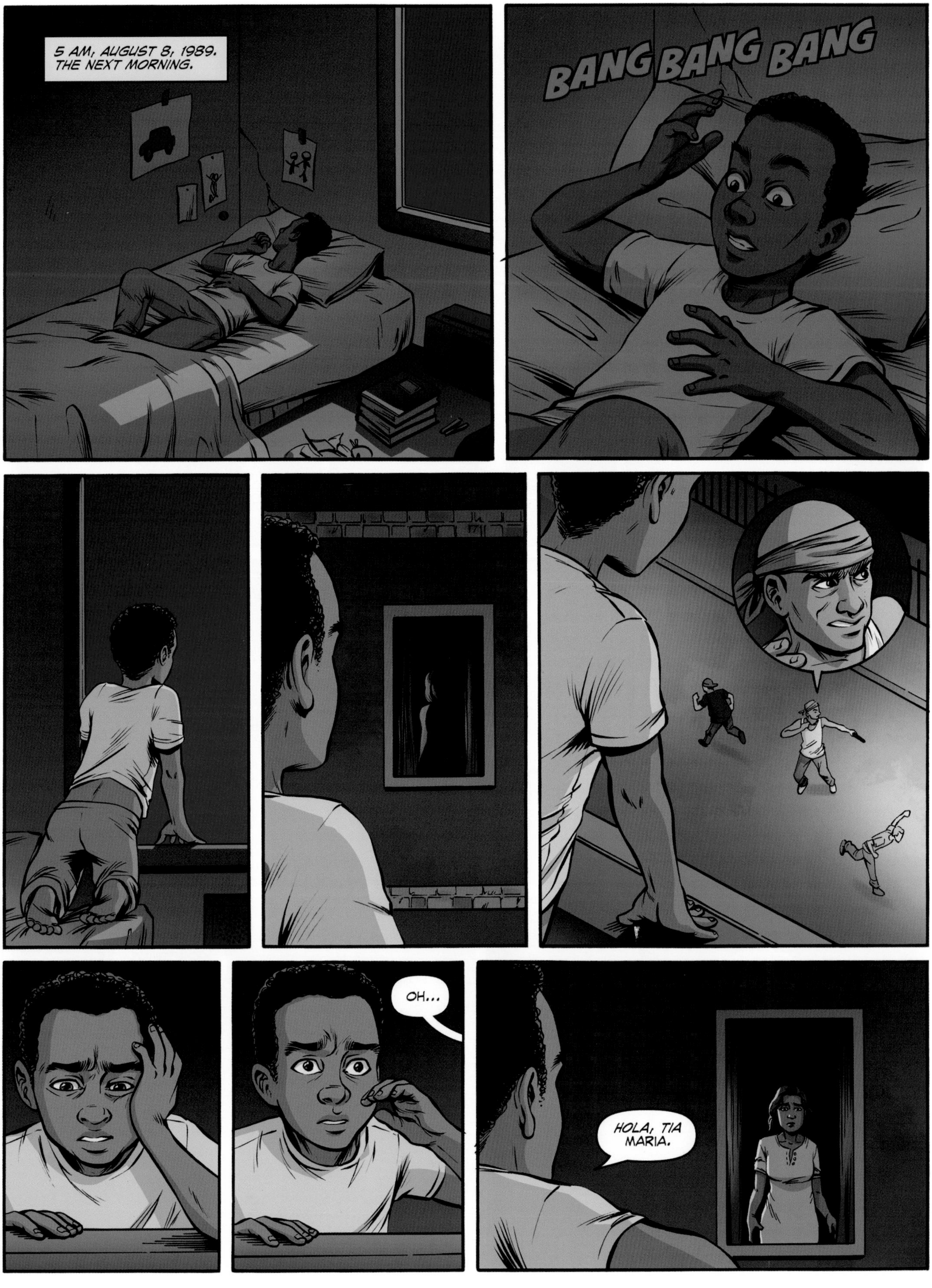
5 AM, AUGUST 8, 1989.
THE NEXT MORNING.
BANG BANG BANG
OH...
HOLA, TIA MARIA.

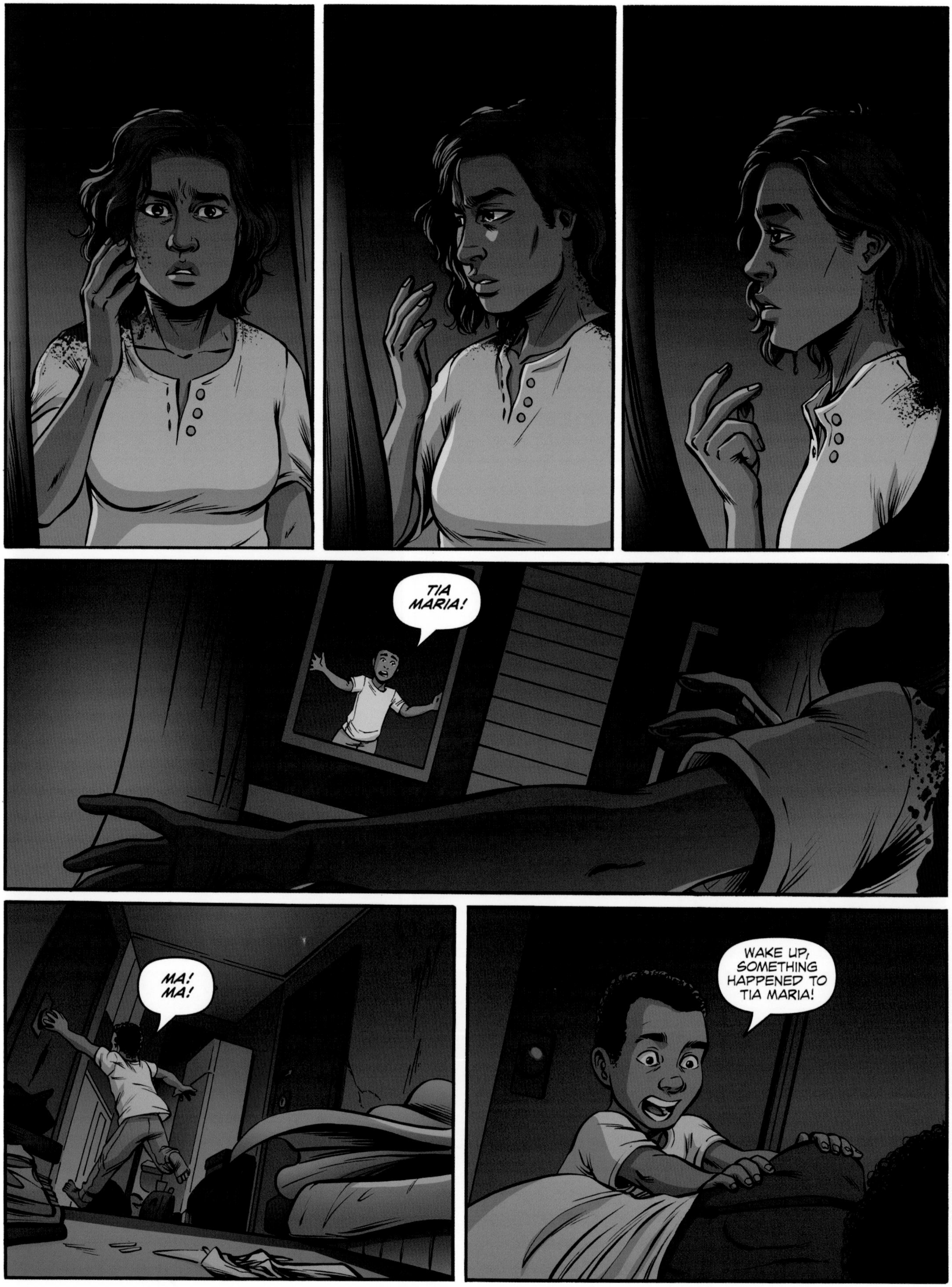
TIA MARIA!
MA! MA!
WAKE UP, SOMETHING HAPPENED TO TIA MARIA!

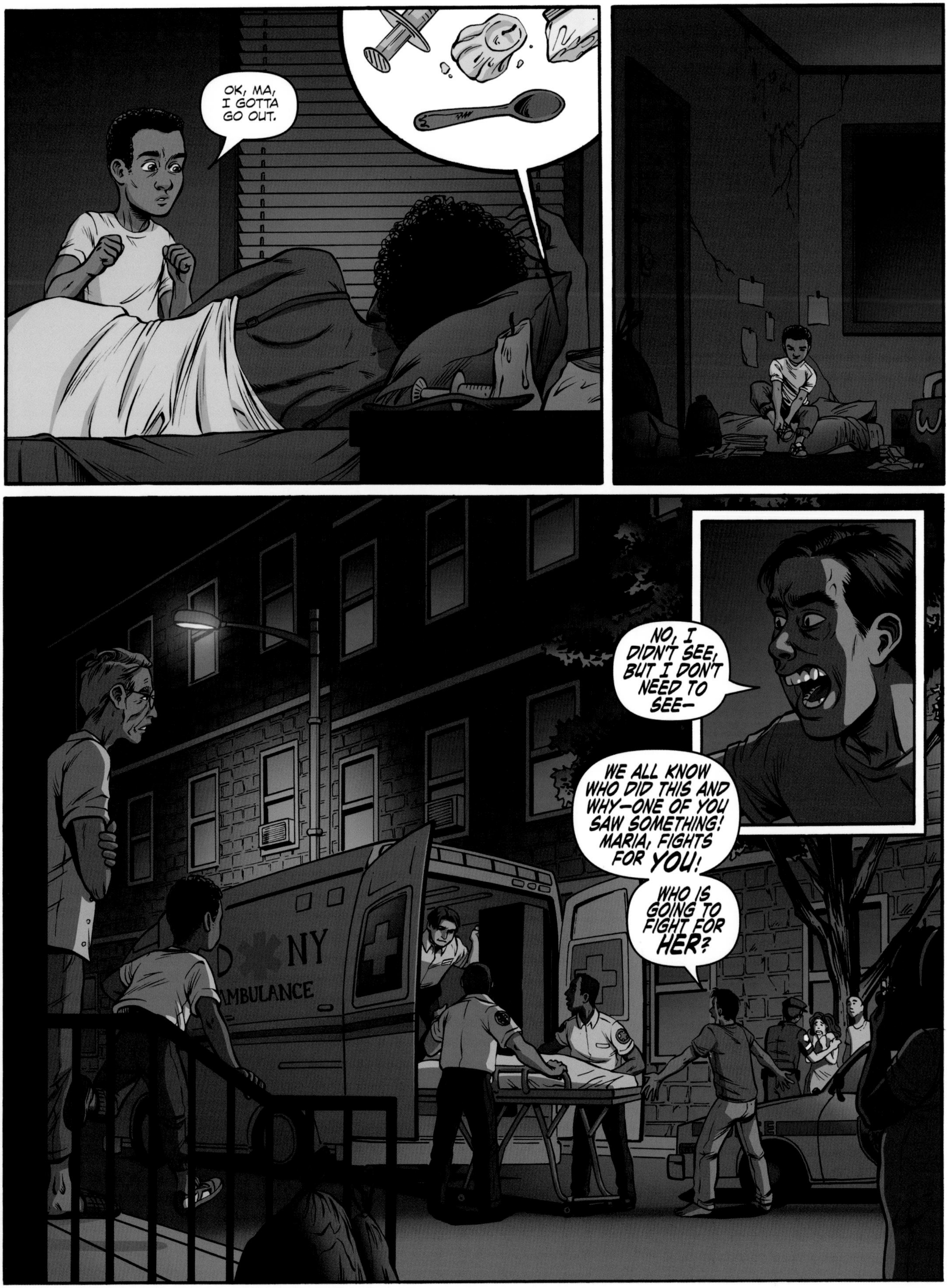
OK, MA, I GOTTA GO OUT.
NO, I DIDN'T SEE, BUT I DON'T NEED TO SEE—
WE ALL KNOW WHO DID THIS AND WHY—ONE OF YOU SAW SOMETHING! MARIA, FIGHTS FOR YOU!
WHO IS GOING TO FIGHT FOR HER?
NY
AMBULANCE

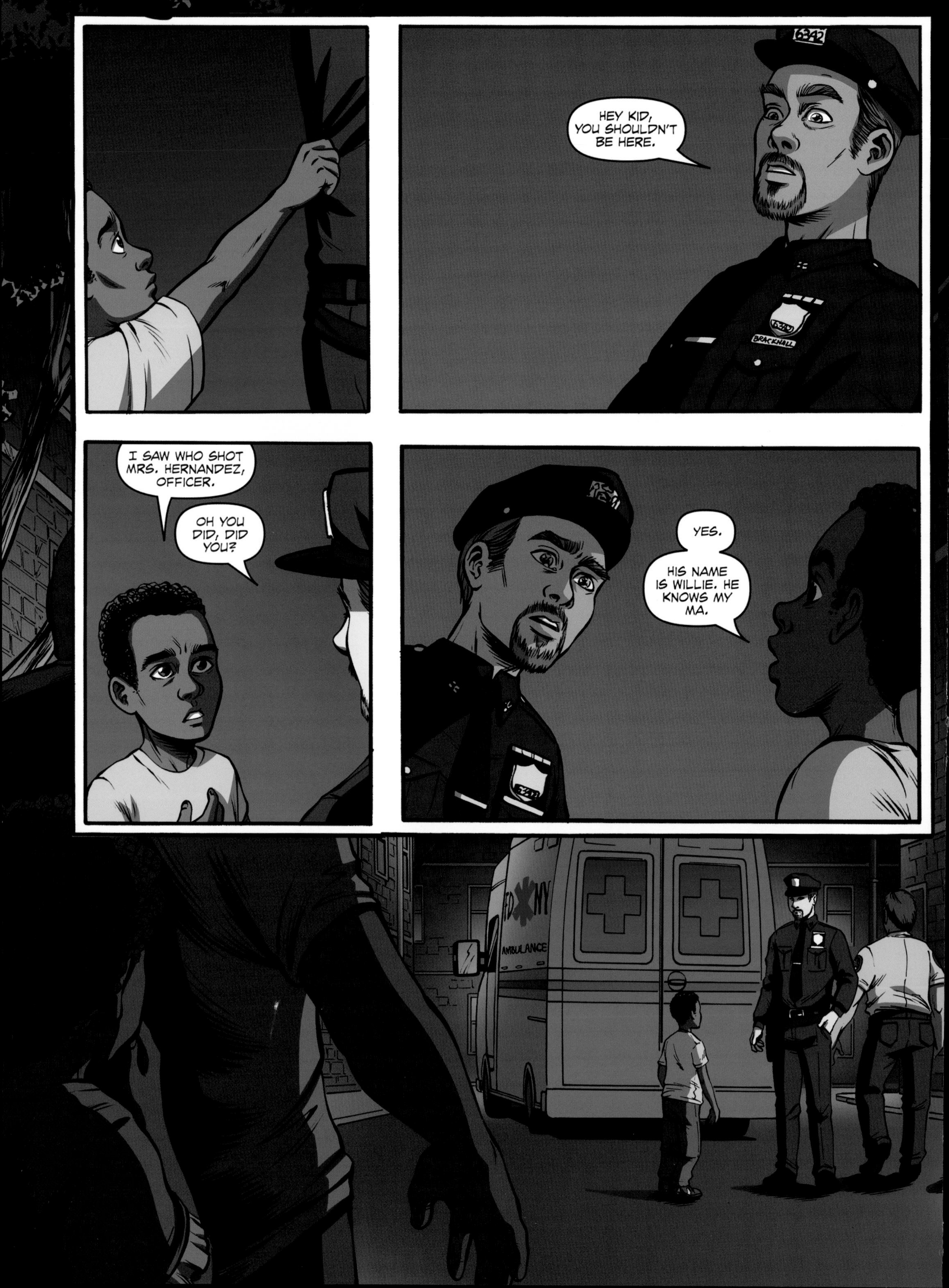
HEY KID, YOU SHOULDN'T BE HERE.
BRACKNALL
I SAW WHO SHOT MRS. HERNANDEZ, OFFICER.
OH YOU DID, DID YOU?
YES.
HIS NAME IS WILLIE. HE KNOWS MY MA.
AMBULANCE

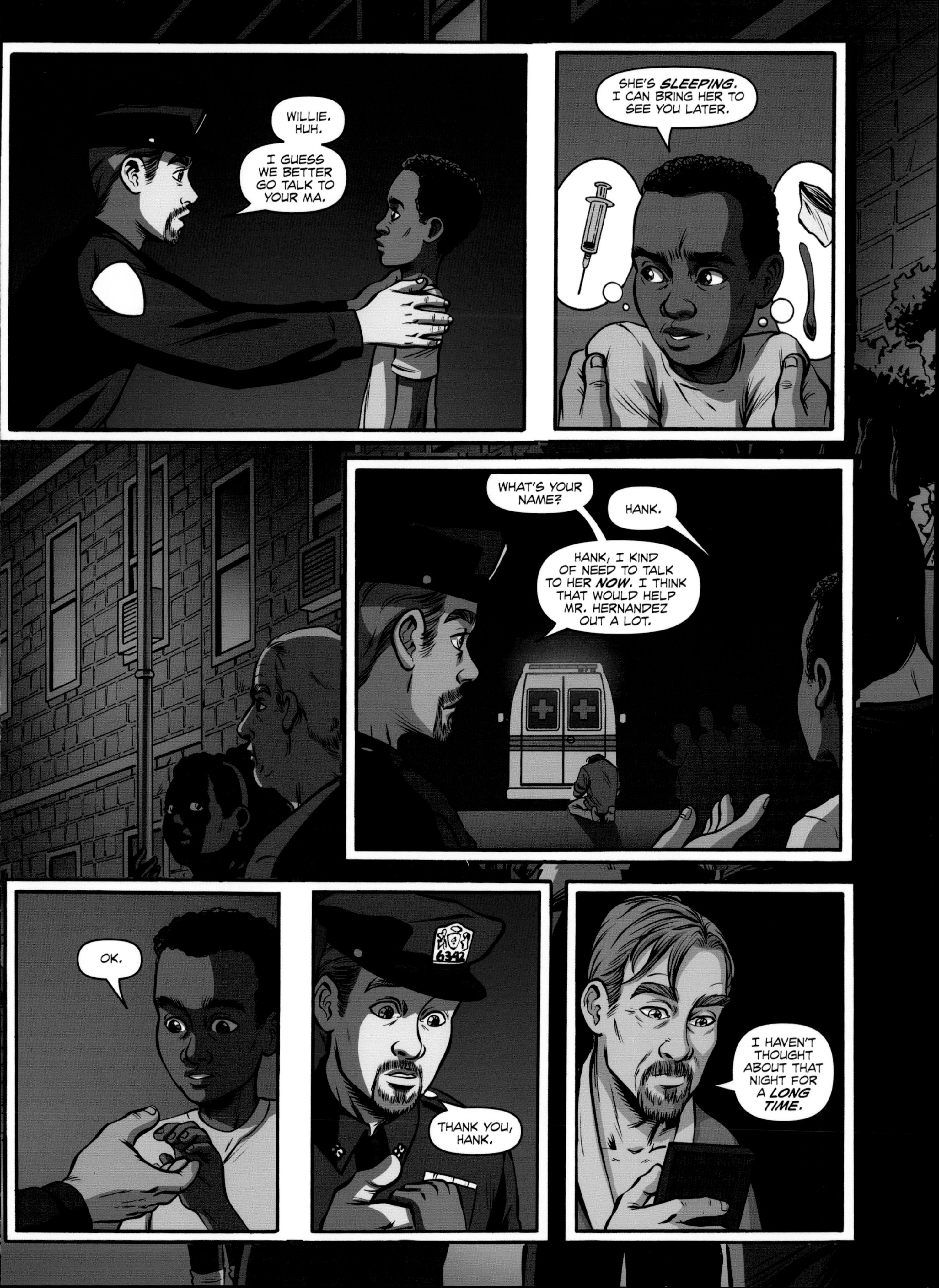
WILLIE. HUH.
I GUESS WE BETTER GO TALK TO YOUR MA.
SHE'S *SLEEPING*. I CAN BRING HER TO SEE YOU LATER.
WHAT'S YOUR NAME?
HANK.
HANK, I KIND OF NEED TO TALK TO HER *NOW*. I THINK THAT WOULD HELP MR. HERNANDEZ OUT A LOT.
OK.
6342
THANK YOU, HANK.
I HAVEN'T THOUGHT ABOUT THAT NIGHT FOR A *LONG TIME*.

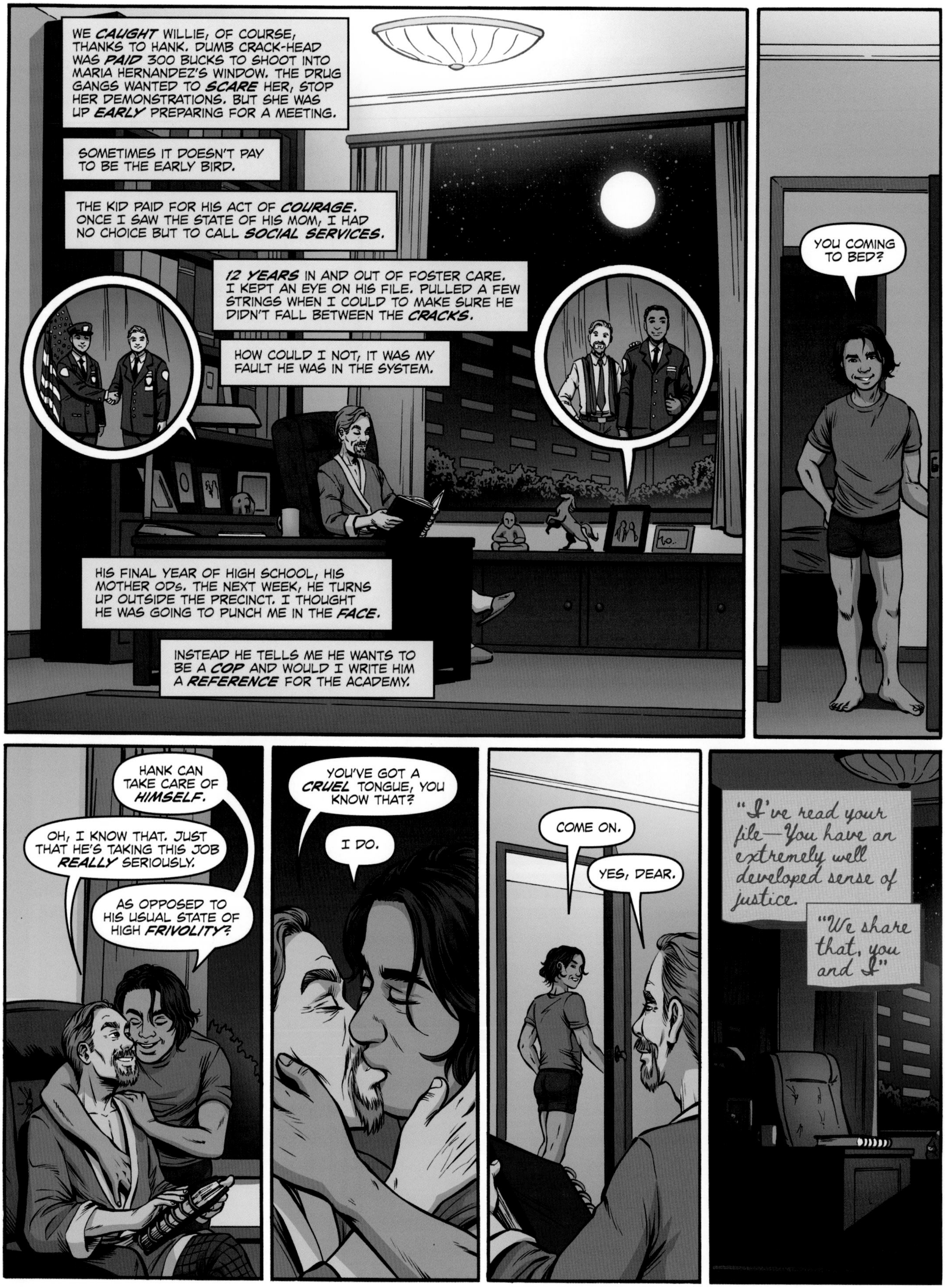

WE CAUGHT WILLIE, OF COURSE, THANKS TO HANK. DUMB CRACK-HEAD WAS PAID 300 BUCKS TO SHOOT INTO MARIA HERNANDEZ'S WINDOW. THE DRUG GANGS WANTED TO SCARE HER, STOP HER DEMONSTRATIONS. BUT SHE WAS UP EARLY PREPARING FOR A MEETING.
SOMETIMES IT DOESN'T PAY TO BE THE EARLY BIRD.
THE KID PAID FOR HIS ACT OF COURAGE. ONCE I SAW THE STATE OF HIS MOM, I HAD NO CHOICE BUT TO CALL SOCIAL SERVICES.
12 YEARS IN AND OUT OF FOSTER CARE. I KEPT AN EYE ON HIS FILE. PULLED A FEW STRINGS WHEN I COULD TO MAKE SURE HE DIDN'T FALL BETWEEN THE CRACKS.
HOW COULD I NOT, IT WAS MY FAULT HE WAS IN THE SYSTEM.
HIS FINAL YEAR OF HIGH SCHOOL, HIS MOTHER ODS. THE NEXT WEEK, HE TURNS UP OUTSIDE THE PRECINCT. I THOUGHT HE WAS GOING TO PUNCH ME IN THE FACE.
INSTEAD HE TELLS ME HE WANTS TO BE A COP AND WOULD I WRITE HIM A REFERENCE FOR THE ACADEMY.
YOU COMING TO BED?
HANK CAN TAKE CARE OF HIMSELF.
OH, I KNOW THAT. JUST THAT HE'S TAKING THIS JOB REALLY SERIOUSLY.
AS OPPOSED TO HIS USUAL STATE OF HIGH FRIVOLITY?
YOU'VE GOT A CRUEL TONGUE, YOU KNOW THAT?
I DO.
COME ON.
YES, DEAR.
"I've read your file—You have an extremely well developed sense of justice.
"We share that, you and I"

REALLY DETECTIVE, YOU SHOULD BE MY ALLY, NOT MY ADVERSARY.
HOW'D YOU FIGURE THAT? I'M A COP, YOU'RE SOME KIND OF CROOK.
ENGLISH ACCENT. EXPENSIVE CLOTHES. SHE'S THE BOSS.
YOU FANCY YOURSELF SOME KIND OF FEMINIST CRUSADER? A ME TOO BATWOMAN, THAT IT?
YOU FIGURE 'CAUSE THESE GUYS ARE ASSHOLES, YOU CAN DO WHAT YOU LIKE TO THEM?
THAT'S NOT JUSTICE, THAT'S REVENGE.
PO-TAE-TO, PO-TA-TO.
YOU THINK THE AMERICAN LEGAL SYSTEM PROVIDES JUSTICE, THEN? EQUAL PROTECTION AND ALL THAT JAZZ?
OUR SYSTEM ISN'T PERFECT, BUT IT'S WHAT WE'VE GOT. YOUR WAY IS CHAOS AND MOB-LAW.
SOME SORT OF SEDATIVE IN THE IV. NEED TO GET IT OUT.
DETECTIVE, THIS IS ALREADY CHAOS...

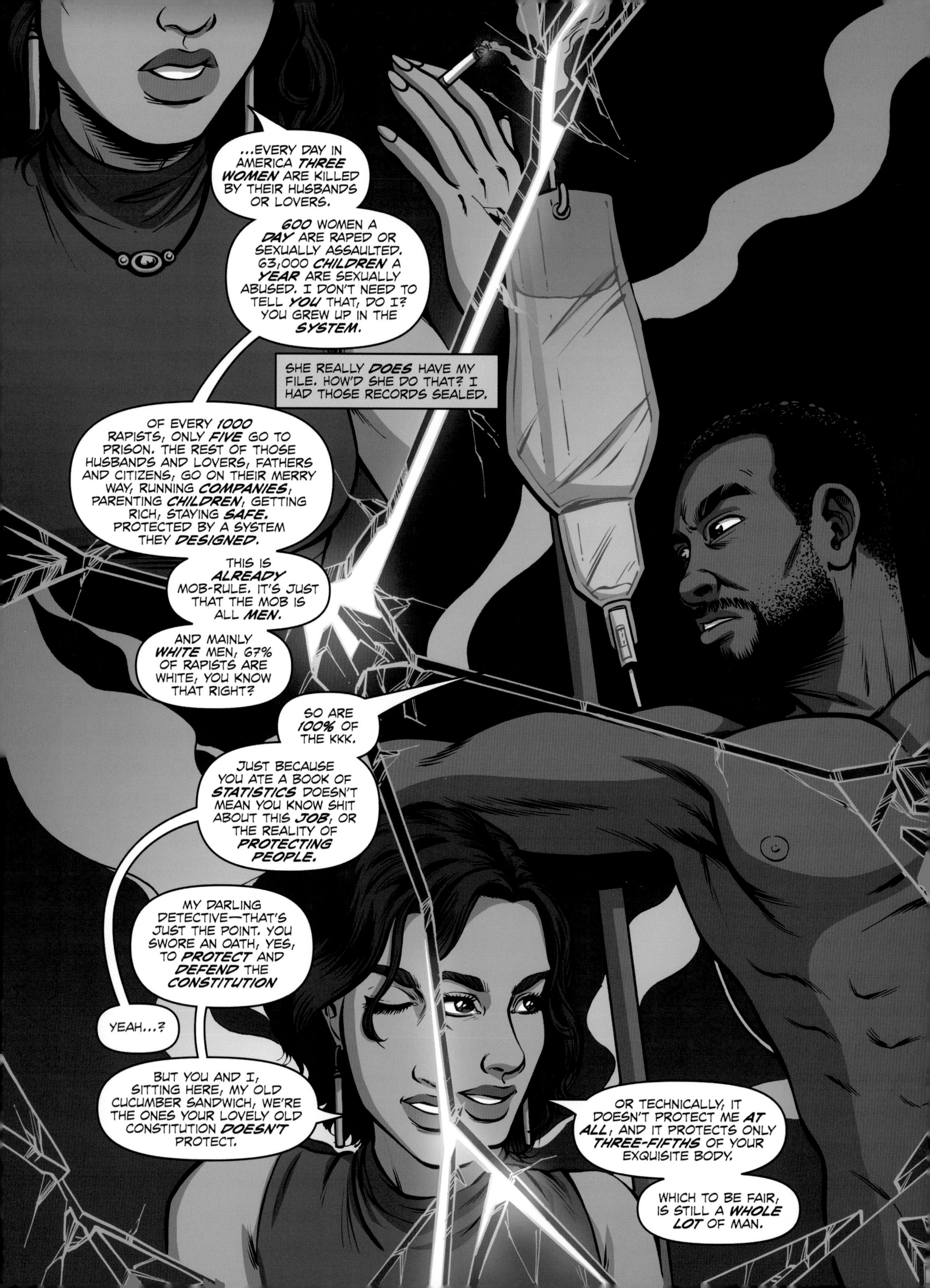

...EVERY DAY IN AMERICA THREE WOMEN ARE KILLED BY THEIR HUSBANDS OR LOVERS.
600 WOMEN A DAY ARE RAPED OR SEXUALLY ASSAULTED. 63,000 CHILDREN A YEAR ARE SEXUALLY ABUSED. I DON'T NEED TO TELL YOU THAT, DO I? YOU GREW UP IN THE SYSTEM.
SHE REALLY DOES HAVE MY FILE. HOW'D SHE DO THAT? I HAD THOSE RECORDS SEALED.
OF EVERY 1000 RAPISTS, ONLY FIVE GO TO PRISON. THE REST OF THOSE HUSBANDS AND LOVERS, FATHERS AND CITIZENS, GO ON THEIR MERRY WAY, RUNNING COMPANIES, PARENTING CHILDREN, GETTING RICH, STAYING SAFE. PROTECTED BY A SYSTEM THEY DESIGNED.
THIS IS ALREADY MOB-RULE. IT'S JUST THAT THE MOB IS ALL MEN.
AND MAINLY WHITE MEN, 67% OF RAPISTS ARE WHITE, YOU KNOW THAT RIGHT?
SO ARE 100% OF THE KKK.
JUST BECAUSE YOU ATE A BOOK OF STATISTICS DOESN'T MEAN YOU KNOW SHIT ABOUT THIS JOB, OR THE REALITY OF PROTECTING PEOPLE.
MY DARLING DETECTIVE—THAT'S JUST THE POINT. YOU SWORE AN OATH, YES, TO PROTECT AND DEFEND THE CONSTITUTION
YEAH...?
BUT YOU AND I, SITTING HERE, MY OLD CUCUMBER SANDWICH, WE'RE THE ONES YOUR LOVELY OLD CONSTITUTION DOESN'T PROTECT.
OR TECHNICALLY, IT DOESN'T PROTECT ME AT ALL, AND IT PROTECTS ONLY THREE-FIFTHS OF YOUR EXQUISITE BODY.
WHICH TO BE FAIR, IS STILL A WHOLE LOT OF MAN.

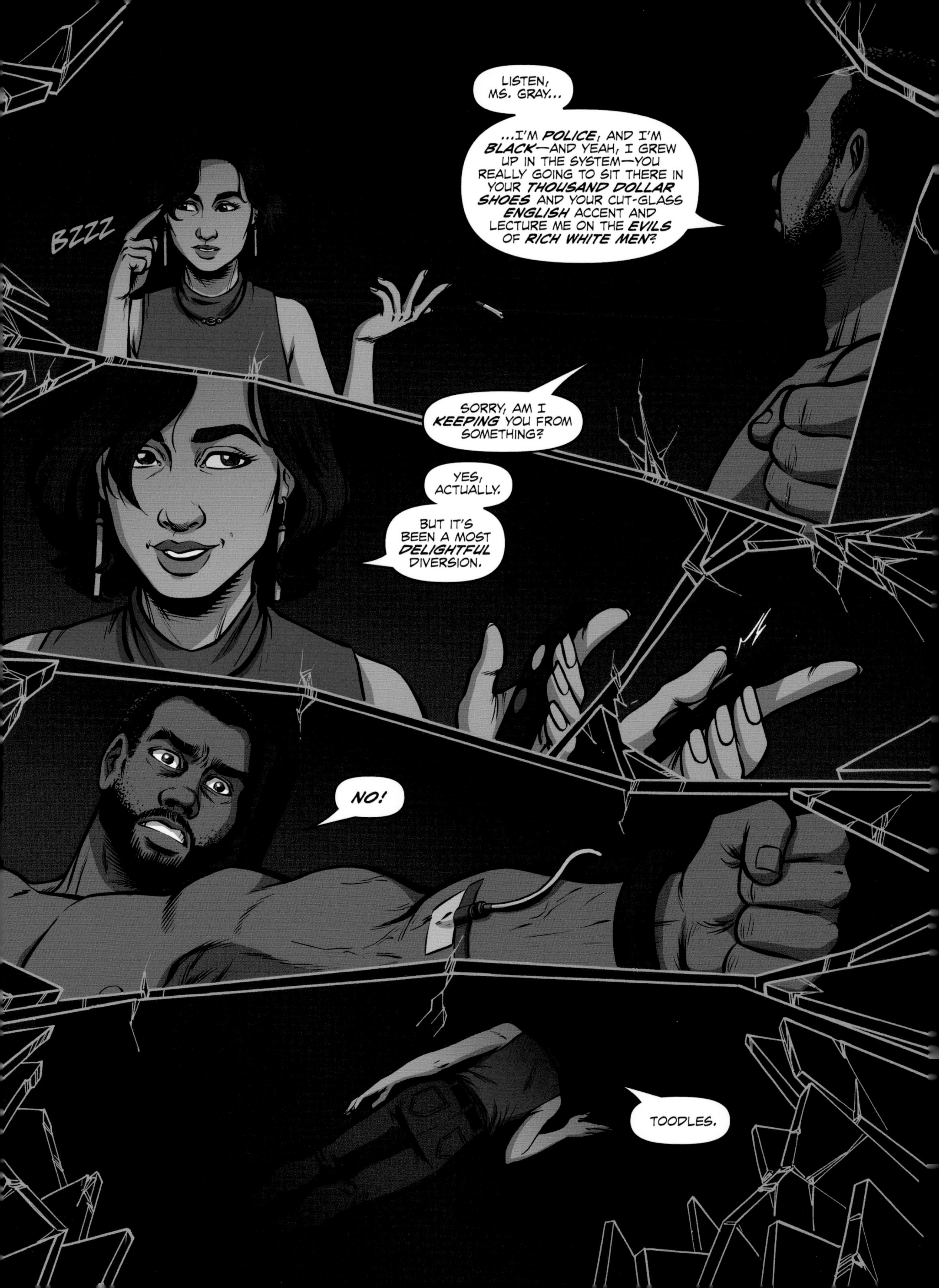
LISTEN, MS. GRAY...
...I'M POLICE, AND I'M BLACK—AND YEAH, I GREW UP IN THE SYSTEM—YOU REALLY GOING TO SIT THERE IN YOUR THOUSAND DOLLAR SHOES AND YOUR CUT-GLASS ENGLISH ACCENT AND LECTURE ME ON THE EVILS OF RICH WHITE MEN?
BZZZ
SORRY, AM I KEEPING YOU FROM SOMETHING?
YES, ACTUALLY.
BUT IT'S BEEN A MOST DELIGHTFUL DIVERSION.
NO!
TOODLES.

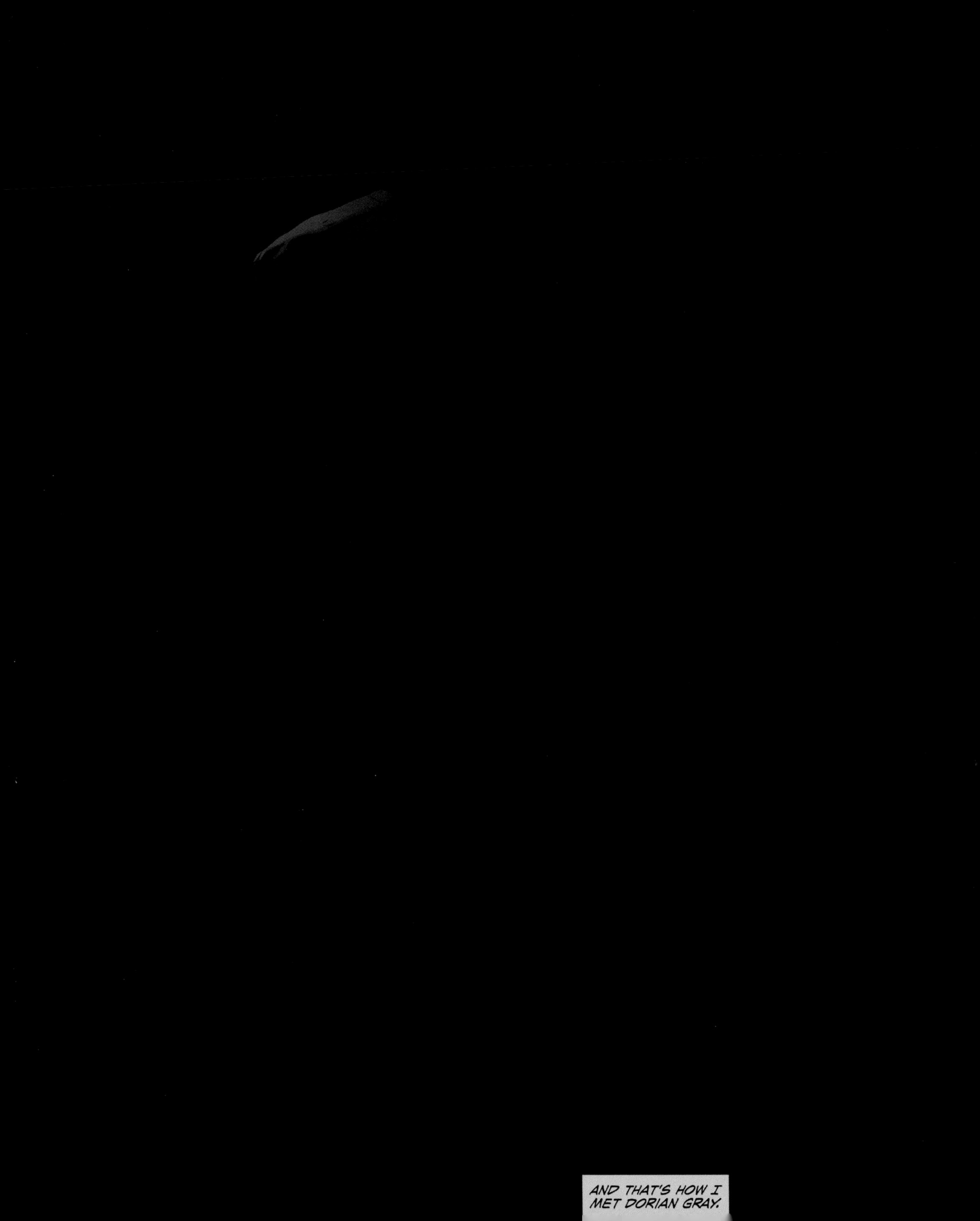
AND THAT'S HOW I MET DORIAN GRAY.

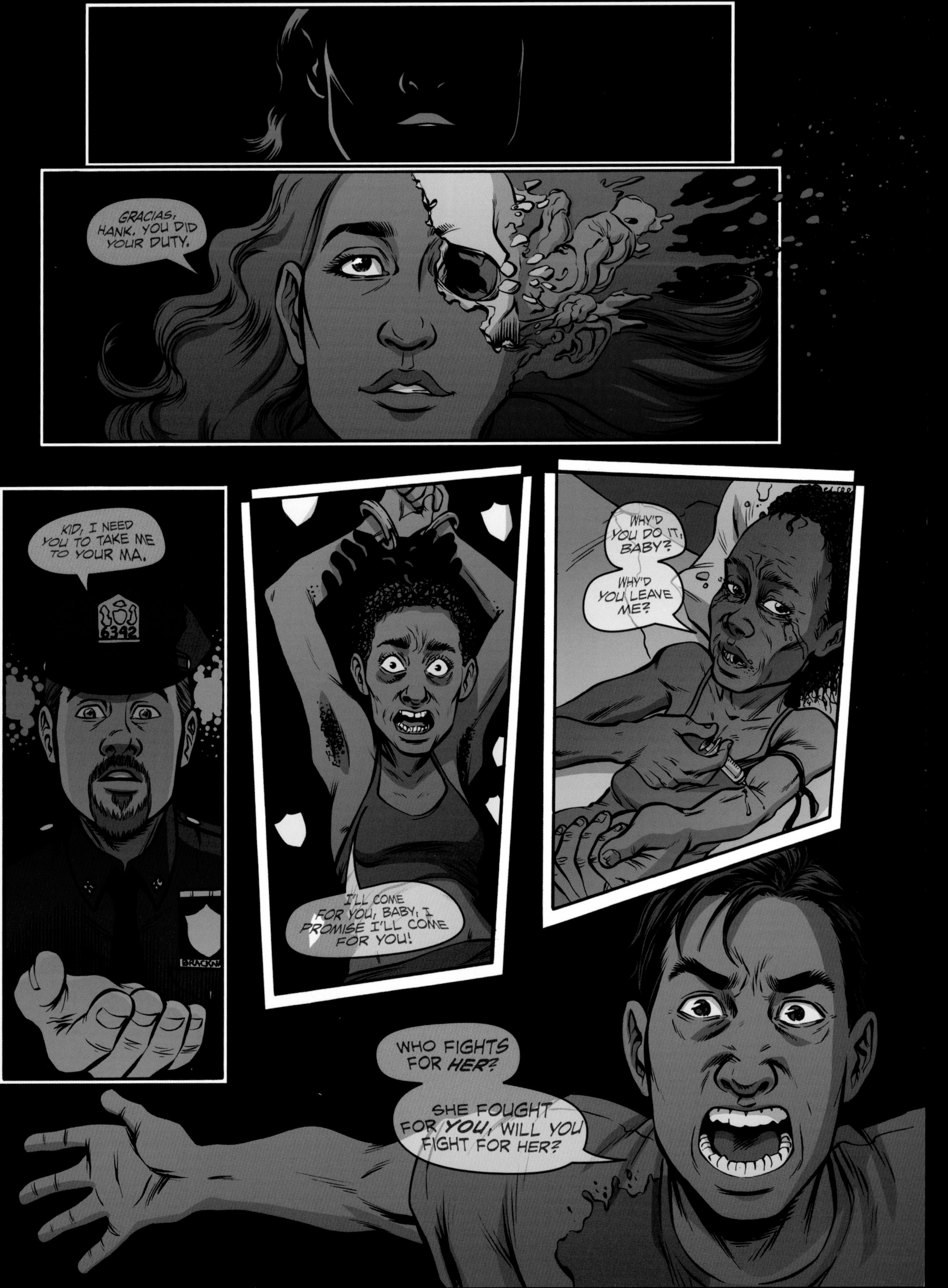
GRACIAS, HANK. YOU DID YOUR DUTY.
KID, I NEED YOU TO TAKE ME TO YOUR MA.
6342
I'LL COME FOR YOU, BABY, I PROMISE I'LL COME FOR YOU!
WHY'D YOU DO IT, BABY?
WHY'D YOU LEAVE ME?
WHO FIGHTS FOR HER?
SHE FOUGHT FOR YOU, WILL YOU FIGHT FOR HER?

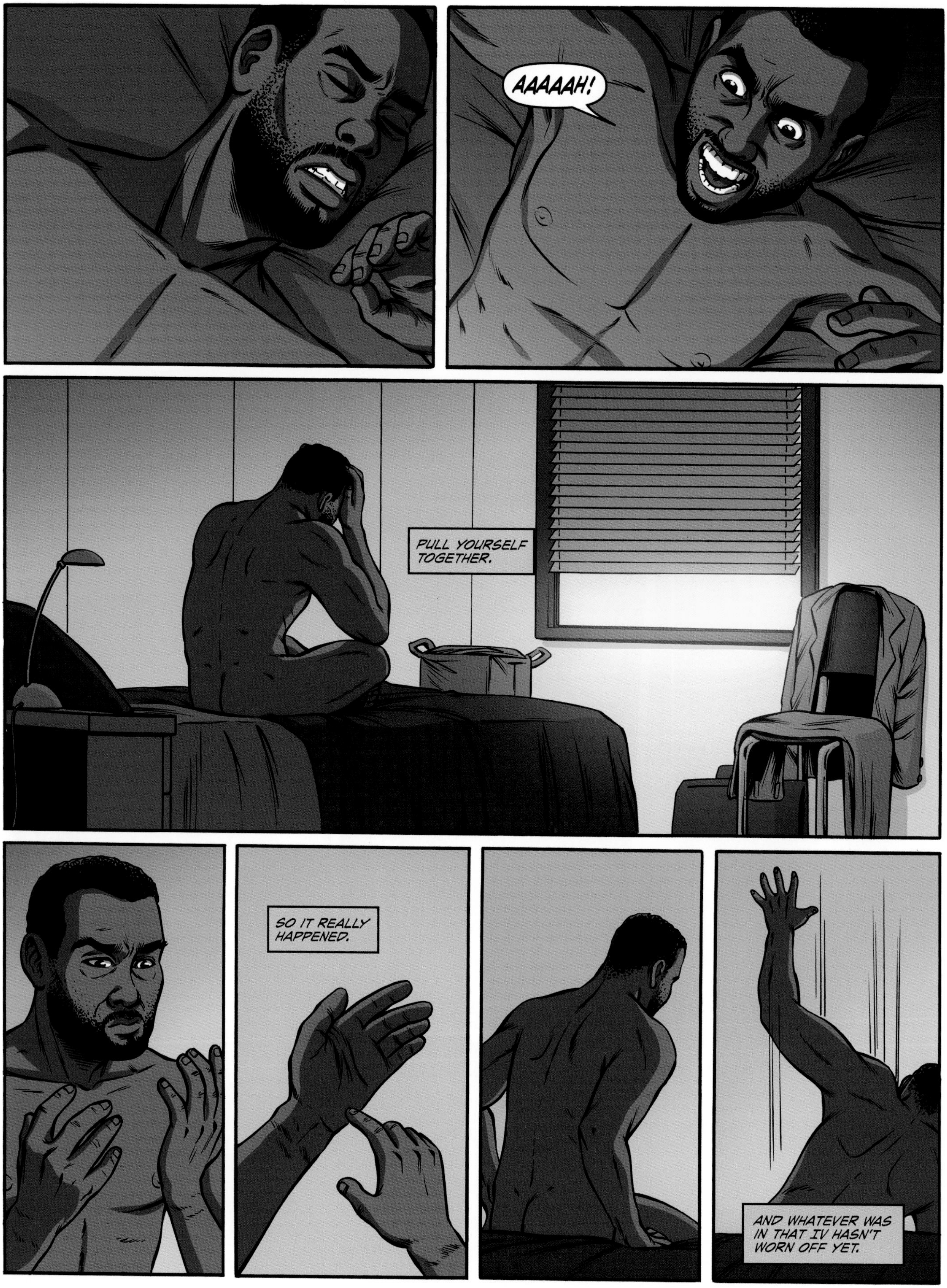
AAAAAH!
PULL YOURSELF TOGETHER.
SO IT REALLY HAPPENED.
AND WHATEVER WAS IN THAT IV HASN'T WORN OFF YET.

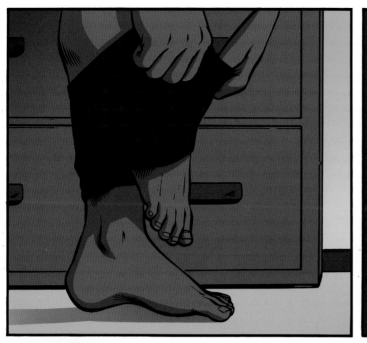

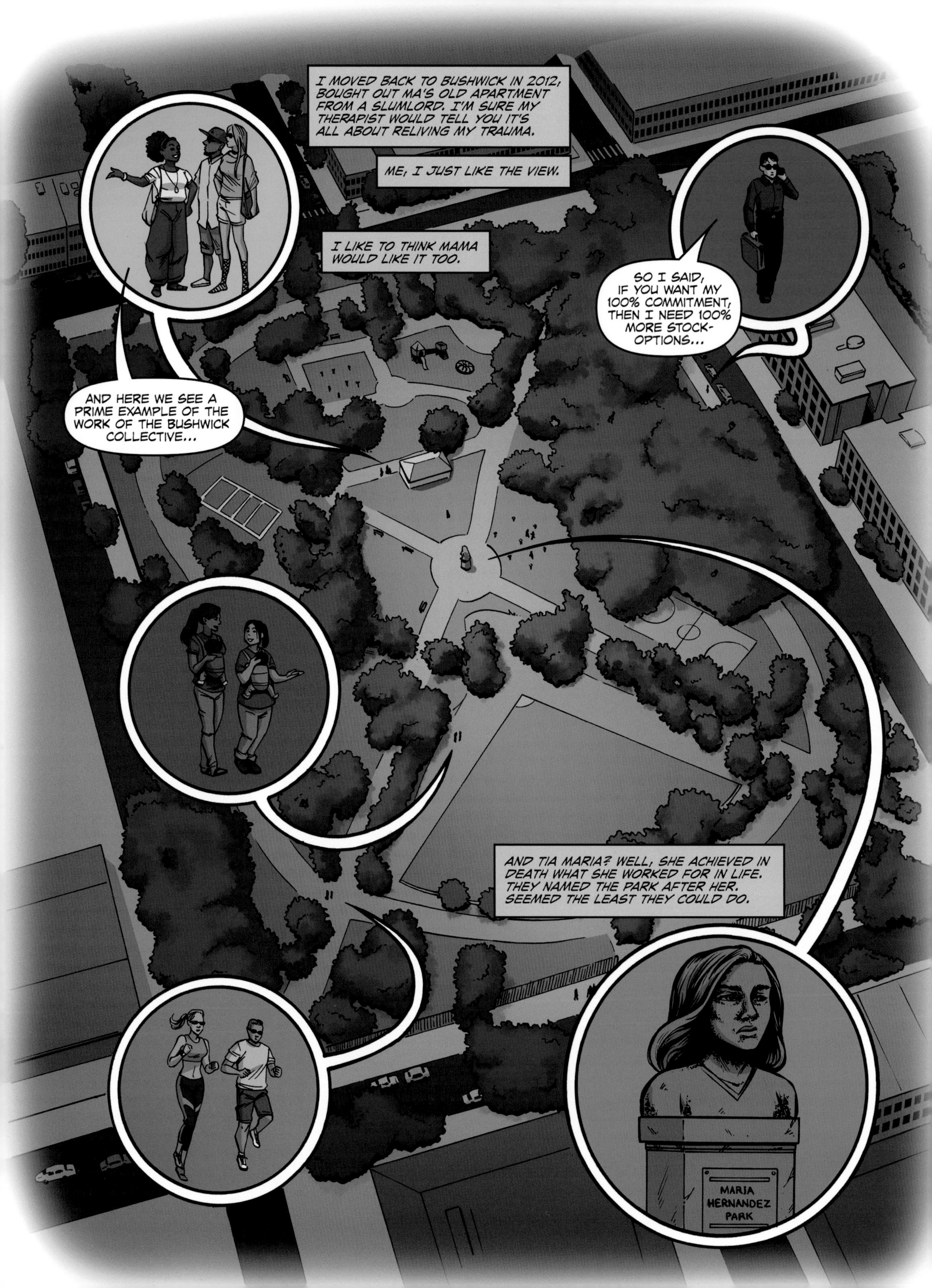
I MOVED BACK TO BUSHWICK IN 2012, BOUGHT OUT MA'S OLD APARTMENT FROM A SLUMLORD. I'M SURE MY THERAPIST WOULD TELL YOU IT'S ALL ABOUT RELIVING MY TRAUMA.
ME, I JUST LIKE THE VIEW.
I LIKE TO THINK MAMA WOULD LIKE IT TOO.
SO I SAID, IF YOU WANT MY 100% COMMITMENT, THEN I NEED 100% MORE STOCK-OPTIONS...
AND HERE WE SEE A PRIME EXAMPLE OF THE WORK OF THE BUSHWICK COLLECTIVE...
AND TIA MARIA? WELL, SHE ACHIEVED IN DEATH WHAT SHE WORKED FOR IN LIFE. THEY NAMED THE PARK AFTER HER. SEEMED THE LEAST THEY COULD DO.
MARIA HERNANDEZ PARK

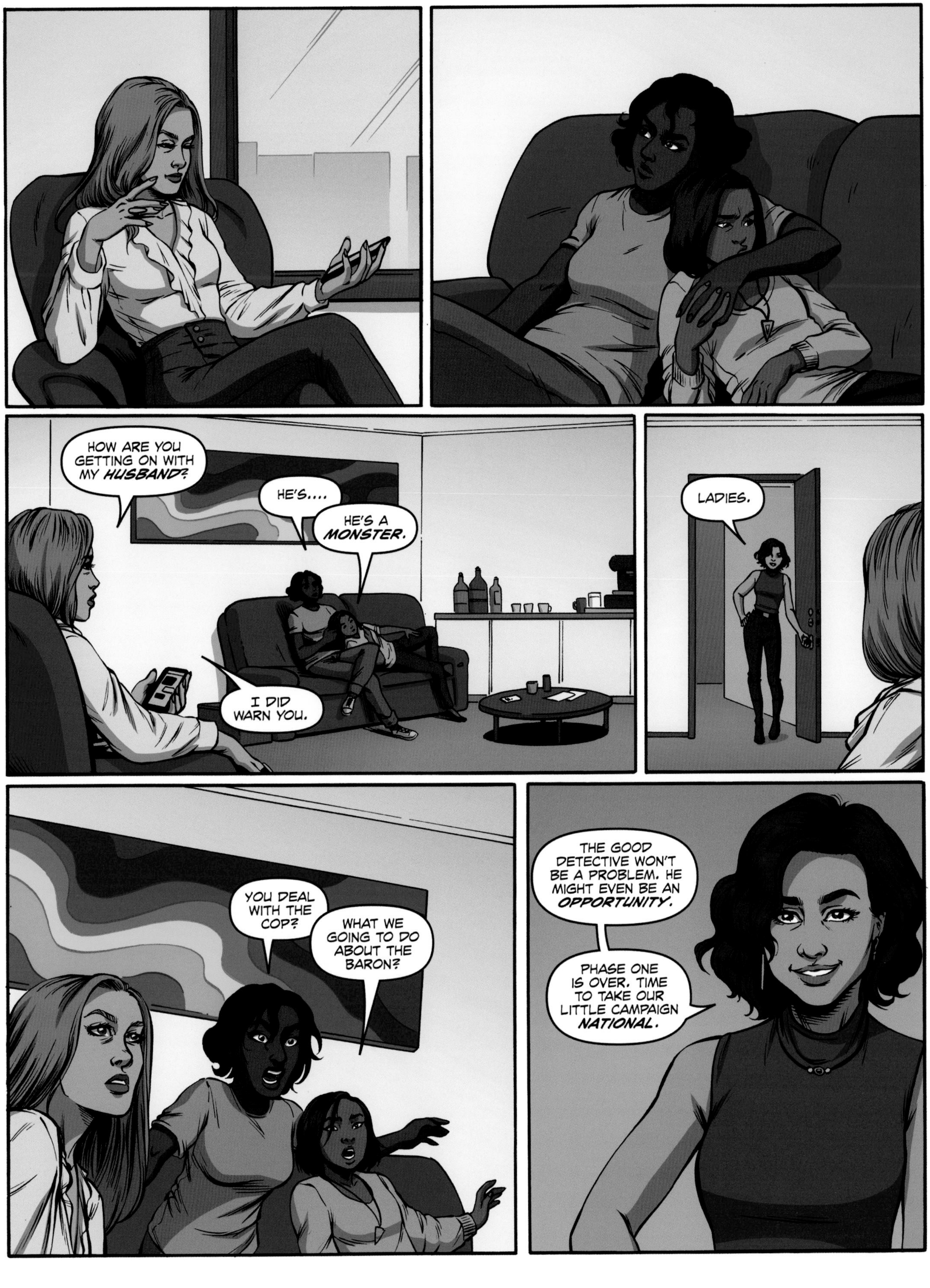
HOW ARE YOU GETTING ON WITH MY *HUSBAND*?
HE'S....
HE'S A *MONSTER*.
I DID WARN YOU.
LADIES.
YOU DEAL WITH THE COP?
WHAT WE GOING TO DO ABOUT THE BARON?
THE GOOD DETECTIVE WON'T BE A PROBLEM. HE MIGHT EVEN BE AN *OPPORTUNITY*.
PHASE ONE IS OVER. TIME TO TAKE OUR LITTLE CAMPAIGN *NATIONAL*.

Chapter 4

"Women are never disarmed by compliments. Men always are. That is the difference between the sexes."

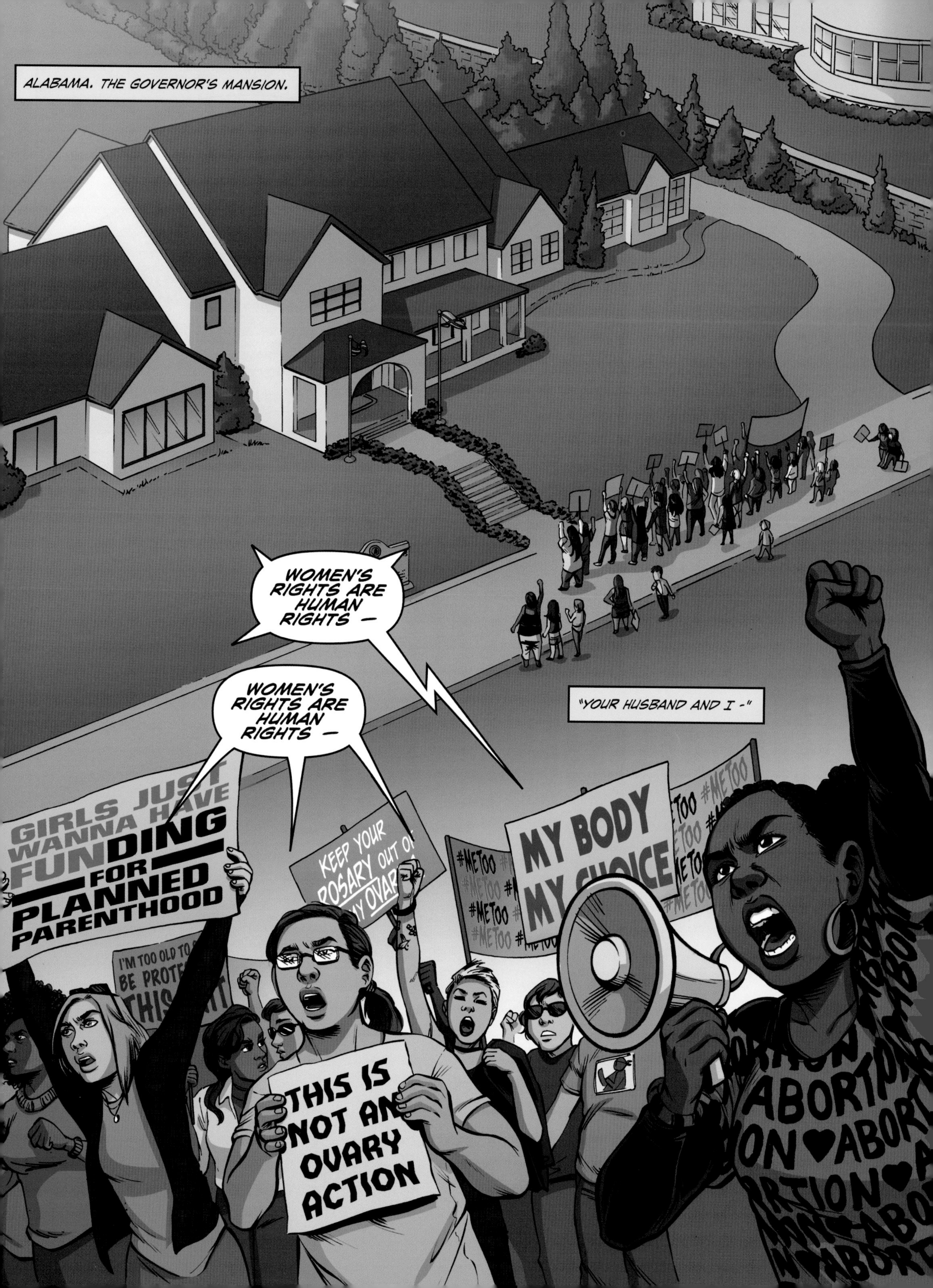
ALABAMA. THE GOVERNOR'S MANSION.
WOMEN'S RIGHTS ARE HUMAN RIGHTS —
WOMEN'S RIGHTS ARE HUMAN RIGHTS —
"YOUR HUSBAND AND I -"
GIRLS JUST WANNA HAVE FUNDING FOR PLANNED PARENTHOOD
KEEP YOUR ROSARY OUT OF
MY BODY MY
#METOO
THIS IS NOT AN OVARY ACTION

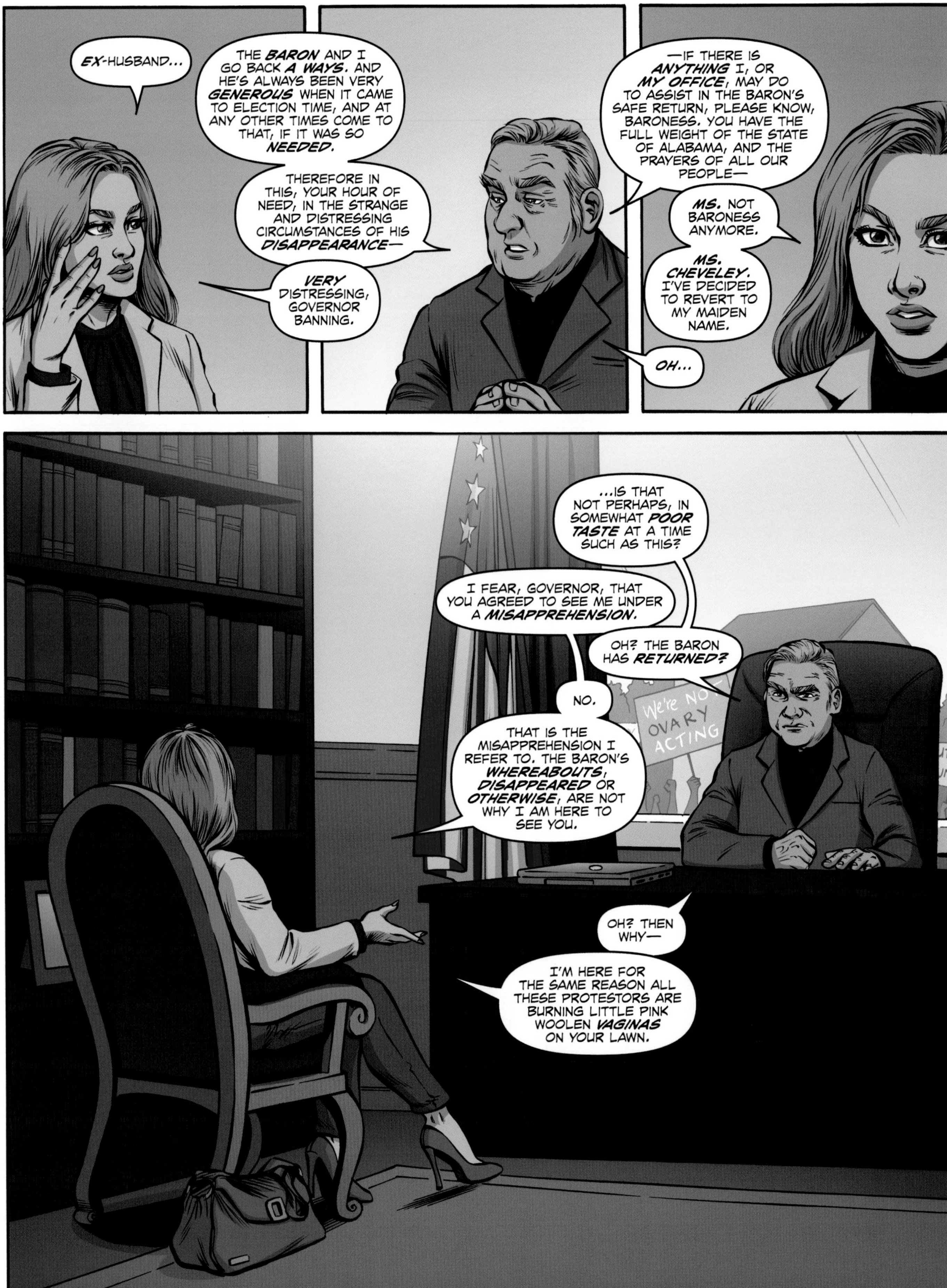
EX-HUSBAND...
THE BARON AND I GO BACK A WAYS. AND HE'S ALWAYS BEEN VERY GENEROUS WHEN IT CAME TO ELECTION TIME, AND AT ANY OTHER TIMES COME TO THAT, IF IT WAS SO NEEDED.
THEREFORE IN THIS, YOUR HOUR OF NEED, IN THE STRANGE AND DISTRESSING CIRCUMSTANCES OF HIS DISAPPEARANCE—
VERY DISTRESSING, GOVERNOR BANNING.
—IF THERE IS ANYTHING I, OR MY OFFICE, MAY DO TO ASSIST IN THE BARON'S SAFE RETURN, PLEASE KNOW, BARONESS. YOU HAVE THE FULL WEIGHT OF THE STATE OF ALABAMA, AND THE PRAYERS OF ALL OUR PEOPLE—
MS. NOT BARONESS ANYMORE.
MS. CHEVELEY. I'VE DECIDED TO REVERT TO MY MAIDEN NAME.
OH...
...IS THAT NOT PERHAPS, IN SOMEWHAT POOR TASTE AT A TIME SUCH AS THIS?
I FEAR, GOVERNOR, THAT YOU AGREED TO SEE ME UNDER A MISAPPREHENSION.
OH? THE BARON HAS RETURNED?
NO.
THAT IS THE MISAPPREHENSION I REFER TO. THE BARON'S WHEREABOUTS, DISAPPEARED OR OTHERWISE, ARE NOT WHY I AM HERE TO SEE YOU.
We're NOT OVARY ACTING
OH? THEN WHY—
I'M HERE FOR THE SAME REASON ALL THESE PROTESTORS ARE BURNING LITTLE PINK WOOLEN VAGINAS ON YOUR LAWN.

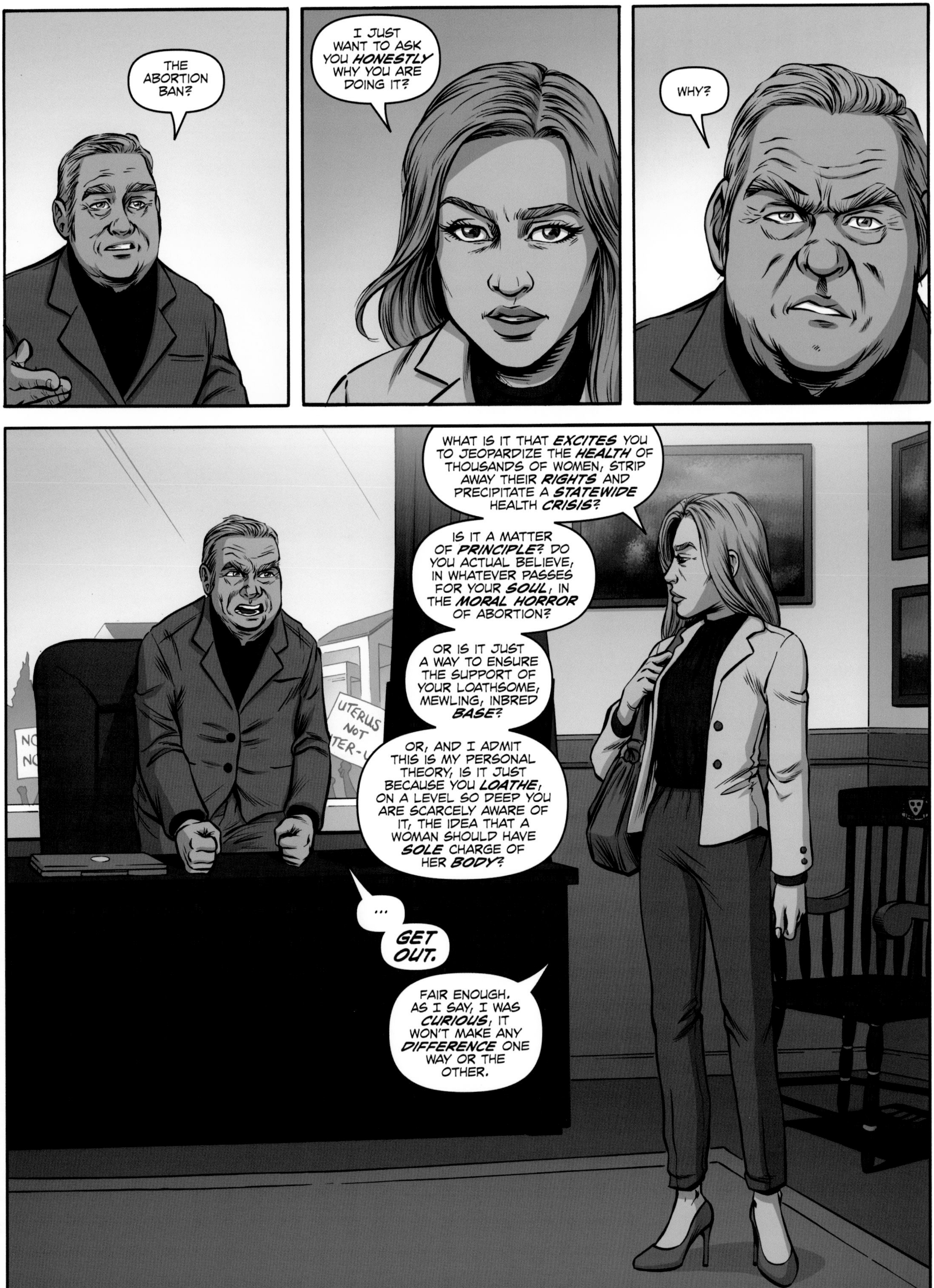

THE ABORTION BAN?
I JUST WANT TO ASK YOU *HONESTLY* WHY YOU ARE DOING IT?
WHY?
WHAT IS IT THAT *EXCITES* YOU TO JEOPARDIZE THE *HEALTH* OF THOUSANDS OF WOMEN, STRIP AWAY THEIR *RIGHTS* AND PRECIPITATE A *STATEWIDE* HEALTH *CRISIS*?
IS IT A MATTER OF *PRINCIPLE*? DO YOU ACTUAL BELIEVE, IN WHATEVER PASSES FOR YOUR *SOUL*, IN THE *MORAL HORROR* OF ABORTION?
OR IS IT JUST A WAY TO ENSURE THE SUPPORT OF YOUR LOATHSOME, MEWLING, INBRED *BASE*?
OR, AND I ADMIT THIS IS MY PERSONAL THEORY, IS IT JUST BECAUSE YOU *LOATHE*, ON A LEVEL SO DEEP YOU ARE SCARCELY AWARE OF IT, THE IDEA THAT A WOMAN SHOULD HAVE *SOLE* CHARGE OF HER *BODY*?
UTERUS NOT
...
GET OUT.
FAIR ENOUGH. AS I SAY, I WAS *CURIOUS*, IT WON'T MAKE ANY *DIFFERENCE* ONE WAY OR THE OTHER.

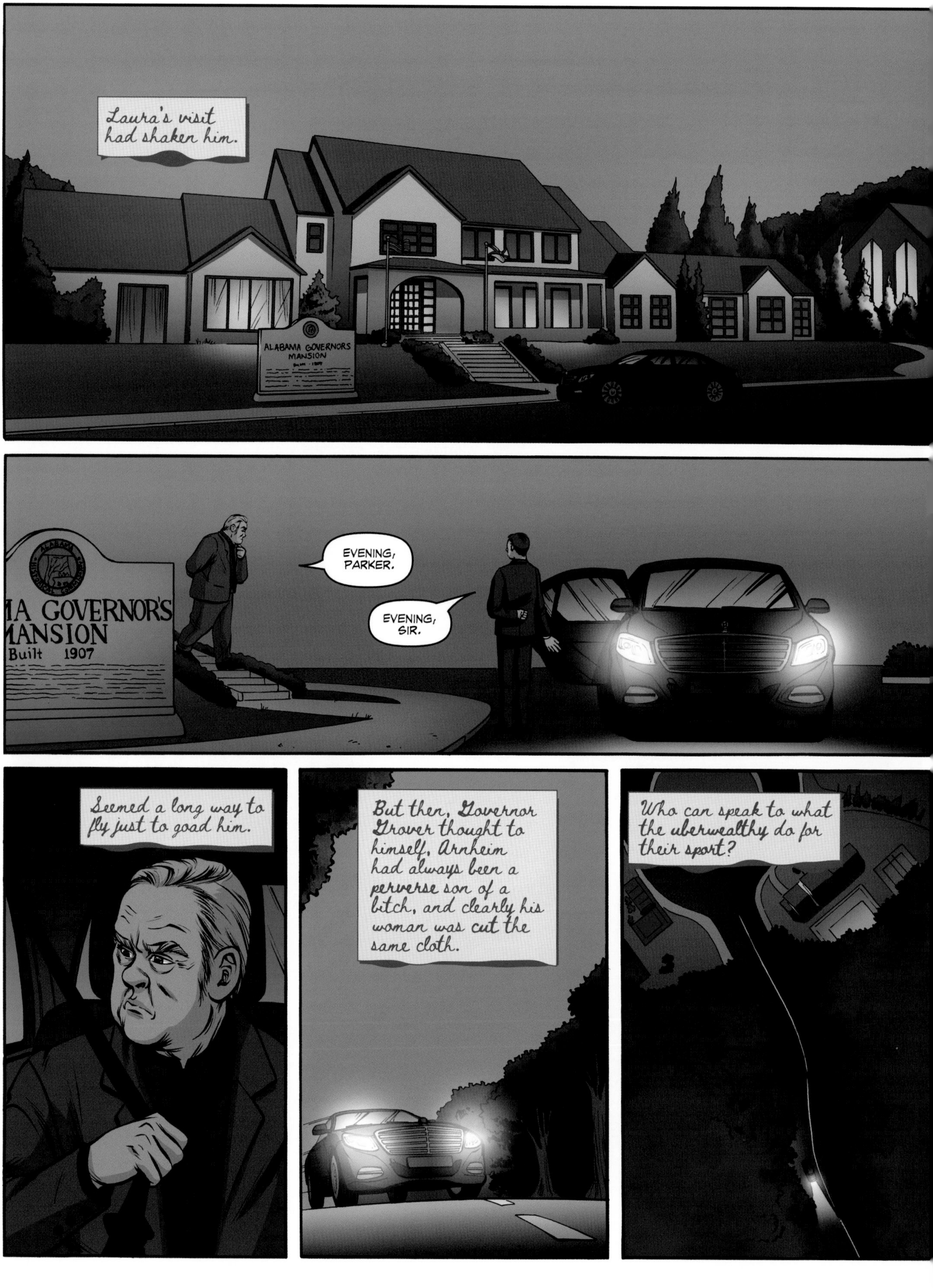
Laura's visit had shaken him.
ALABAMA GOVERNORS MANSION
EVENING, PARKER.
EVENING, SIR.
MA GOVERNOR'S MANSION
Built 1907
Seemed a long way to fly just to goad him.
But then, Governor Grover thought to himself, Arnheim had always been a perverse son of a bitch, and clearly his woman was cut the same cloth.
Who can speak to what the uberwealthy do for their sport?

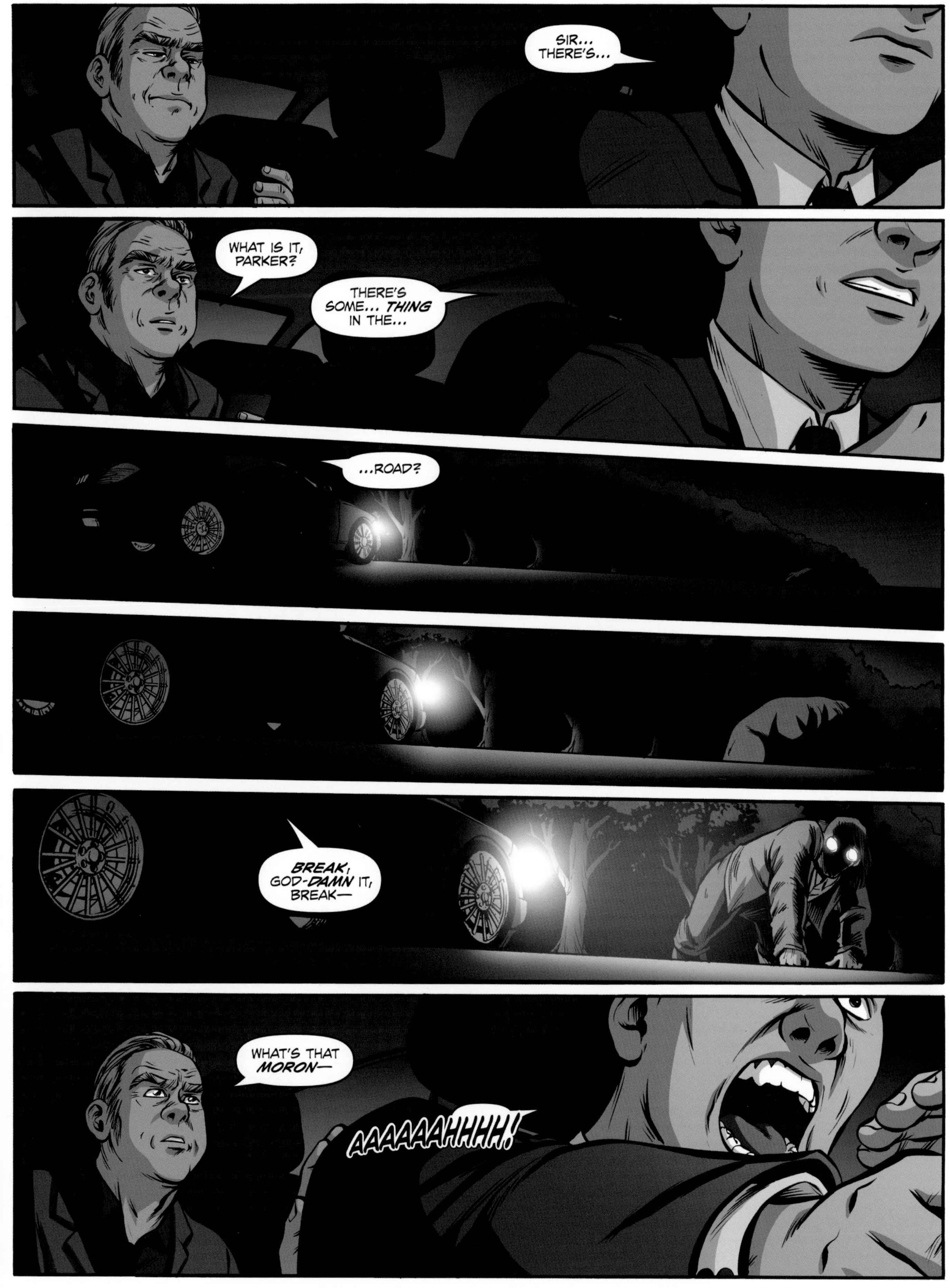
SIR... THERE'S...
WHAT IS IT, PARKER?
THERE'S SOME... THING IN THE...
...ROAD?
BREAK, GOD-DAMN IT, BREAK—
WHAT'S THAT MORON—
AAAAAAHHHH!

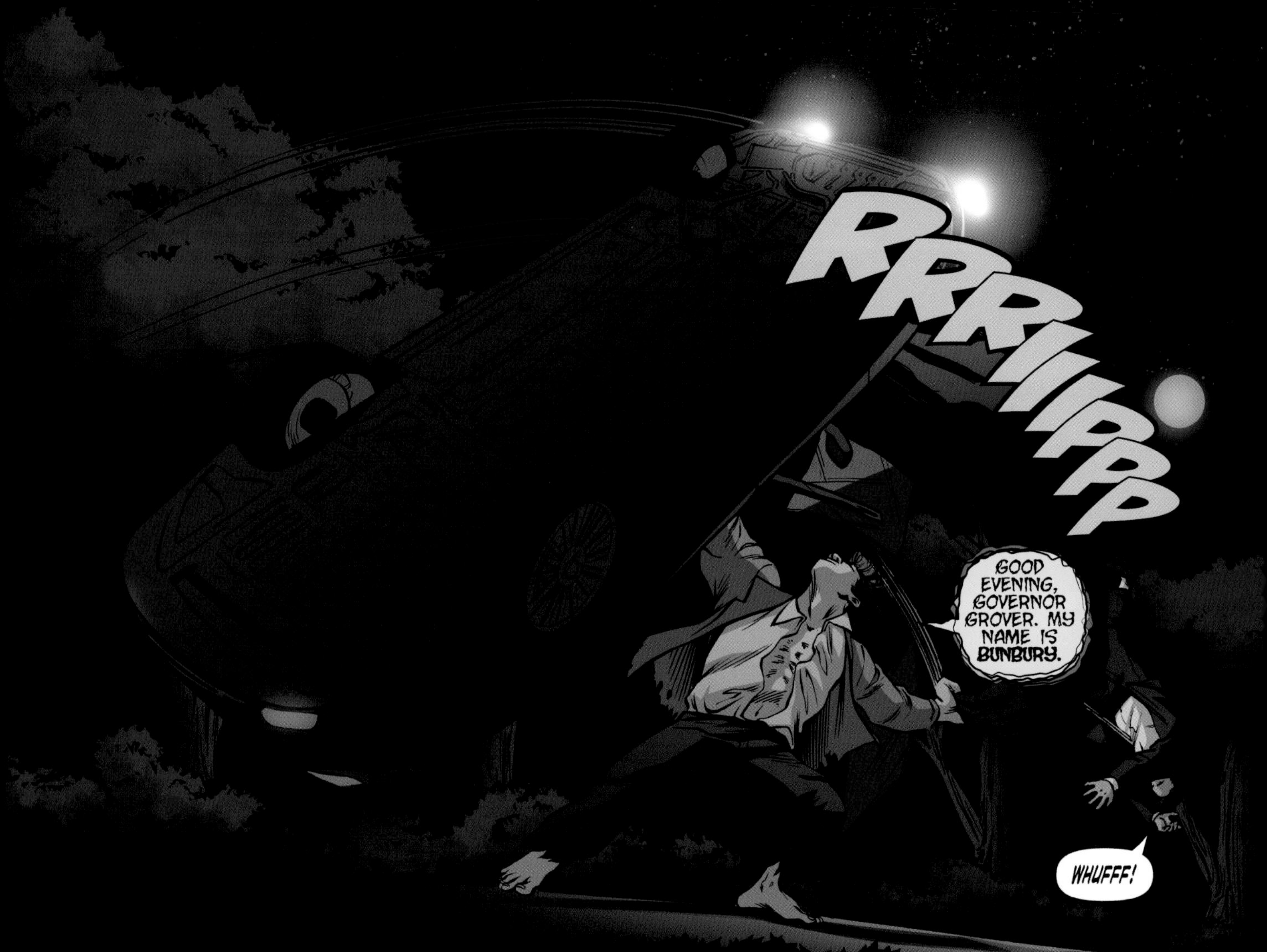
RRRIIIPPP
GOOD EVENING, GOVERNOR GROVER. MY NAME IS BUNBURY.
WHUFFF!

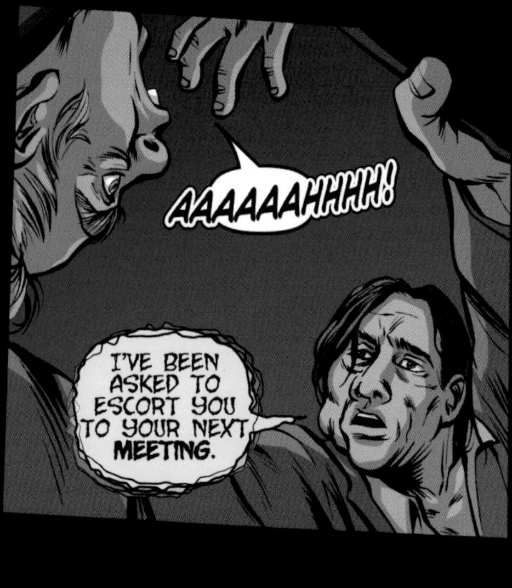
AAAAAAHHHH!
I'VE BEEN ASKED TO ESCORT YOU TO YOUR NEXT MEETING.

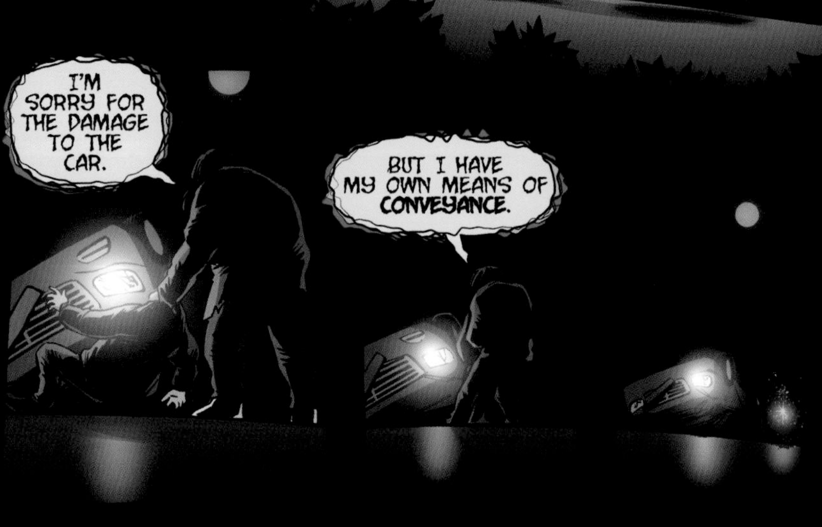
I'M SORRY FOR THE DAMAGE TO THE CAR.
BUT I HAVE MY OWN MEANS OF CONVEYANCE.

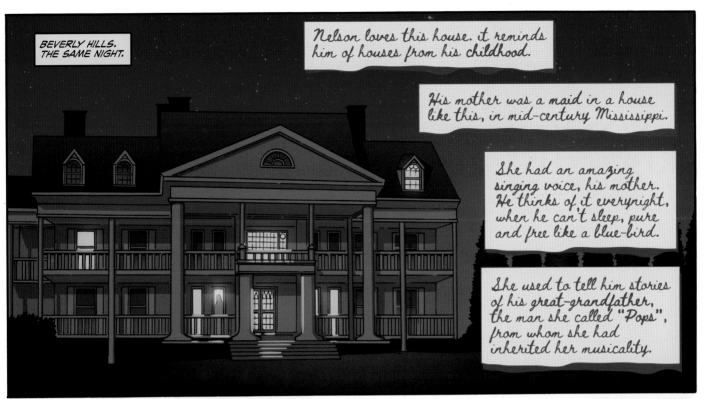

BEVERLY HILLS.
THE SAME NIGHT.

Nelson loves this house. it reminds him of houses from his childhood.

His mother was a maid in a house like this, in mid-century Mississippi.

She had an amazing singing voice, his mother. He thinks of it everynight, when he can't sleep, pure and free like a blue-bird.

She used to tell him stories of his great-grandfather, the man she called "Pops", from whom she had inherited her musicality.

As Nelson grew older, he came to realize that Pops had started out as a slave. A prized slave.

At every party, his owners would proudly show off his singing voice and talents on the piano.

But he was a slave none the less.

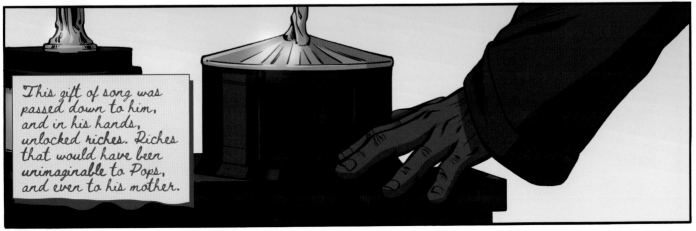

This gift of song was passed down to him, and in his hands, unlocked riches. Riches that would have been unimaginable to Pops, and even to his mother.

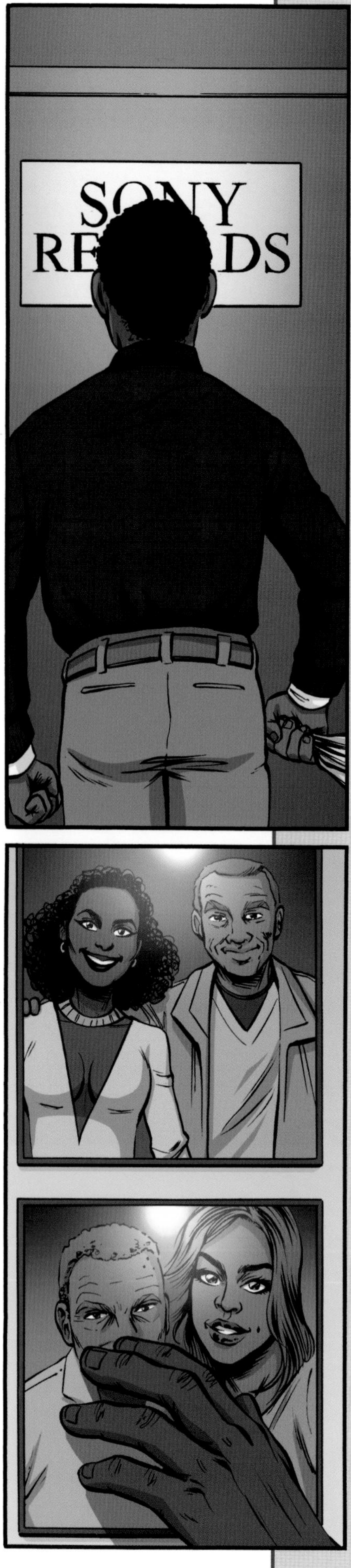
SONY

For the first few decades, he seemed to be getting **nowhere**, despite his certainty in his own talent.

But then, a breakthrough. In 1982 a crossover album that went **triple Platinum**.

That success seemed to **supercharge** his creativity, and in the decades thereafter, hits flowed from him, like water to the sea. He was **unstoppable**.

By the time of his 11th and final album, he was in a category of his own.

A **legend** with enough number ones to fill a three hour set, head of his own **record label** and **media empire**, a cross-over television star from variety to sitcoms.

Someone whose music and very personality defined the coming of age of two generations.

He had become the sort of man who gets called "**icon**" and "**Trailblazer**."

He did not dispute those tributes. And he enjoyed the idea that his example and enabled the generations of Black artists who came after him.

He thinks of his **legacy** more and more now, in his **retirement**, for at 70 he no longer makes hit songs, not even for others.

Now he mainly stays at home, with his **memories**. He has become a creature of habit.

In his age, Nelson requires the energy of **youth**. And he likes **routine**.

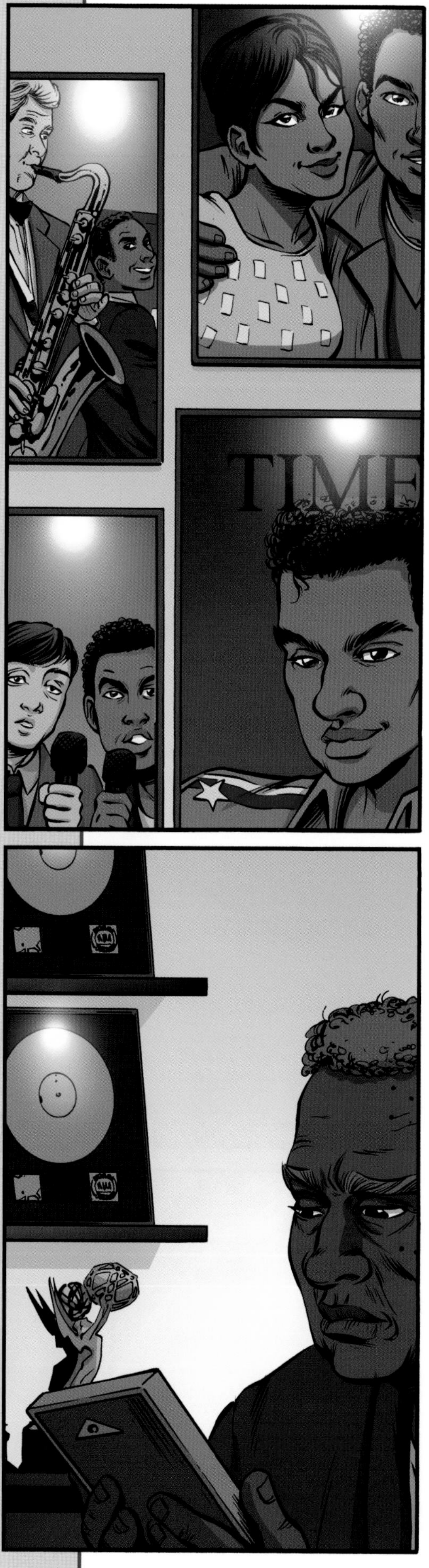
TIME

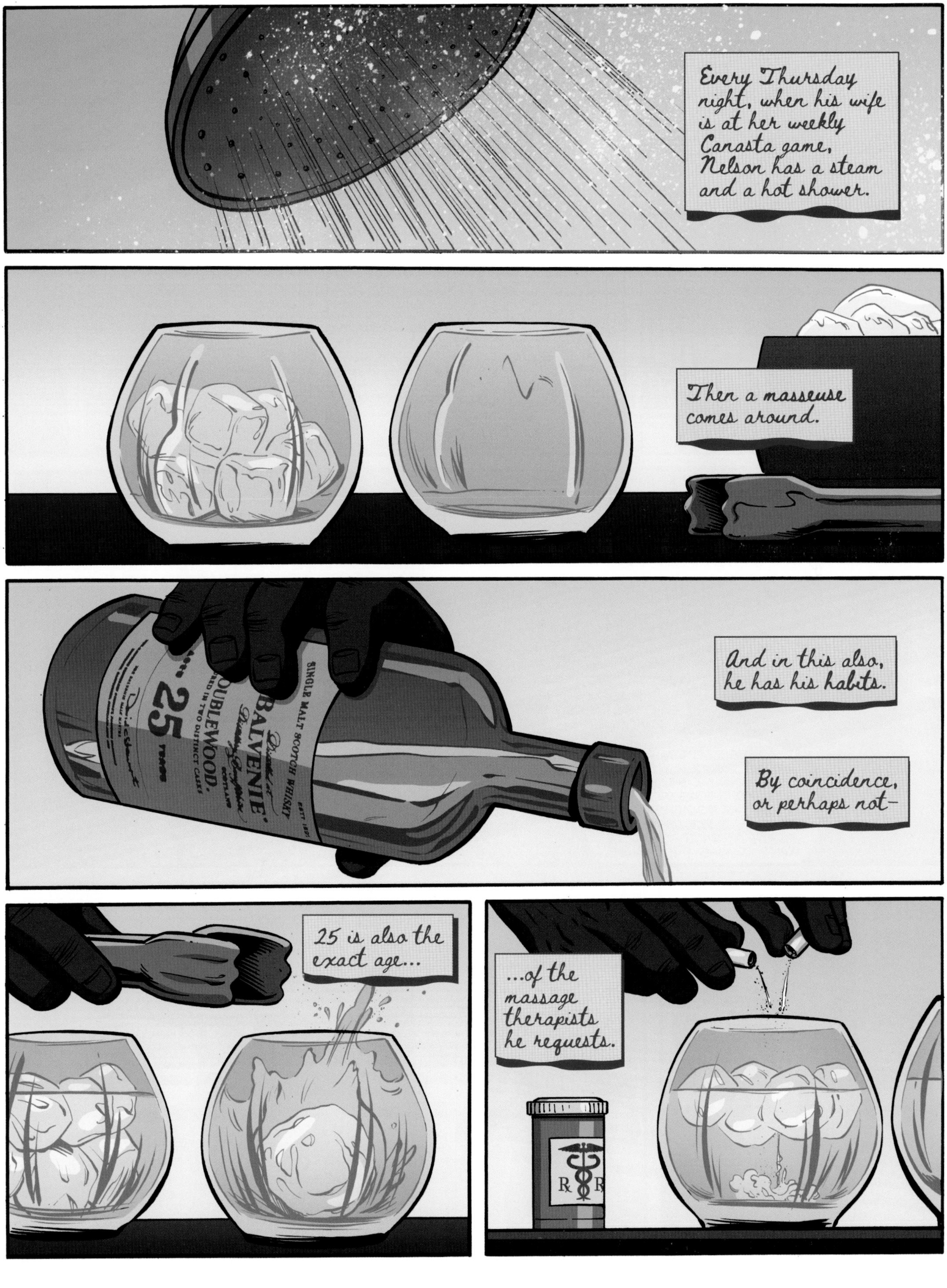
Every Thursday night, when his wife is at her weekly Canasta game, Nelson has a steam and a hot shower.
Then a masseuse comes around.
SINGLE MALT SCOTCH WHISKY
25
And in this also, he has his habits.
By coincidence, or perhaps not–
25 is also the exact age...
...of the massage therapists he requests.

DING DONG

SNIFF SNIFF

GOOD EVENING, MY DEAR. YOU'RE JUST ON TIME.

THE AGENCY SAID YOU VALUED PUNCTUALITY.

BESIDES, I'M A *HUGE* FAN. I HOPE YOU DON'T MIND ME SAYING, I'M *NEW* TO THE AGENCY, BUT WHEN THE BOOKING CAME THROUGH, I *VOLUNTEERED* FOR IT AT ONCE—I DIDN'T WANT TO MISS THE CHANCE.

YOU'RE VERY KIND TO AN OLD MAN.

COME IN, COME IN.

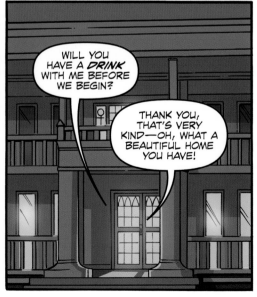

WILL YOU HAVE A *DRINK* WITH ME BEFORE WE BEGIN?

THANK YOU, THAT'S VERY KIND—OH, WHAT A BEAUTIFUL HOME YOU HAVE!

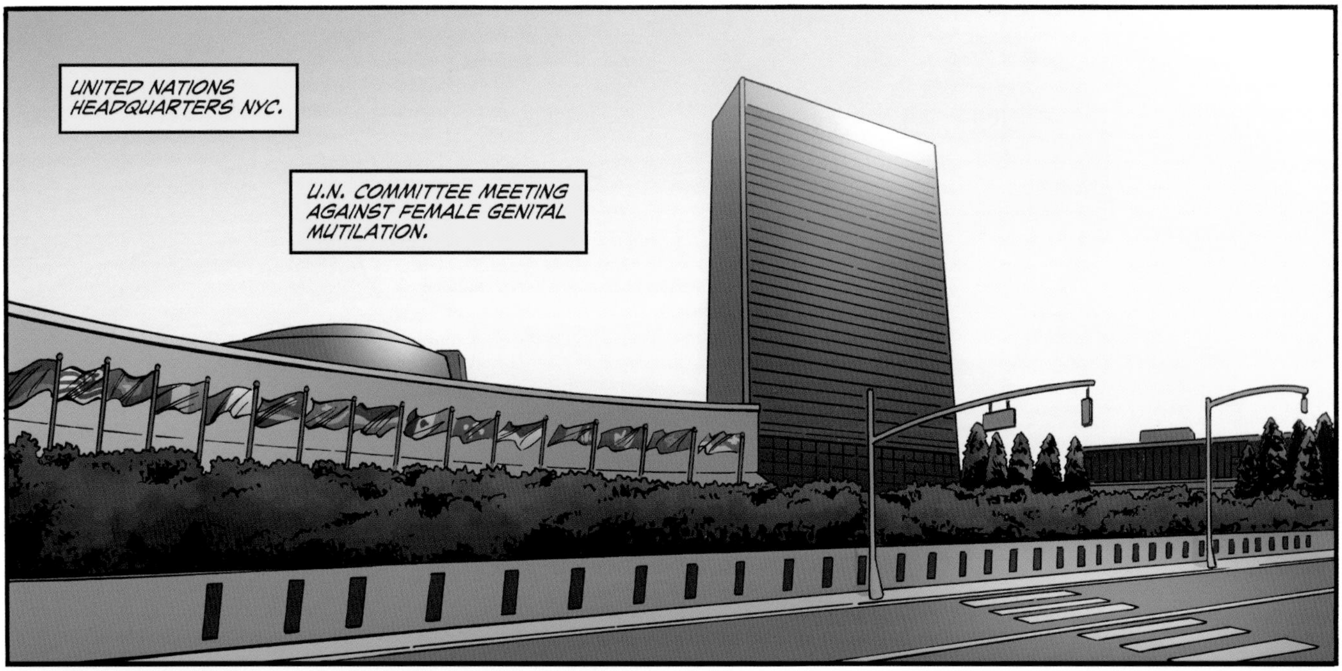
UNITED NATIONS HEADQUARTERS NYC.
U.N. COMMITTEE MEETING AGAINST FEMALE GENITAL MUTILATION.

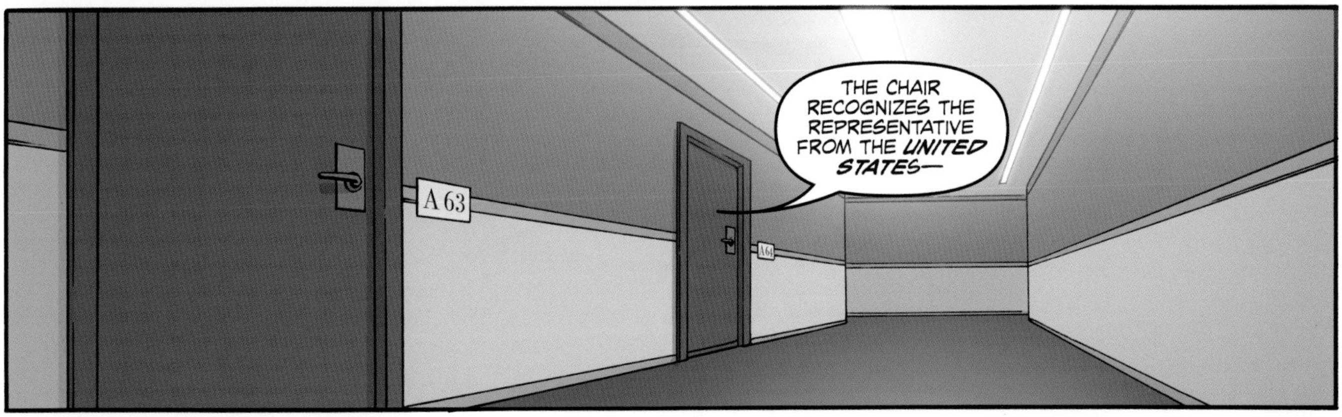
A 63
THE CHAIR RECOGNIZES THE REPRESENTATIVE FROM THE UNITED STATES—

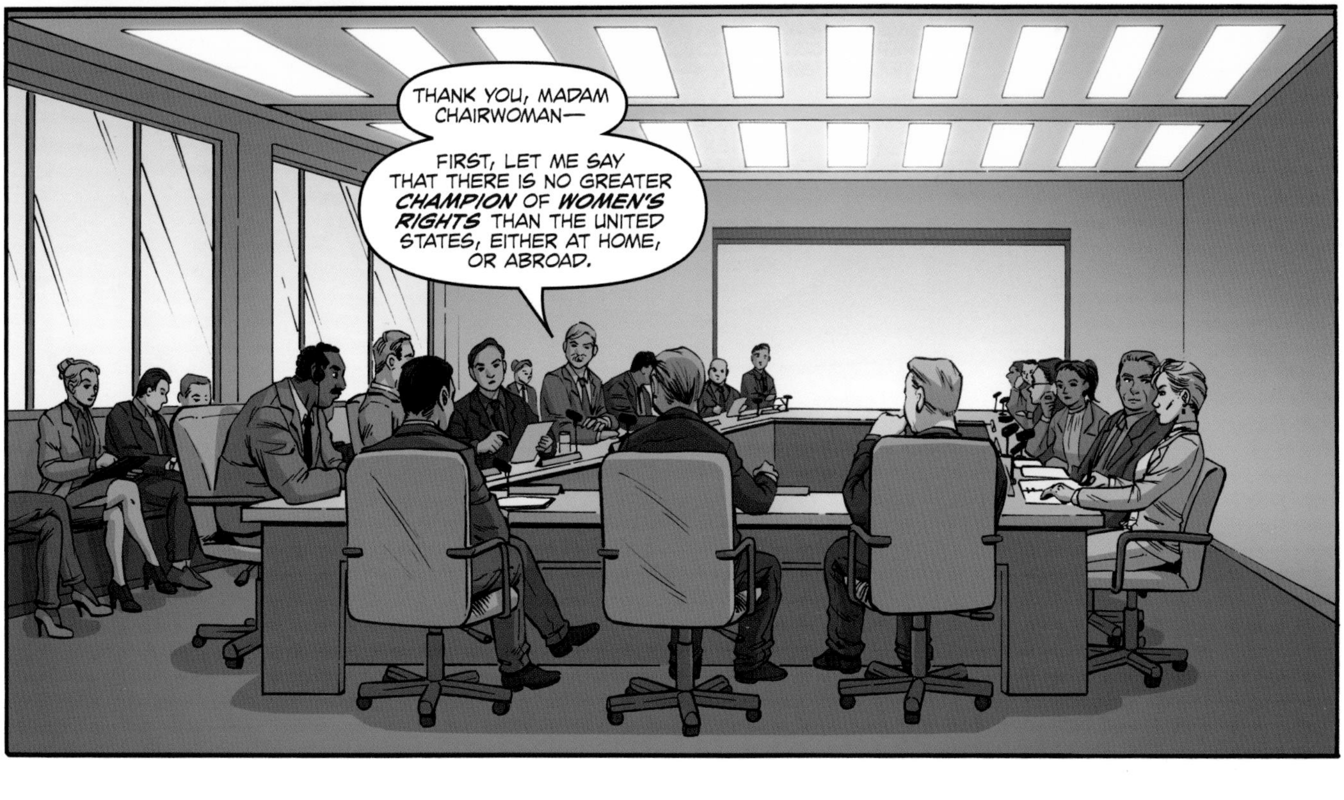
THANK YOU, MADAM CHAIRWOMAN—
FIRST, LET ME SAY THAT THERE IS NO GREATER CHAMPION OF WOMEN'S RIGHTS THAN THE UNITED STATES, EITHER AT HOME, OR ABROAD.

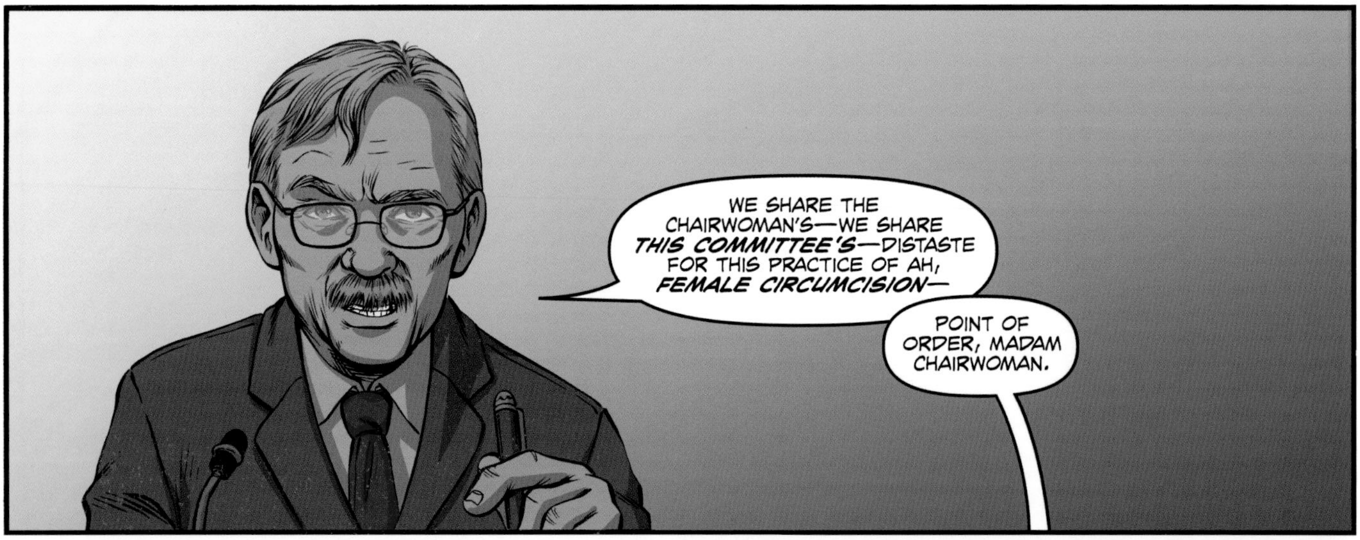
WE SHARE THE CHAIRWOMAN'S—WE SHARE THIS COMMITTEE'S—DISTASTE FOR THIS PRACTICE OF AH, FEMALE CIRCUMCISION—
POINT OF ORDER, MADAM CHAIRWOMAN.

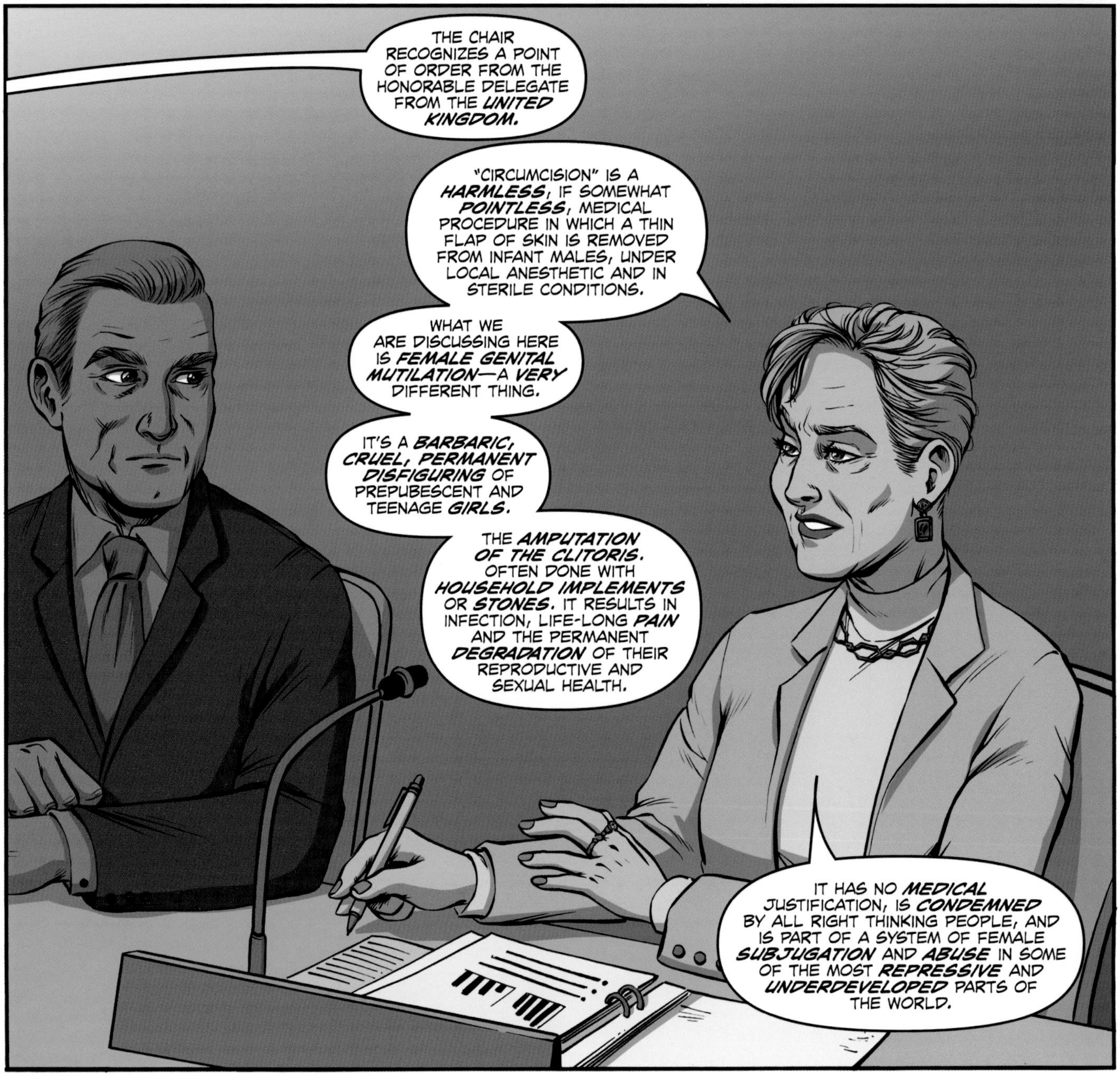
THE CHAIR RECOGNIZES A POINT OF ORDER FROM THE HONORABLE DELEGATE FROM THE UNITED KINGDOM.
"CIRCUMCISION" IS A HARMLESS, IF SOMEWHAT POINTLESS, MEDICAL PROCEDURE IN WHICH A THIN FLAP OF SKIN IS REMOVED FROM INFANT MALES, UNDER LOCAL ANESTHETIC AND IN STERILE CONDITIONS.
WHAT WE ARE DISCUSSING HERE IS FEMALE GENITAL MUTILATION—A VERY DIFFERENT THING.
IT'S A BARBARIC, CRUEL, PERMANENT DISFIGURING OF PREPUBESCENT AND TEENAGE GIRLS.
THE AMPUTATION OF THE CLITORIS. OFTEN DONE WITH HOUSEHOLD IMPLEMENTS OR STONES. IT RESULTS IN INFECTION, LIFE-LONG PAIN AND THE PERMANENT DEGRADATION OF THEIR REPRODUCTIVE AND SEXUAL HEALTH.
IT HAS NO MEDICAL JUSTIFICATION, IS CONDEMNED BY ALL RIGHT THINKING PEOPLE, AND IS PART OF A SYSTEM OF FEMALE SUBJUGATION AND ABUSE IN SOME OF THE MOST REPRESSIVE AND UNDERDEVELOPED PARTS OF THE WORLD.

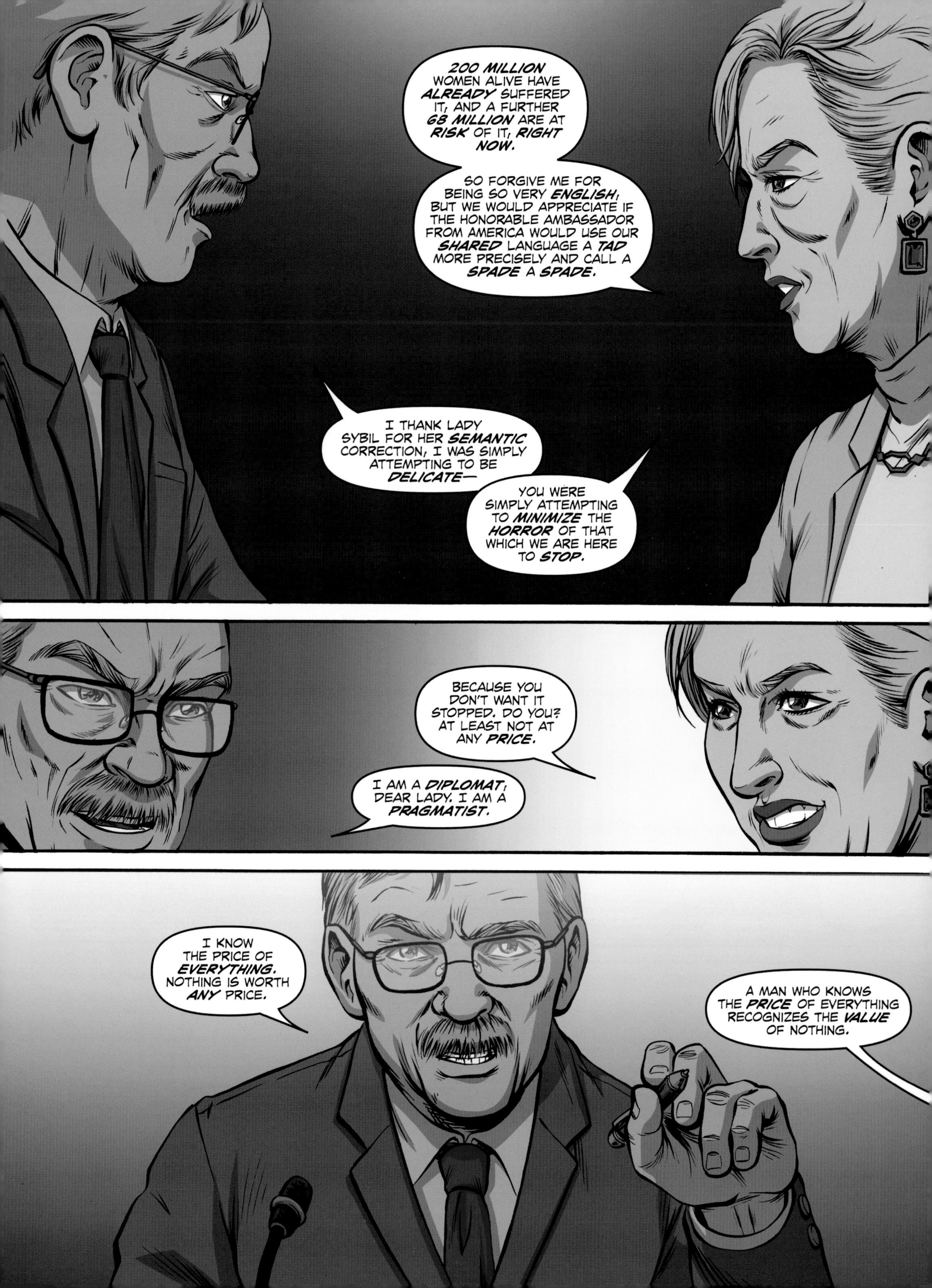
200 MILLION WOMEN ALIVE HAVE ALREADY SUFFERED IT, AND A FURTHER 68 MILLION ARE AT RISK OF IT, RIGHT NOW.
SO FORGIVE ME FOR BEING SO VERY ENGLISH, BUT WE WOULD APPRECIATE IF THE HONORABLE AMBASSADOR FROM AMERICA WOULD USE OUR SHARED LANGUAGE A TAD MORE PRECISELY AND CALL A SPADE A SPADE.
I THANK LADY SYBIL FOR HER SEMANTIC CORRECTION, I WAS SIMPLY ATTEMPTING TO BE DELICATE—
YOU WERE SIMPLY ATTEMPTING TO MINIMIZE THE HORROR OF THAT WHICH WE ARE HERE TO STOP.
BECAUSE YOU DON'T WANT IT STOPPED. DO YOU? AT LEAST NOT AT ANY PRICE.
I AM A DIPLOMAT, DEAR LADY. I AM A PRAGMATIST.
I KNOW THE PRICE OF EVERYTHING. NOTHING IS WORTH ANY PRICE.
A MAN WHO KNOWS THE PRICE OF EVERYTHING RECOGNIZES THE VALUE OF NOTHING.

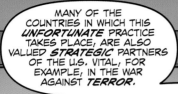

MANY OF THE COUNTRIES IN WHICH THIS *UNFORTUNATE* PRACTICE TAKES PLACE, ARE ALSO VALUED *STRATEGIC* PARTNERS OF THE U.S. VITAL, FOR EXAMPLE, IN THE WAR AGAINST *TERROR.*

THEREFORE WHILE I PERSONALLY SHARE OUR COLLEAGUES VIEWS AS TO THE *REPREHENSIBLE* NATURE OF *FGM,* I WOULD URGE THE COMMITTEE TO A SENSE OF *PROPORTIONALITY,* AND TO SEE THE *WHOLE BOARD.*

PERHAPS THIS IS AN *UNFORTUNATE* METAPHOR IN THE CIRCUMSTANCES, BUT WE MUST BE CAREFUL NOT TO *CUT* OFF OUR *NOSE* TO SPITE OUR *FACE.*

THIS MEASURE, AS DRAFTED, DOES *NOT* HAVE THE *SUPPORT* OF THE UNITED STATES OF AMERICA.

DING

YOU KNOW THERE WAS NOTHING *PERSONAL* IN THAT VOTE—

PERHAPS WE SHOULD MAKE IT PERSONAL.

SORRY, *WHAT?*

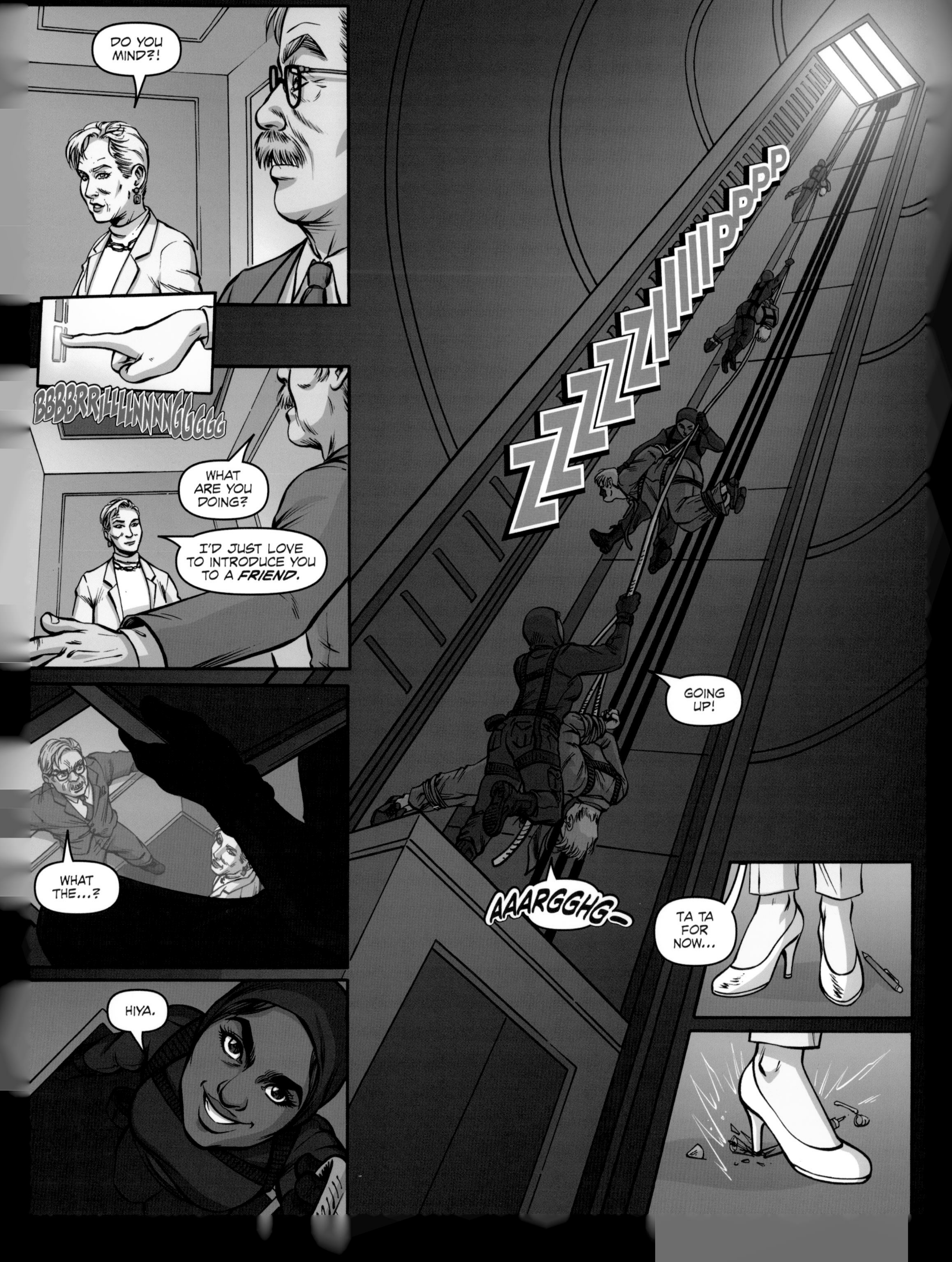
DO YOU MIND?!
BBBBRRILLLLNNNNGGGGG
WHAT ARE YOU DOING?
I'D JUST LOVE TO INTRODUCE YOU TO A FRIEND.
WHAT THE...?
HIYA.
ZZZZZIIIIIIPPPPP
GOING UP!
AAARGGHG-
TA TA FOR NOW...

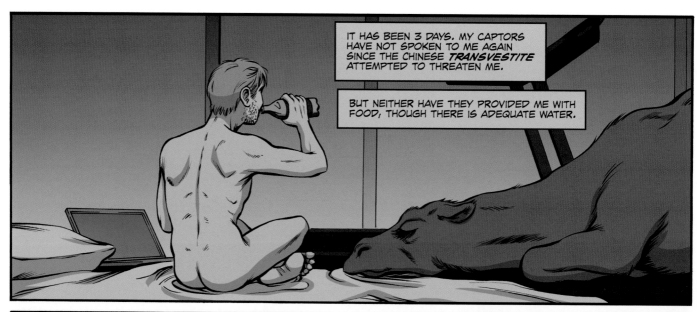

IT HAS BEEN 3 DAYS. MY CAPTORS HAVE NOT SPOKEN TO ME AGAIN SINCE THE CHINESE *TRANSVESTITE* ATTEMPTED TO THREATEN ME.

BUT NEITHER HAVE THEY PROVIDED ME WITH FOOD, THOUGH THERE IS ADEQUATE WATER.

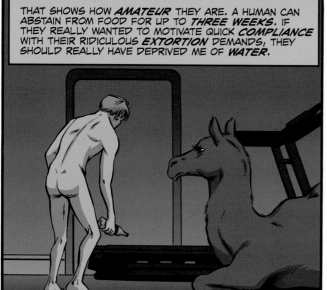

THAT SHOWS HOW *AMATEUR* THEY ARE. A HUMAN CAN ABSTAIN FROM FOOD FOR UP TO *THREE WEEKS*. IF THEY REALLY WANTED TO MOTIVATE QUICK *COMPLIANCE* WITH THEIR RIDICULOUS *EXTORTION* DEMANDS, THEY SHOULD REALLY HAVE DEPRIVED ME OF *WATER*.

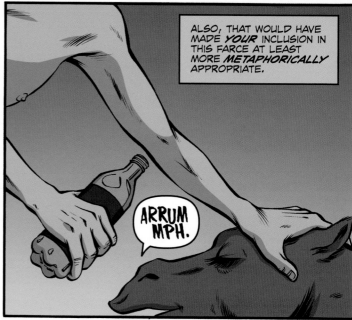

ALSO, THAT WOULD HAVE MADE *YOUR* INCLUSION IN THIS FARCE AT LEAST MORE *METAPHORICALLY* APPROPRIATE.

ARRUM MPH.

YOU FEEL IT *TOO*, DON'T YOU OLD BOY?

THERE WAS A LOT OF *ACTIVITY* LAST NIGHT. AND NOW, SOMETHING HAS *CHANGED* IN THIS BUILDING.

WE ARE NO LONGER THE ONLY *PRISONERS* HERE.

WE HAVE *COMPANY*. WHICH MEANS WE HAVE *ALLIES*.

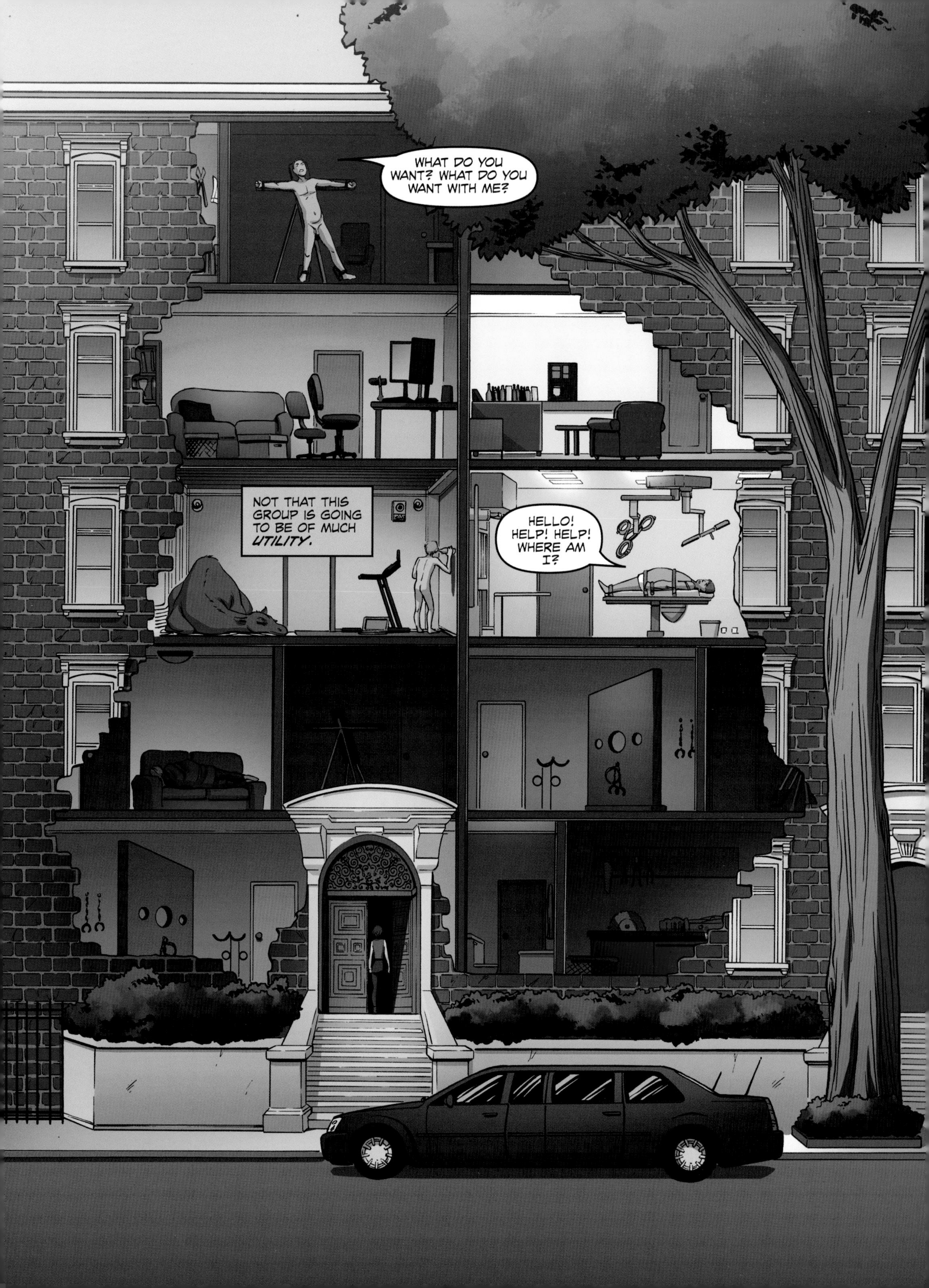
WHAT DO YOU WANT? WHAT DO YOU WANT WITH ME?
NOT THAT THIS GROUP IS GOING TO BE OF MUCH *UTILITY*.
HELLO! HELP! HELP! WHERE AM I?

THE FOOLS LEFT ME A
COMPUTER, THROUGH WHICH
TO GIVE AWAY MY FORTUNE.

MY CAPTORS *UNDERESTIMATE* ME. I AM NO
SKILLESS MANIPULATOR OF STOCK MARKETS.
NO *MERE-MANAGER* OF OTHER PEOPLE'S
MONEY. MY FORTUNE IS FOUNDED ON *CRAFT*.

I *BUILT* THE SYSTEM THAT BEARS
MY *NAME*, THE MOST *SECURE*, THE
FASTEST, MOST *ADAPTABLE CLOSED
NETWORK* IN THE HISTORY OF *FINANCE*.

IT IS ON MY *CODE*
THAT THE WORLD'S
MARKETS RUN.

WHICH MEANS, AMONGST OTHER
THINGS, I KNOW HOW TO *HACK*.

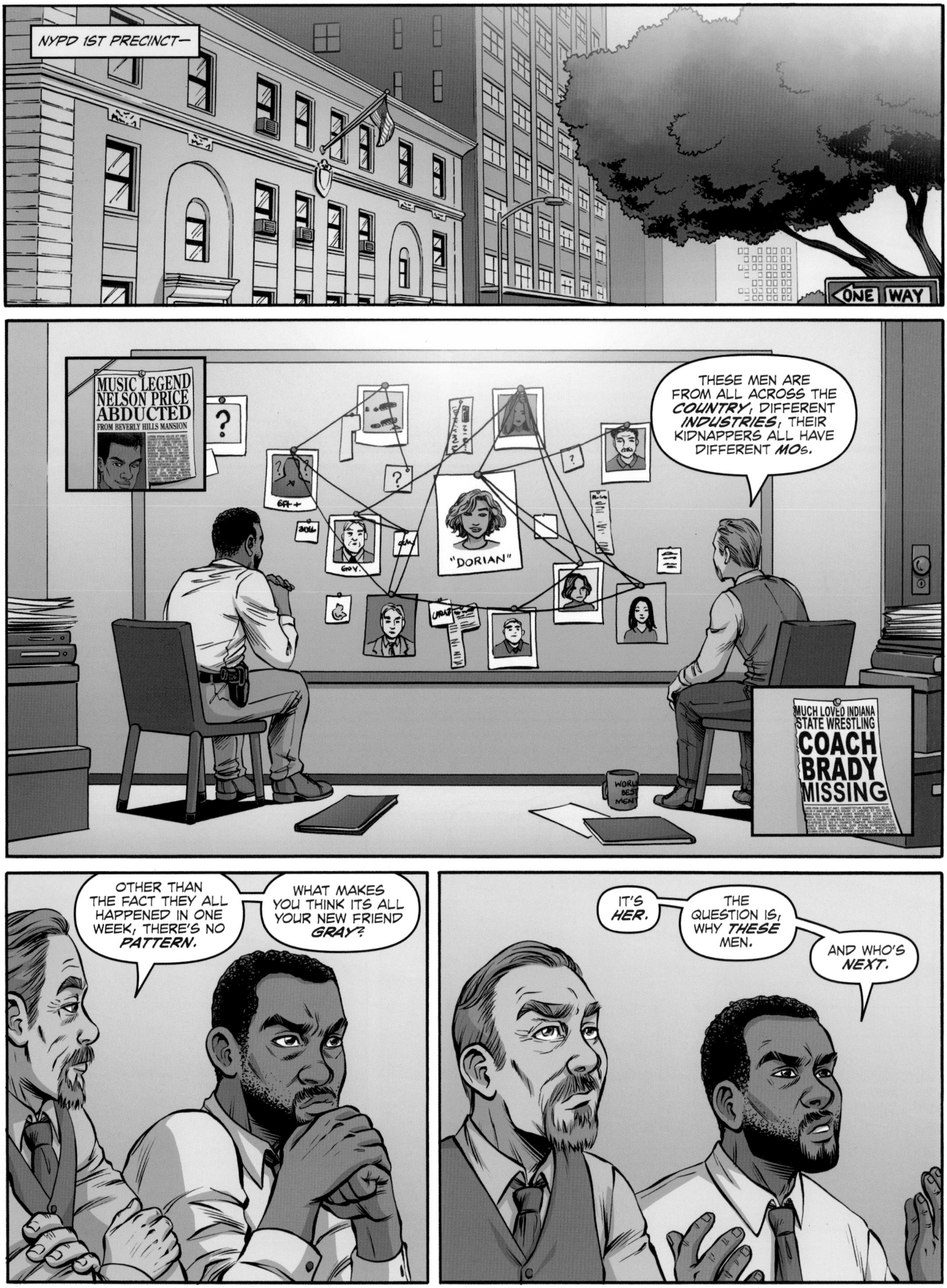
NYPD 1ST PRECINCT—
ONE WAY
MUSIC LEGEND NELSON PRICE ABDUCTED
FROM BEVERLY HILLS MANSION
"DORIAN"
GOV.
THESE MEN ARE FROM ALL ACROSS THE COUNTRY, DIFFERENT INDUSTRIES, THEIR KIDNAPPERS ALL HAVE DIFFERENT MOs.
MUCH LOVED INDIANA STATE WRESTLING COACH BRADY MISSING
OTHER THAN THE FACT THEY ALL HAPPENED IN ONE WEEK, THERE'S NO PATTERN.
WHAT MAKES YOU THINK ITS ALL YOUR NEW FRIEND GRAY?
IT'S HER.
THE QUESTION IS, WHY THESE MEN.
AND WHO'S NEXT.

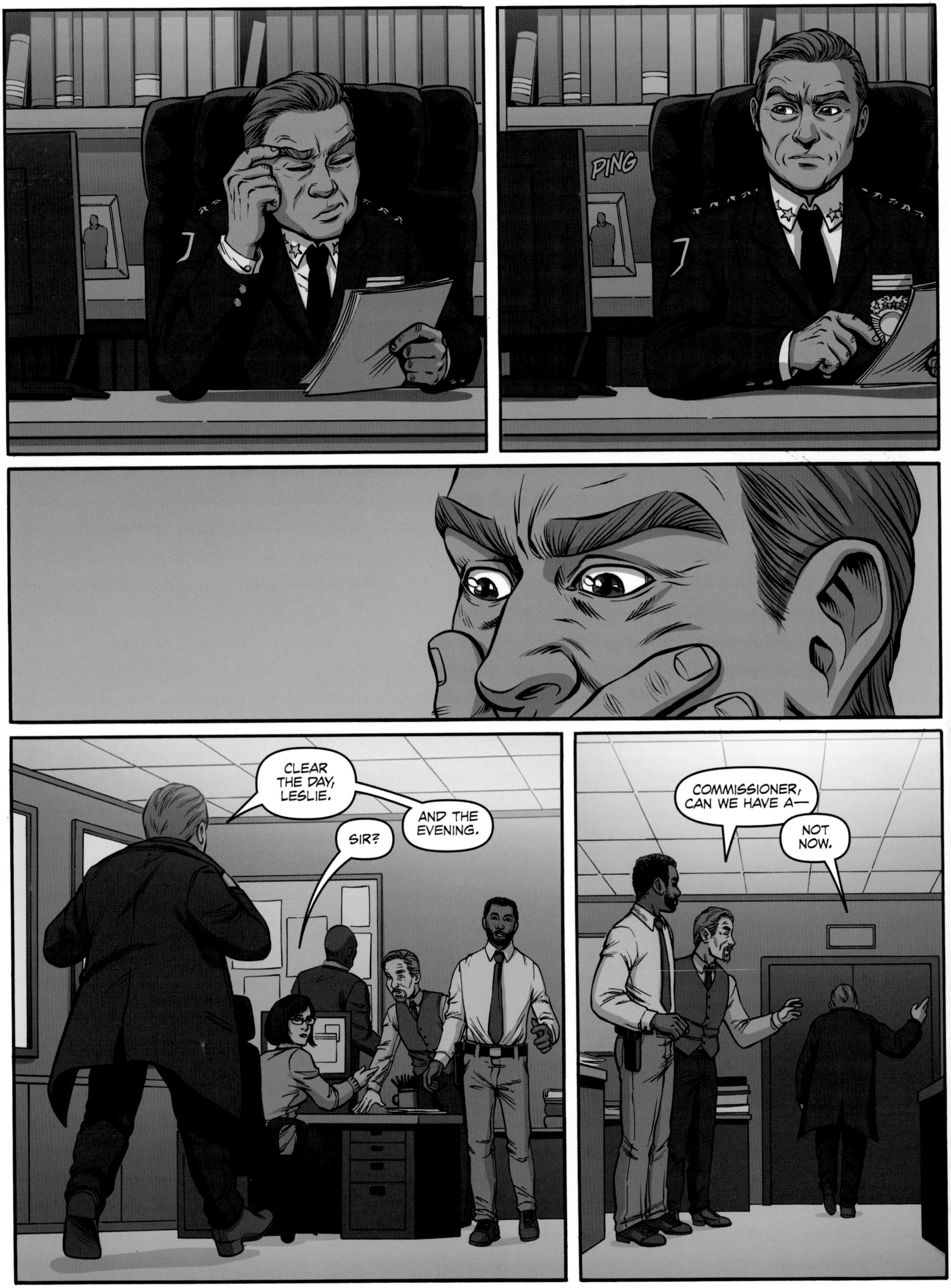
PING
CLEAR THE DAY, LESLIE.
AND THE EVENING.
SIR?
COMMISSIONER, CAN WE HAVE A—
NOT NOW.

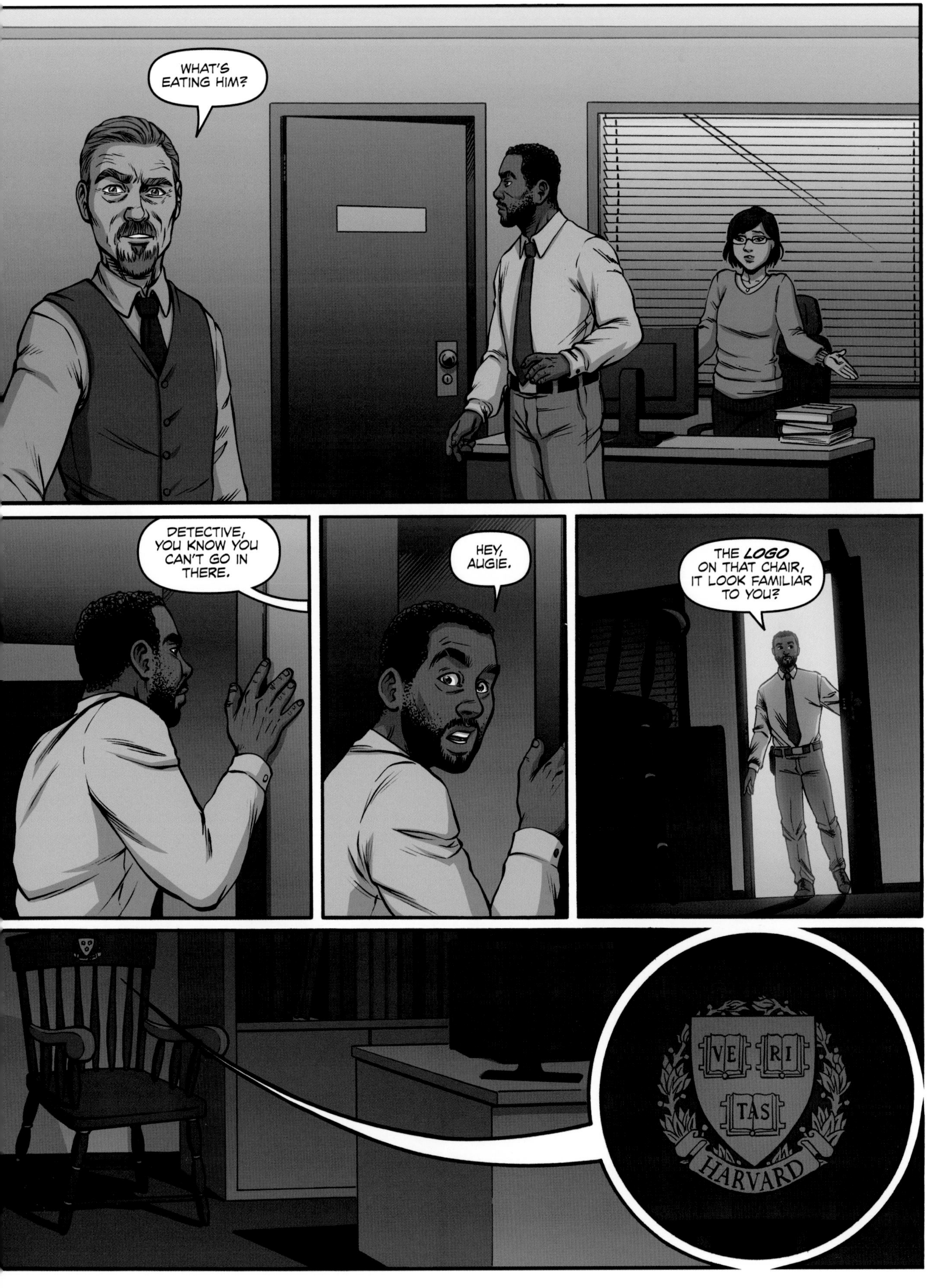
WHAT'S EATING HIM?
DETECTIVE, YOU KNOW YOU CAN'T GO IN THERE.
HEY, AUGIE.
THE LOGO ON THAT CHAIR, IT LOOK FAMILIAR TO YOU?
VE RI TAS
HARVARD

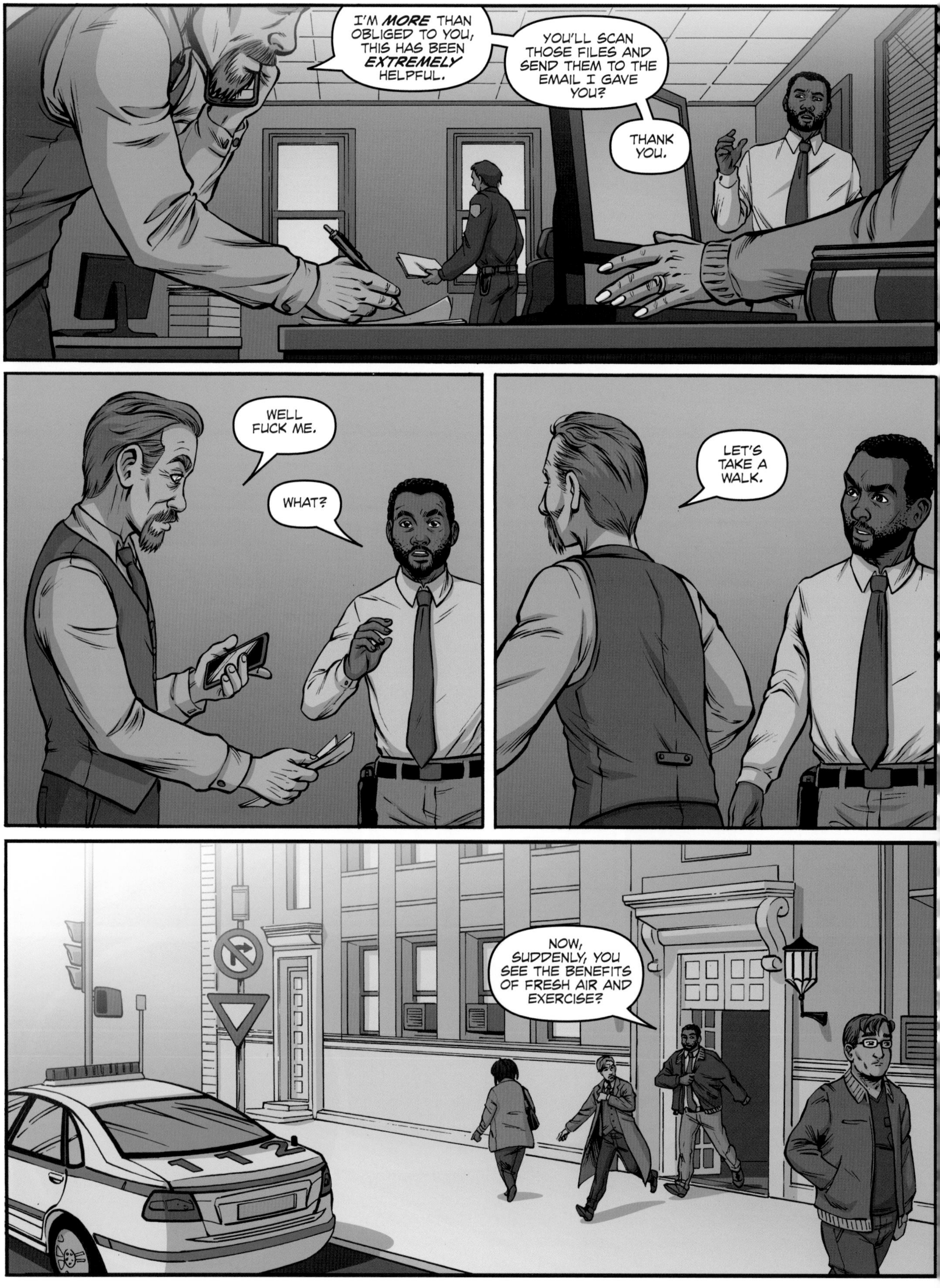
I'M MORE THAN OBLIGED TO YOU, THIS HAS BEEN EXTREMELY HELPFUL.
YOU'LL SCAN THOSE FILES AND SEND THEM TO THE EMAIL I GAVE YOU?
THANK YOU.
WELL FUCK ME.
WHAT?
LET'S TAKE A WALK.
NOW, SUDDENLY, YOU SEE THE BENEFITS OF FRESH AIR AND EXERCISE?

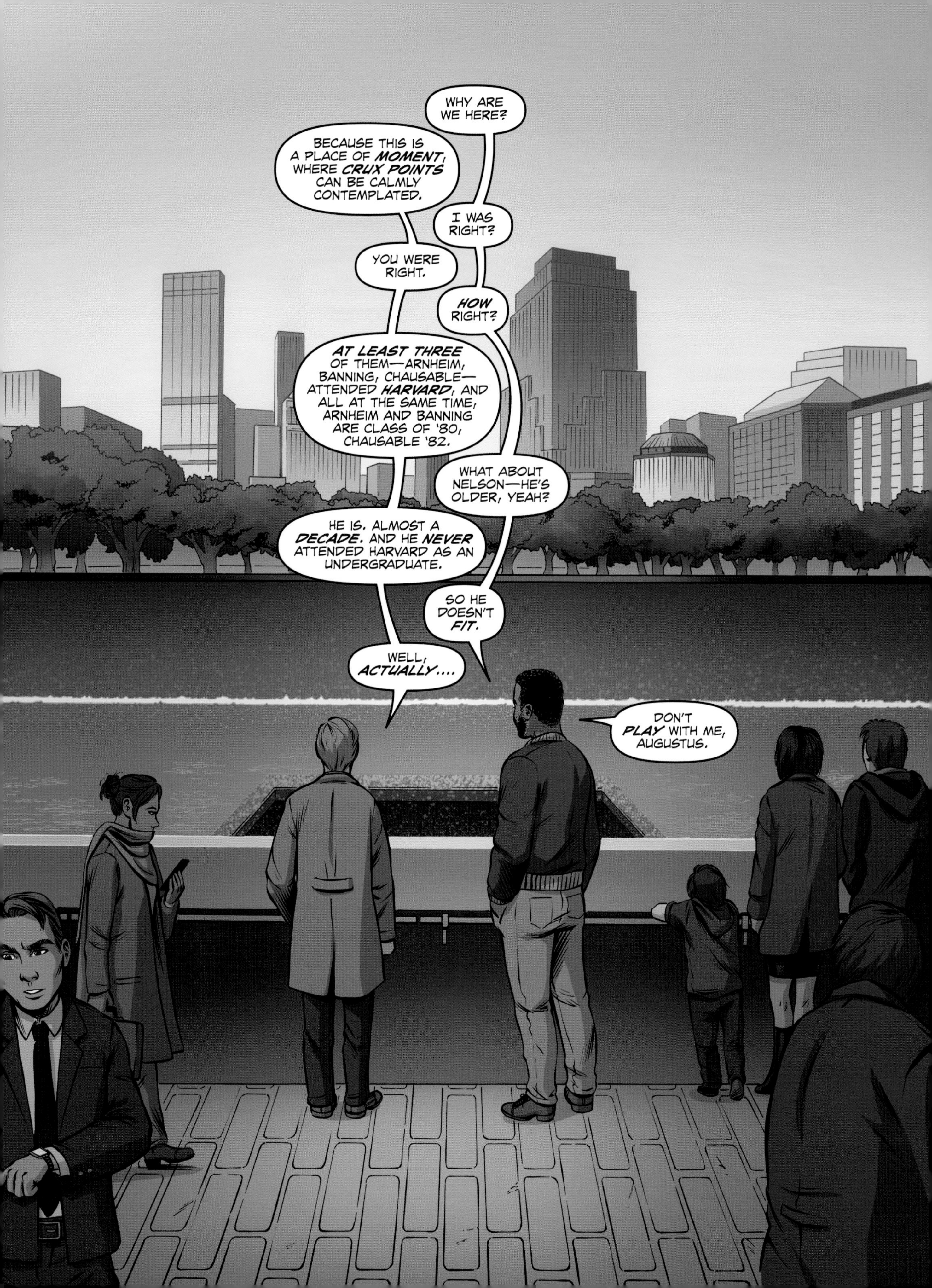
WHY ARE WE HERE?
BECAUSE THIS IS A PLACE OF MOMENT, WHERE CRUX POINTS CAN BE CALMLY CONTEMPLATED.
I WAS RIGHT?
YOU WERE RIGHT.
HOW RIGHT?
AT LEAST THREE OF THEM—ARNHEIM, BANNING, CHAUSABLE—ATTENDED HARVARD, AND ALL AT THE SAME TIME. ARNHEIM AND BANNING ARE CLASS OF '80, CHAUSABLE '82.
WHAT ABOUT NELSON—HE'S OLDER, YEAH?
HE IS. ALMOST A DECADE. AND HE NEVER ATTENDED HARVARD AS AN UNDERGRADUATE.
SO HE DOESN'T FIT.
WELL, ACTUALLY....
DON'T PLAY WITH ME, AUGUSTUS.

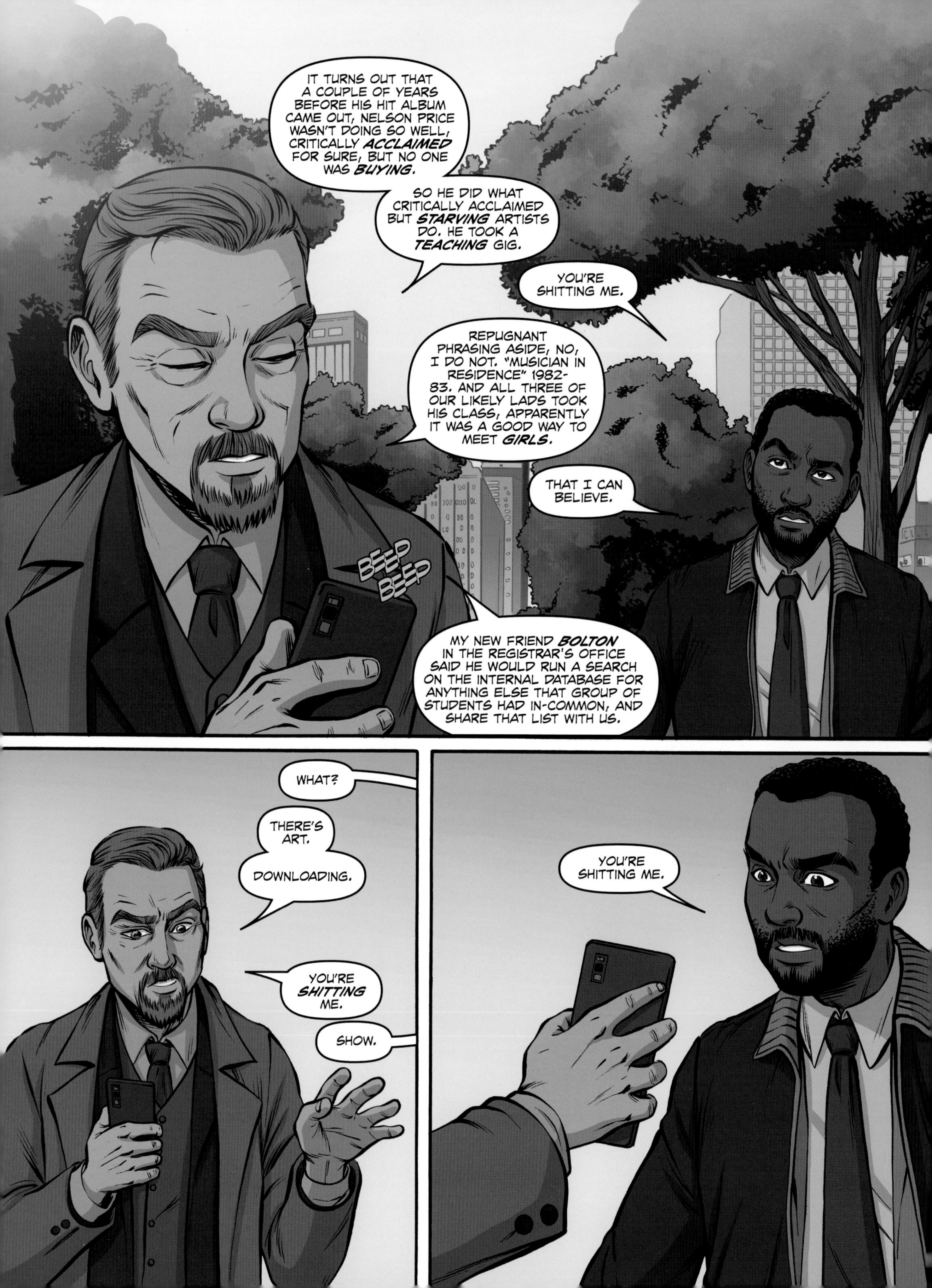
IT TURNS OUT THAT A COUPLE OF YEARS BEFORE HIS HIT ALBUM CAME OUT, NELSON PRICE WASN'T DOING SO WELL, CRITICALLY ACCLAIMED FOR SURE, BUT NO ONE WAS BUYING.
SO HE DID WHAT CRITICALLY ACCLAIMED BUT STARVING ARTISTS DO. HE TOOK A TEACHING GIG.
YOU'RE SHITTING ME.
REPUGNANT PHRASING ASIDE, NO, I DO NOT. "MUSICIAN IN RESIDENCE" 1982-83. AND ALL THREE OF OUR LIKELY LADS TOOK HIS CLASS, APPARENTLY IT WAS A GOOD WAY TO MEET GIRLS.
THAT I CAN BELIEVE.
BEEP BEEP
MY NEW FRIEND BOLTON IN THE REGISTRAR'S OFFICE SAID HE WOULD RUN A SEARCH ON THE INTERNAL DATABASE FOR ANYTHING ELSE THAT GROUP OF STUDENTS HAD IN-COMMON, AND SHARE THAT LIST WITH US.
WHAT?
THERE'S ART.
DOWNLOADING.
YOU'RE SHITTING ME.
SHOW.
YOU'RE SHITTING ME.

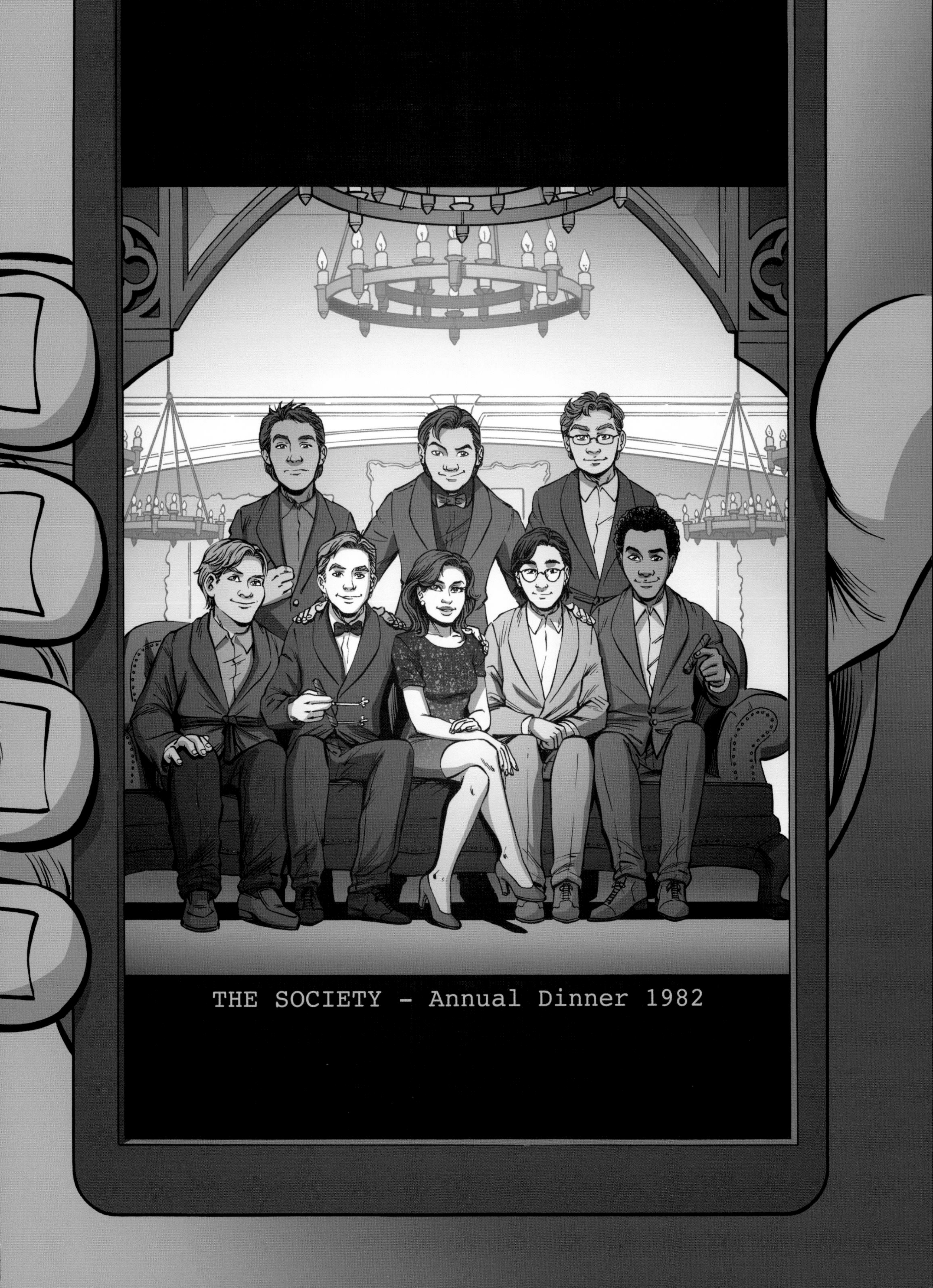
THE SOCIETY - Annual Dinner 1982

Chapter 5

"If you want to know what a woman really means—which, by the way, is always a dangerous thing to do—look at her, don't listen to her."

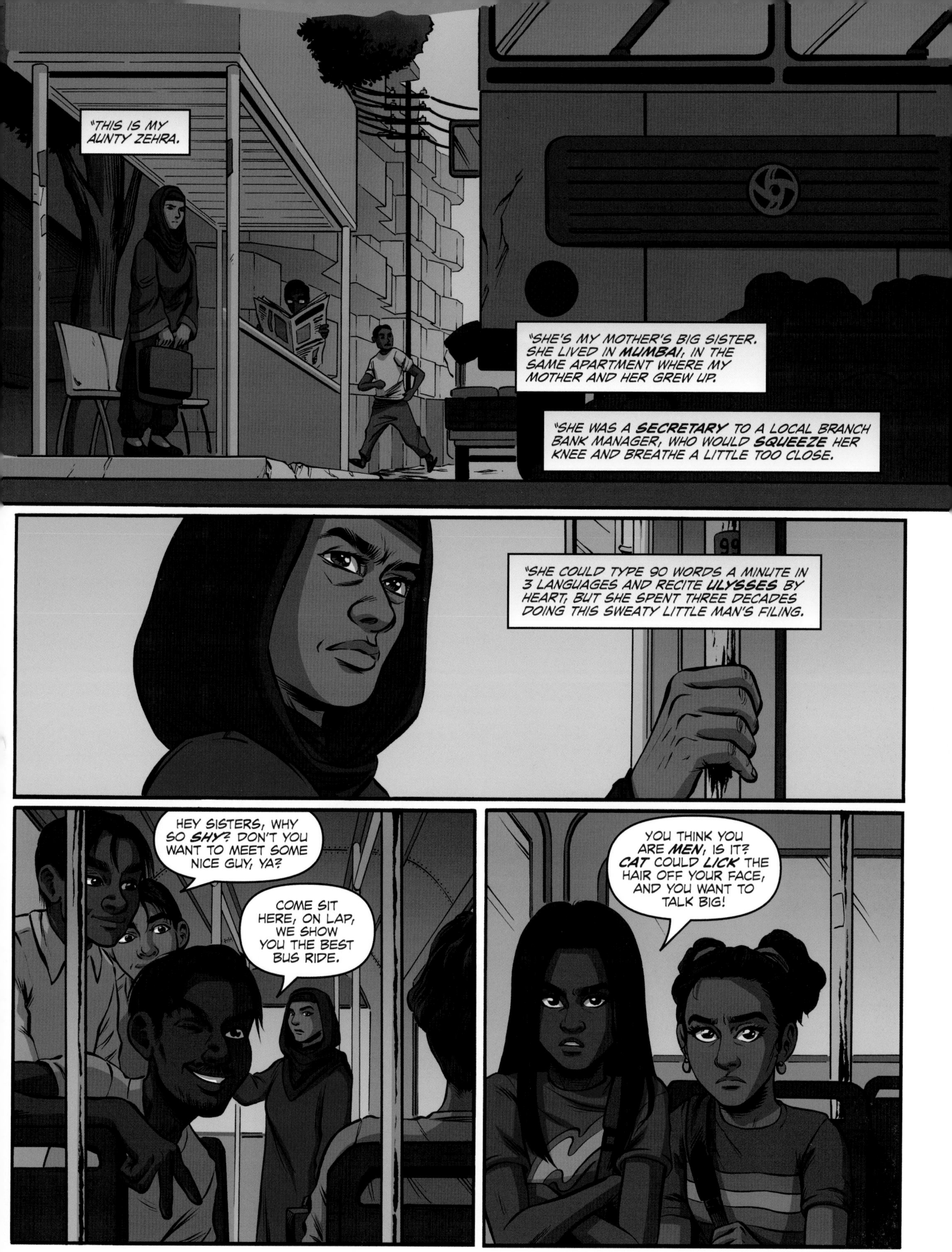

"THIS IS MY AUNTY ZEHRA.
"SHE'S MY MOTHER'S BIG SISTER. SHE LIVED IN MUMBAI, IN THE SAME APARTMENT WHERE MY MOTHER AND HER GREW UP.
"SHE WAS A SECRETARY TO A LOCAL BRANCH BANK MANAGER, WHO WOULD SQUEEZE HER KNEE AND BREATHE A LITTLE TOO CLOSE.
"SHE COULD TYPE 90 WORDS A MINUTE IN 3 LANGUAGES AND RECITE ULYSSES BY HEART, BUT SHE SPENT THREE DECADES DOING THIS SWEATY LITTLE MAN'S FILING.
HEY SISTERS, WHY SO SHY? DON'T YOU WANT TO MEET SOME NICE GUY, YA?
COME SIT HERE, ON LAP, WE SHOW YOU THE BEST BUS RIDE.
YOU THINK YOU ARE MEN, IS IT? CAT COULD LICK THE HAIR OFF YOUR FACE, AND YOU WANT TO TALK BIG!

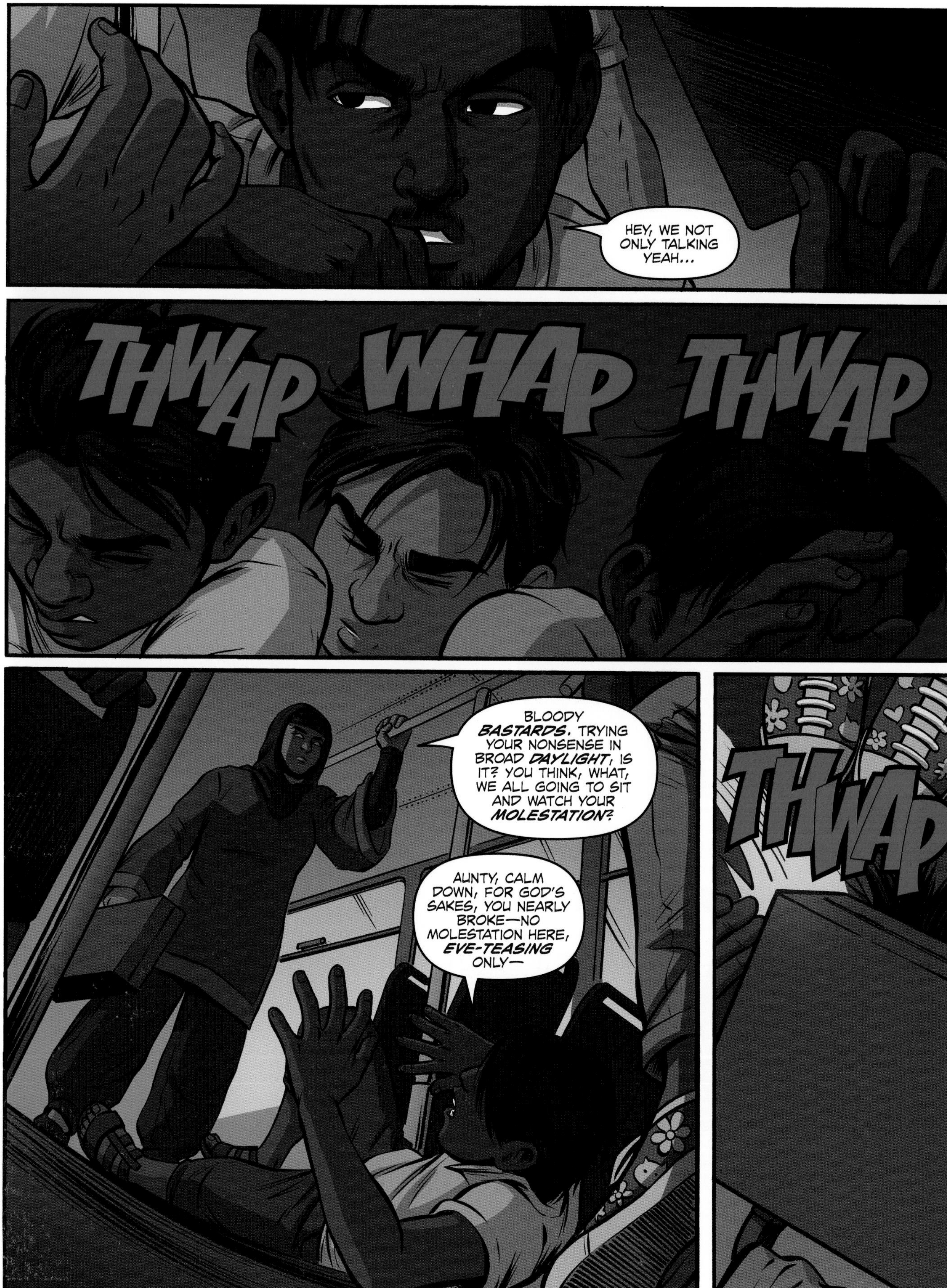
HEY, WE NOT ONLY TALKING YEAH...
THWAP
WHAP
THWAP
BLOODY BASTARDS. TRYING YOUR NONSENSE IN BROAD DAYLIGHT, IS IT? YOU THINK, WHAT, WE ALL GOING TO SIT AND WATCH YOUR MOLESTATION?
AUNTY, CALM DOWN, FOR GOD'S SAKES, YOU NEARLY BROKE—NO MOLESTATION HERE, EVE-TEASING ONLY—
THWAP

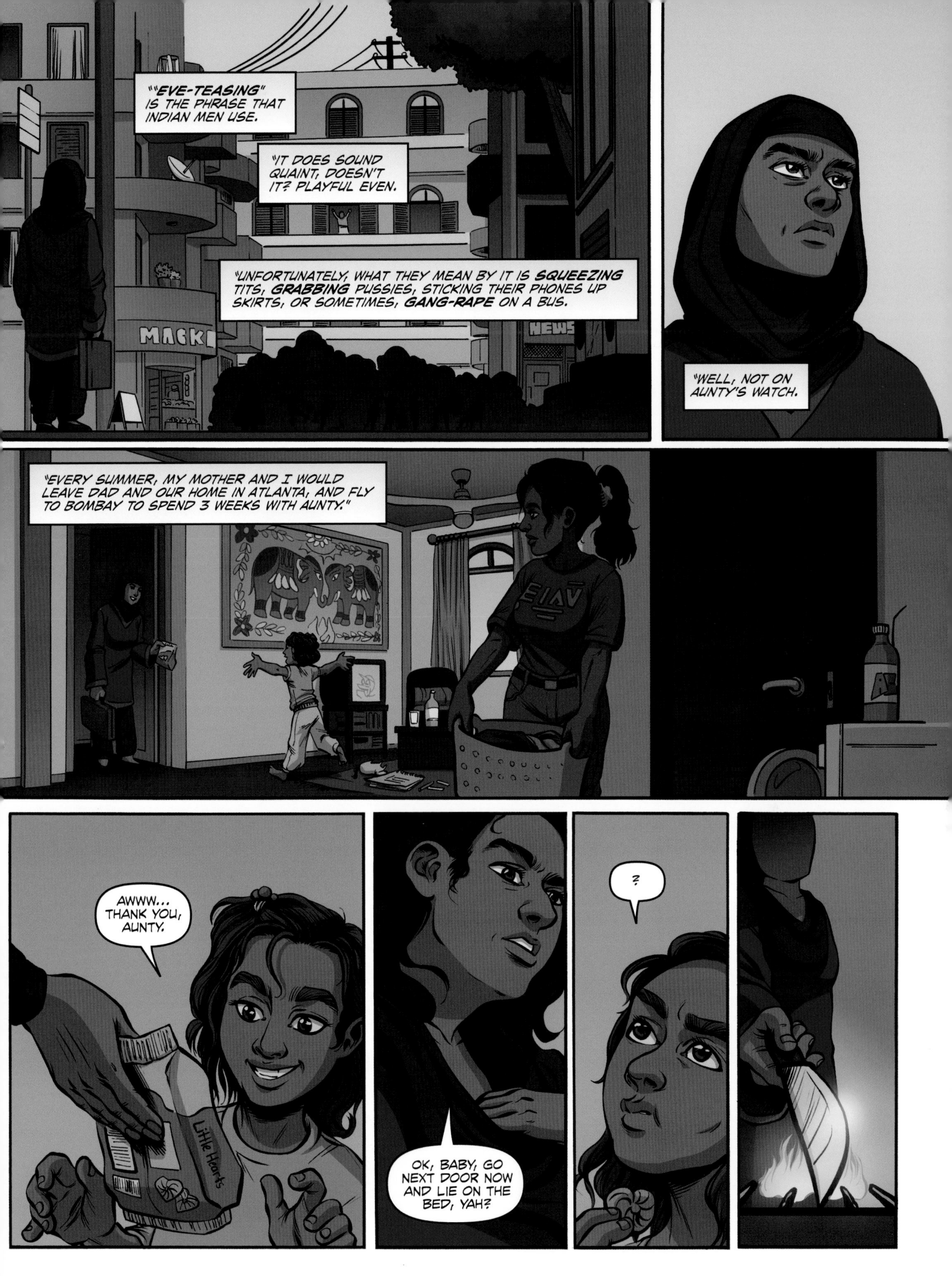
"“EVE-TEASING” IS THE PHRASE THAT INDIAN MEN USE.
"IT DOES SOUND QUAINT, DOESN'T IT? PLAYFUL EVEN.
"UNFORTUNATELY, WHAT THEY MEAN BY IT IS SQUEEZING TITS, GRABBING PUSSIES, STICKING THEIR PHONES UP SKIRTS, OR SOMETIMES, GANG-RAPE ON A BUS.
MACK
NEWS
"WELL, NOT ON AUNTY'S WATCH.
"EVERY SUMMER, MY MOTHER AND I WOULD LEAVE DAD AND OUR HOME IN ATLANTA, AND FLY TO BOMBAY TO SPEND 3 WEEKS WITH AUNTY."
AWWW... THANK YOU, AUNTY.
Little Hearts
OK, BABY, GO NEXT DOOR NOW AND LIE ON THE BED, YAH?
?

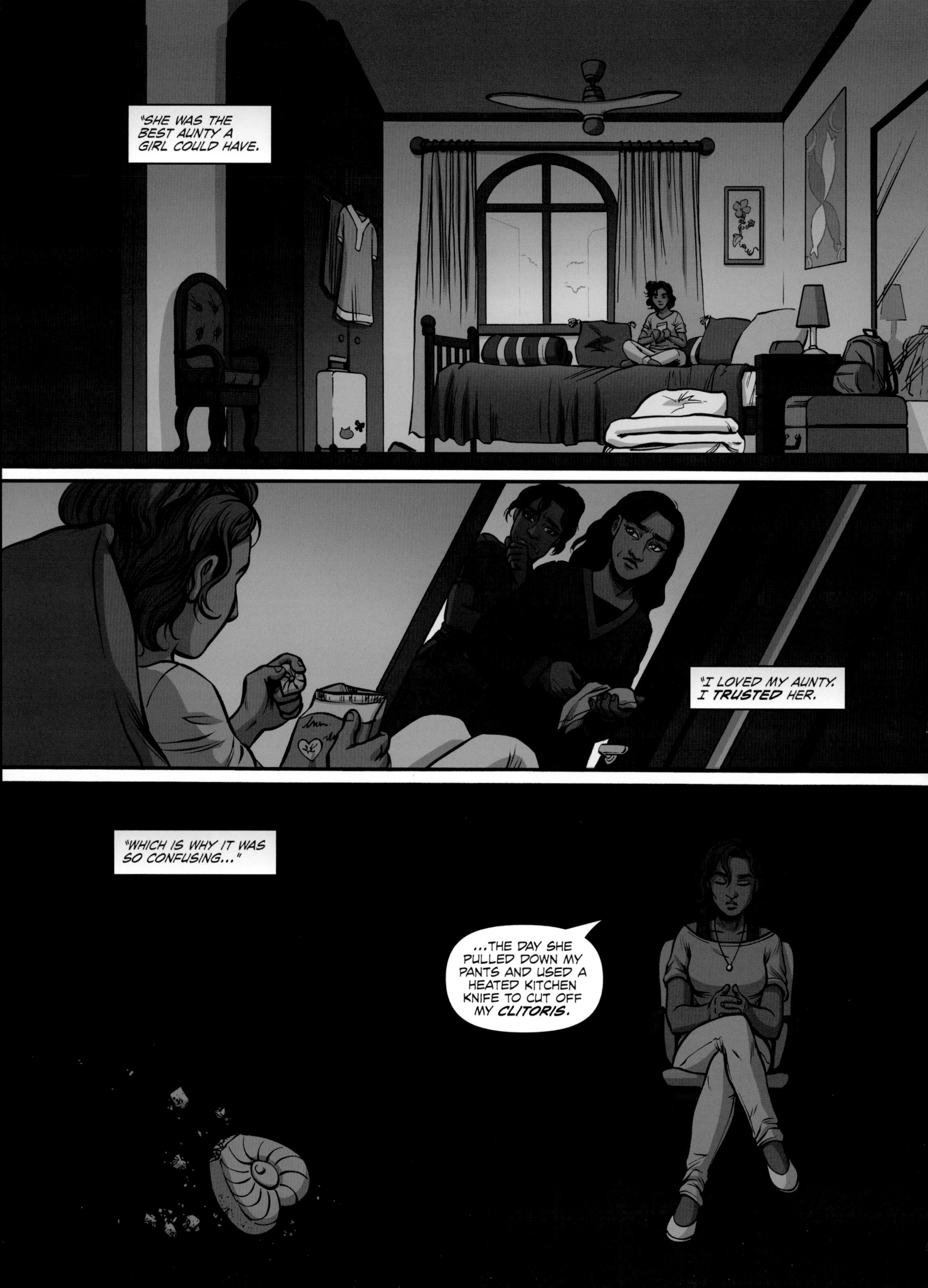
"SHE WAS THE BEST AUNTY A GIRL COULD HAVE.
"I LOVED MY AUNTY. I TRUSTED HER.
"WHICH IS WHY IT WAS SO CONFUSING..."
...THE DAY SHE PULLED DOWN MY PANTS AND USED A HEATED KITCHEN KNIFE TO CUT OFF MY CLITORIS.

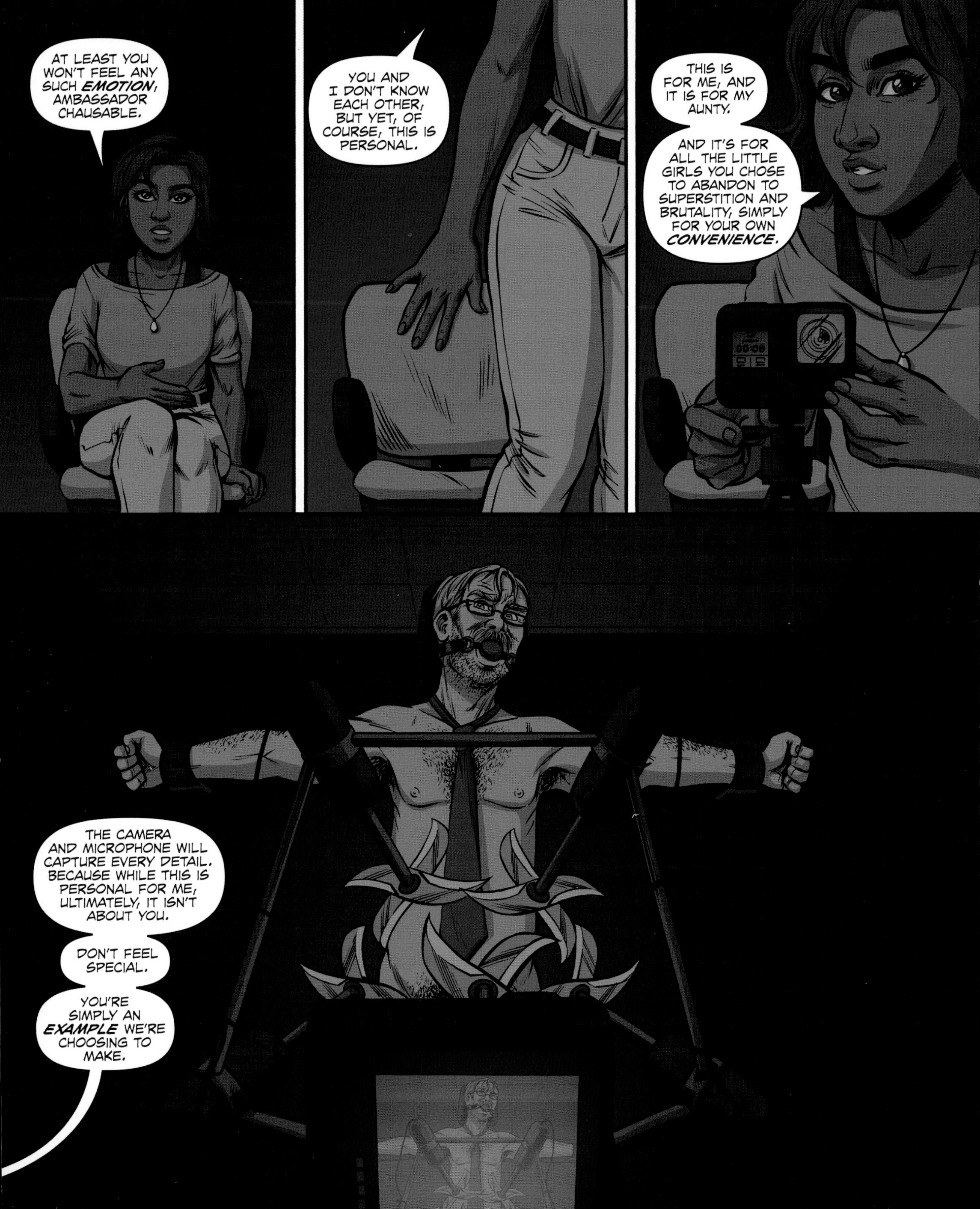

AT LEAST YOU WON'T FEEL ANY SUCH *EMOTION*, AMBASSADOR CHAUSABLE.
YOU AND I DON'T KNOW EACH OTHER, BUT YET, OF COURSE, THIS IS PERSONAL.
THIS IS FOR ME, AND IT IS FOR MY AUNTY.
AND IT'S FOR ALL THE LITTLE GIRLS YOU CHOSE TO ABANDON TO SUPERSTITION AND BRUTALITY, SIMPLY FOR YOUR OWN *CONVENIENCE*.
THE CAMERA AND MICROPHONE WILL CAPTURE EVERY DETAIL. BECAUSE WHILE THIS IS PERSONAL FOR ME, ULTIMATELY, IT ISN'T ABOUT YOU.
DON'T FEEL SPECIAL.
YOU'RE SIMPLY AN *EXAMPLE* WE'RE CHOOSING TO MAKE.

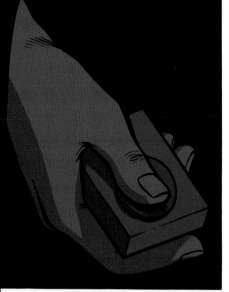

WWHHIIIIZZZZ

WWHHIIIIZZZZ

AHHHHHH

YOU'RE THE COLLATERAL DAMAGE IN FIXING SOMETHING THAT NEEDS FIXING.

EH HEH EHE HEH EHEHE HEH HHEH!

THAT'S ALL ANY OF YOU ARE.

WWHHIIIIZZZZ

WWHHIIIIZZZZ

AHHHHHH

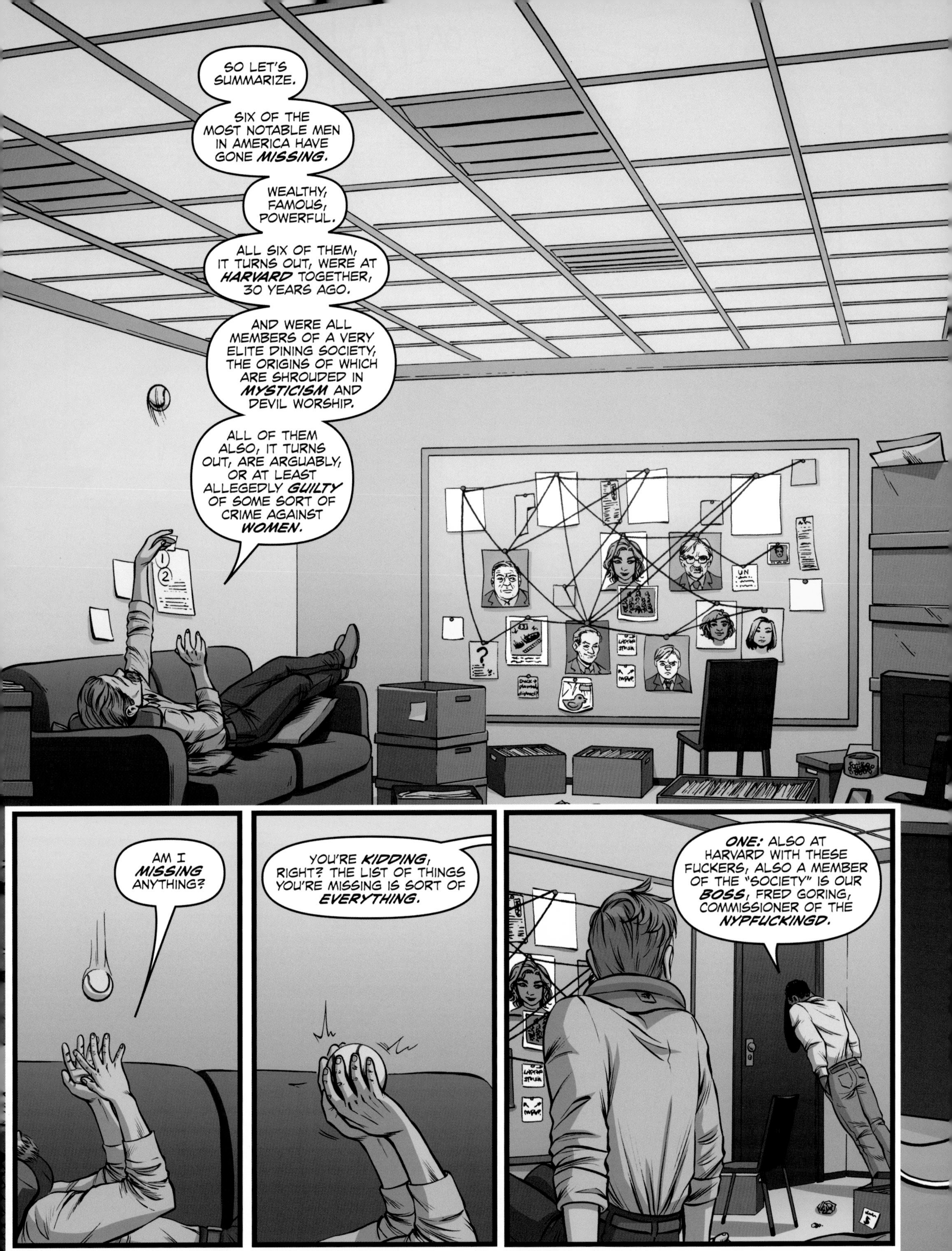
SO LET'S SUMMARIZE.
SIX OF THE MOST NOTABLE MEN IN AMERICA HAVE GONE MISSING.
WEALTHY, FAMOUS, POWERFUL.
ALL SIX OF THEM, IT TURNS OUT, WERE AT HARVARD TOGETHER, 30 YEARS AGO.
AND WERE ALL MEMBERS OF A VERY ELITE DINING SOCIETY, THE ORIGINS OF WHICH ARE SHROUDED IN MYSTICISM AND DEVIL WORSHIP.
ALL OF THEM ALSO, IT TURNS OUT, ARE ARGUABLY, OR AT LEAST ALLEGEDLY GUILTY OF SOME SORT OF CRIME AGAINST WOMEN.
AM I MISSING ANYTHING?
YOU'RE KIDDING, RIGHT? THE LIST OF THINGS YOU'RE MISSING IS SORT OF EVERYTHING.
ONE: ALSO AT HARVARD WITH THESE FUCKERS, ALSO A MEMBER OF THE "SOCIETY" IS OUR BOSS, FRED GORING, COMMISSIONER OF THE NYPFUCKINGD.

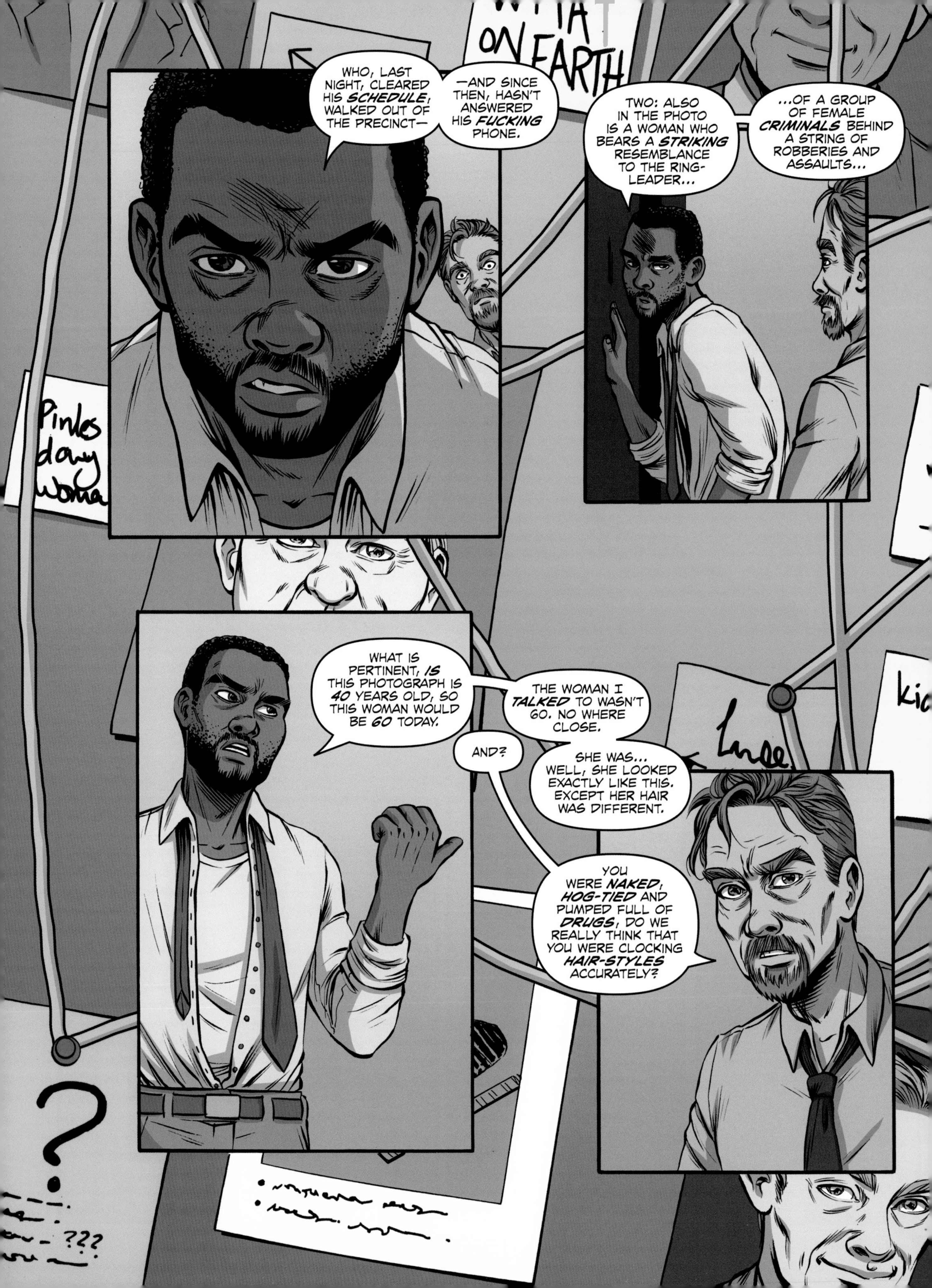
ON EARTH
WHO, LAST NIGHT, CLEARED HIS SCHEDULE, WALKED OUT OF THE PRECINCT—
—AND SINCE THEN, HASN'T ANSWERED HIS FUCKING PHONE.
TWO: ALSO IN THE PHOTO IS A WOMAN WHO BEARS A STRIKING RESEMBLANCE TO THE RING-LEADER...
...OF A GROUP OF FEMALE CRIMINALS BEHIND A STRING OF ROBBERIES AND ASSAULTS...
WHAT IS PERTINENT, IS THIS PHOTOGRAPH IS 40 YEARS OLD, SO THIS WOMAN WOULD BE 60 TODAY.
THE WOMAN I TALKED TO WASN'T 60. NO WHERE CLOSE.
AND?
SHE WAS... WELL, SHE LOOKED EXACTLY LIKE THIS. EXCEPT HER HAIR WAS DIFFERENT.
YOU WERE NAKED, HOG-TIED AND PUMPED FULL OF DRUGS, DO WE REALLY THINK THAT YOU WERE CLOCKING HAIR-STYLES ACCURATELY?
???

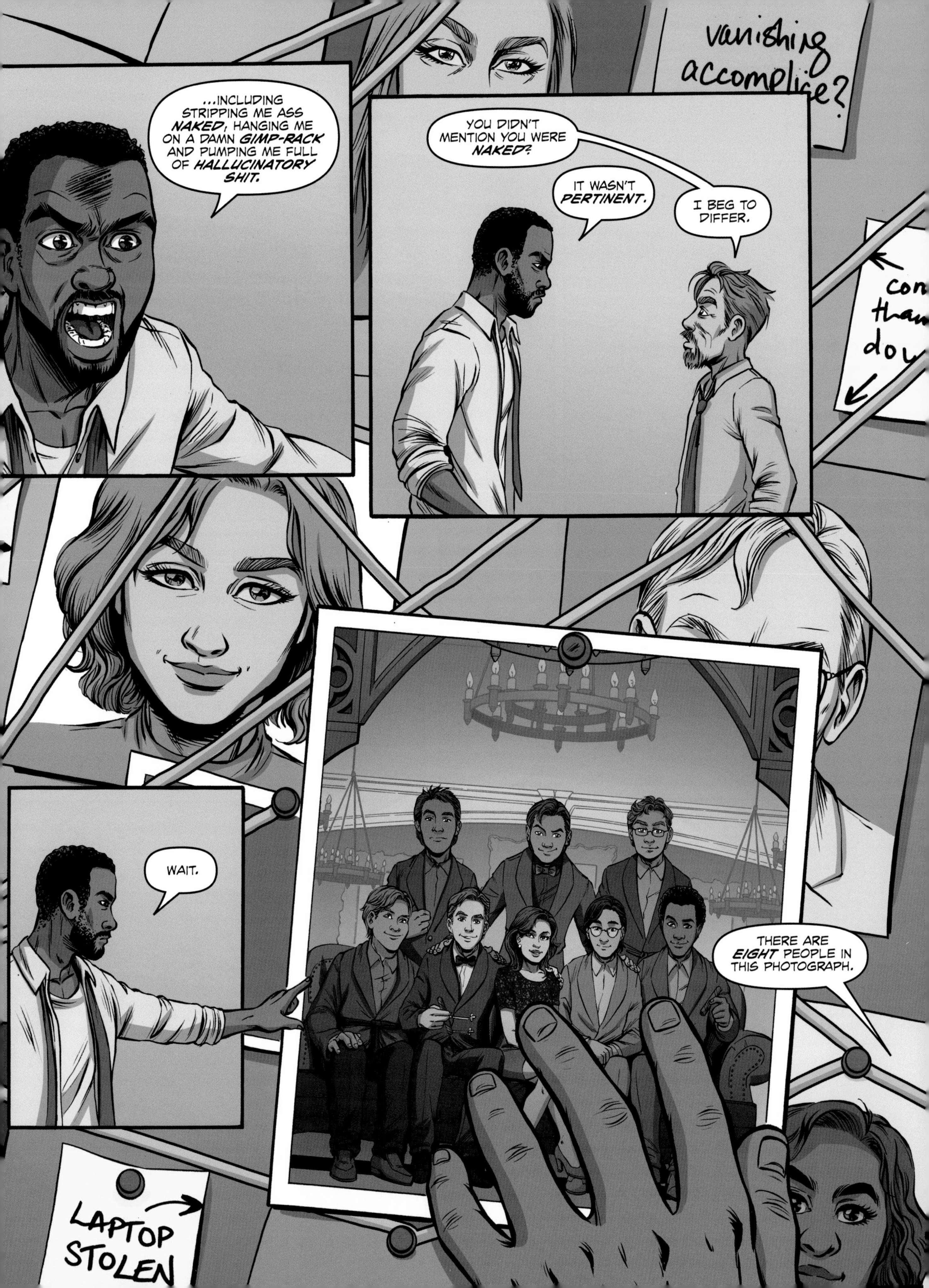
vanishing accomplice?
...INCLUDING STRIPPING ME ASS NAKED, HANGING ME ON A DAMN GIMP-RACK AND PUMPING ME FULL OF HALLUCINATORY SHIT.
YOU DIDN'T MENTION YOU WERE NAKED?
IT WASN'T PERTINENT.
I BEG TO DIFFER.
WAIT.
THERE ARE EIGHT PEOPLE IN THIS PHOTOGRAPH.
LAPTOP STOLEN

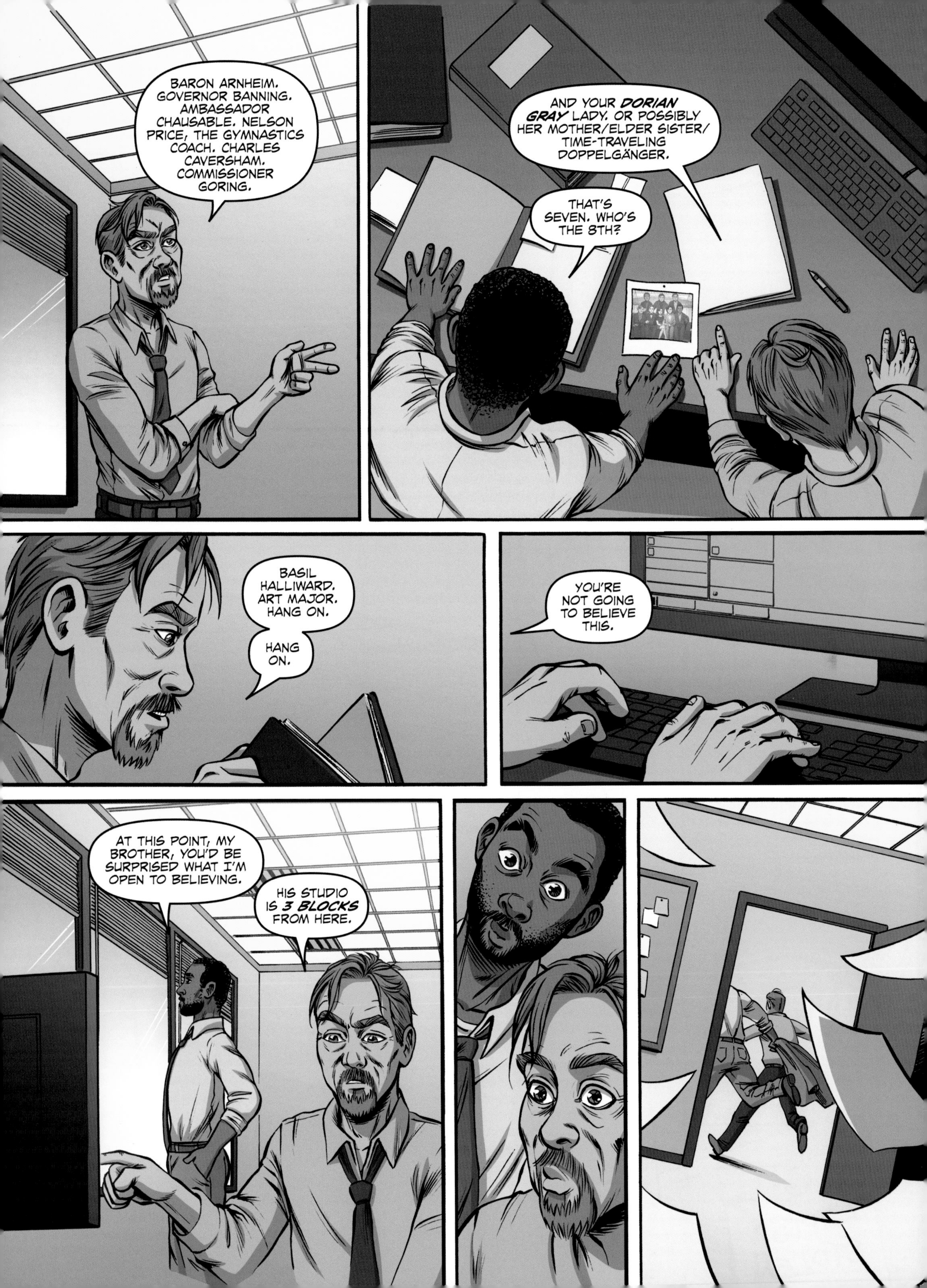
BARON ARNHEIM. GOVERNOR BANNING. AMBASSADOR CHAUSABLE. NELSON PRICE, THE GYMNASTICS COACH. CHARLES CAVERSHAM. COMMISSIONER GORING.
AND YOUR DORIAN GRAY LADY. OR POSSIBLY HER MOTHER/ELDER SISTER/ TIME-TRAVELING DOPPELGÄNGER.
THAT'S SEVEN. WHO'S THE 8TH?
BASIL HALLIWARD. ART MAJOR. HANG ON.
HANG ON.
YOU'RE NOT GOING TO BELIEVE THIS.
AT THIS POINT, MY BROTHER, YOU'D BE SURPRISED WHAT I'M OPEN TO BELIEVING.
HIS STUDIO IS 3 BLOCKS FROM HERE.

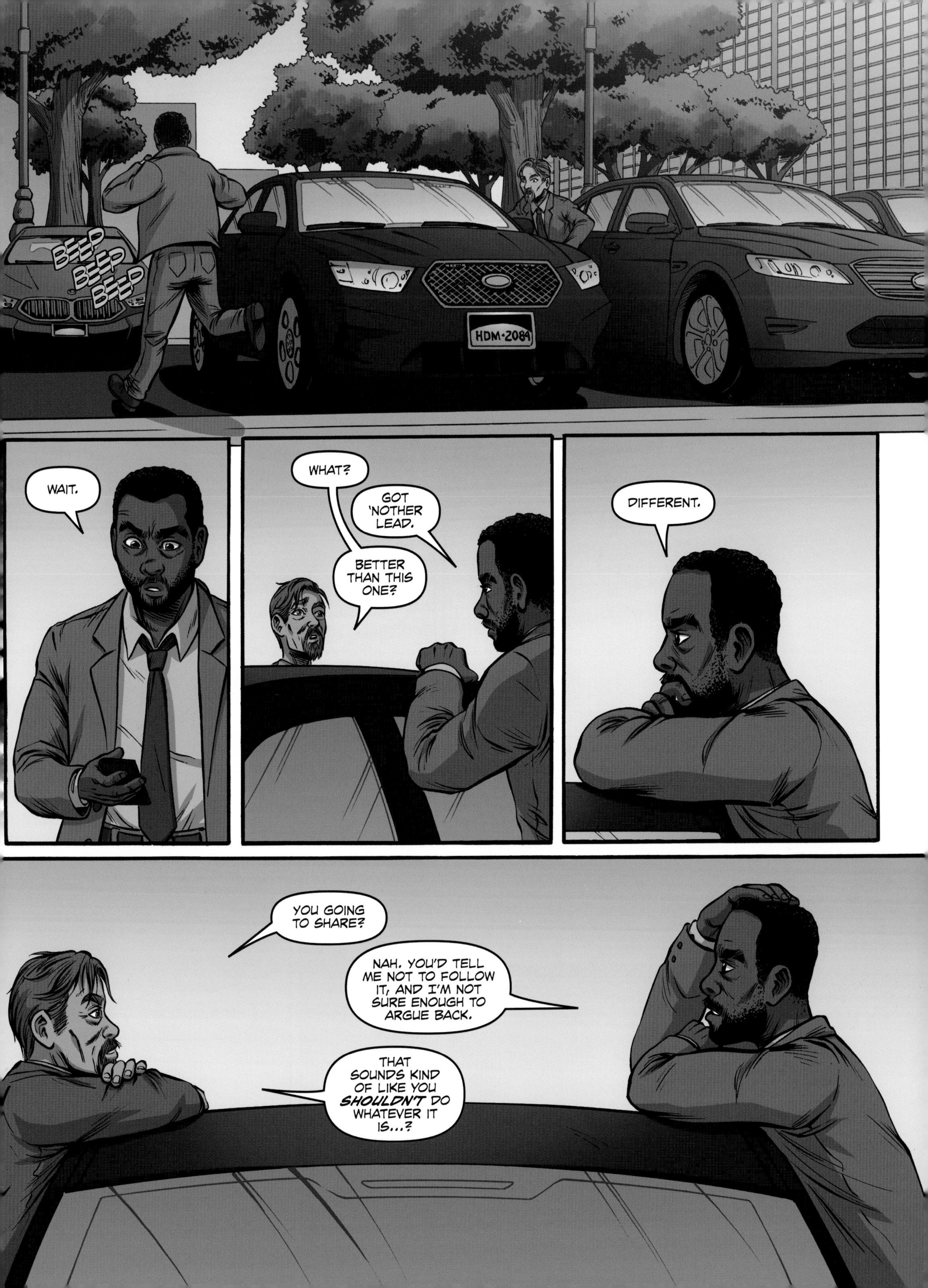
BEEP BEEP BEEP
HDM-2084
WAIT.
WHAT?
GOT 'NOTHER LEAD.
BETTER THAN THIS ONE?
DIFFERENT.
YOU GOING TO SHARE?
NAH. YOU'D TELL ME NOT TO FOLLOW IT, AND I'M NOT SURE ENOUGH TO ARGUE BACK.
THAT SOUNDS KIND OF LIKE YOU SHOULDN'T DO WHATEVER IT IS...?

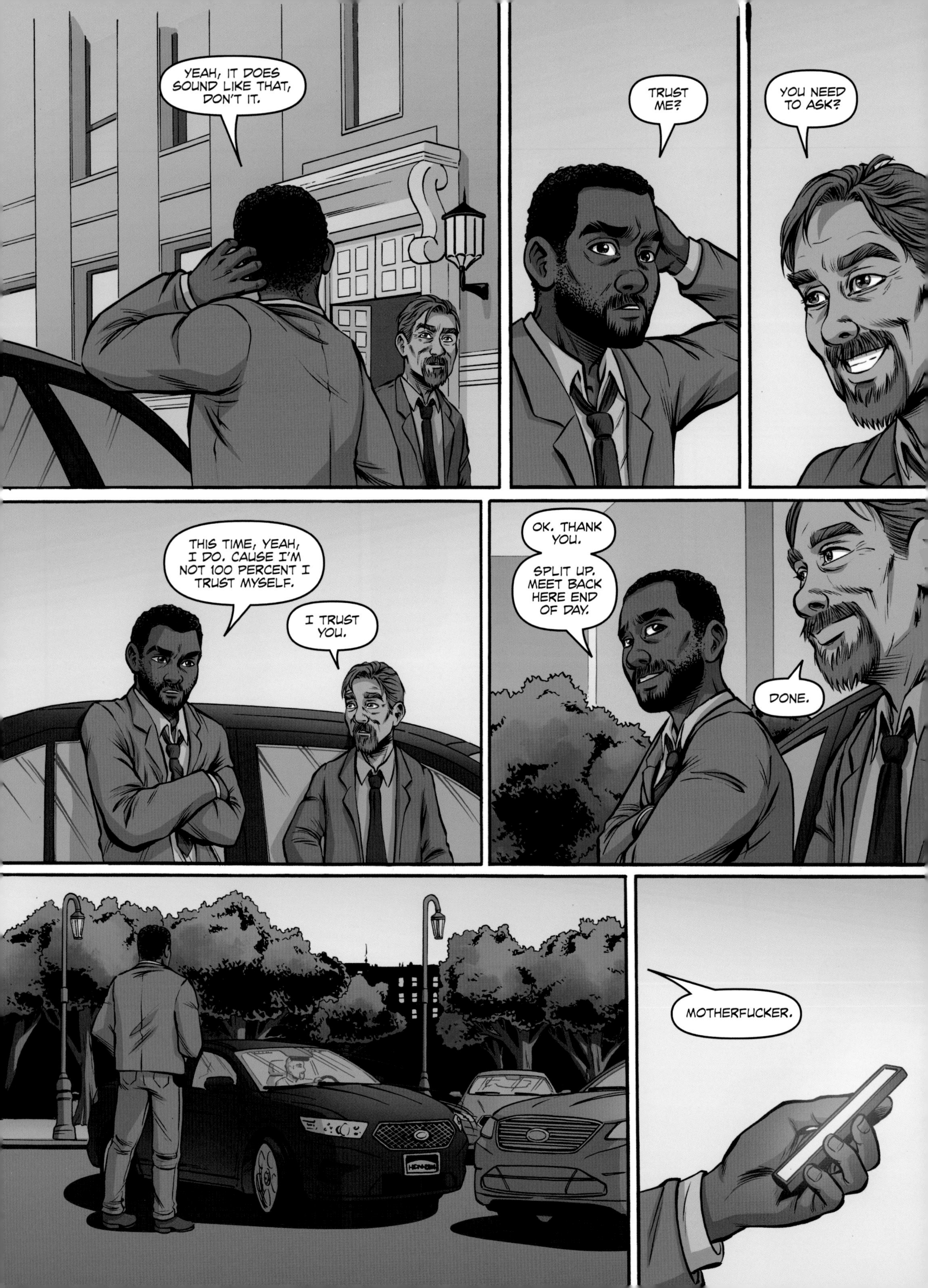
YEAH, IT DOES SOUND LIKE THAT, DON'T IT.
TRUST ME?
YOU NEED TO ASK?
THIS TIME, YEAH, I DO. CAUSE I'M NOT 100 PERCENT I TRUST MYSELF.
I TRUST YOU.
OK. THANK YOU.
SPLIT UP. MEET BACK HERE END OF DAY.
DONE.
MOTHERFUCKER.

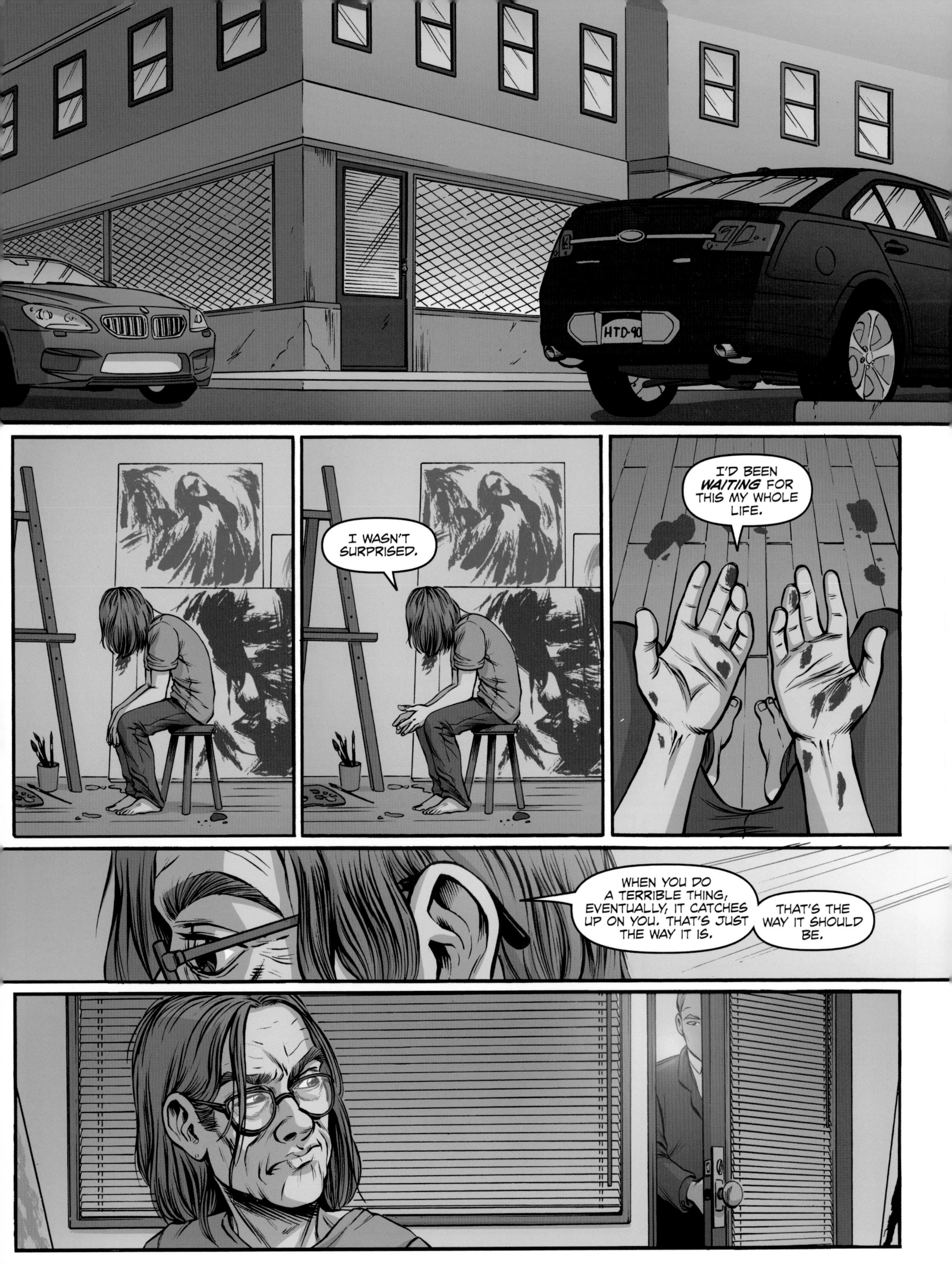
HTD-90
I WASN'T SURPRISED.
I'D BEEN WAITING FOR THIS MY WHOLE LIFE.
WHEN YOU DO A TERRIBLE THING, EVENTUALLY, IT CATCHES UP ON YOU. THAT'S JUST THE WAY IT IS.
THAT'S THE WAY IT SHOULD BE.

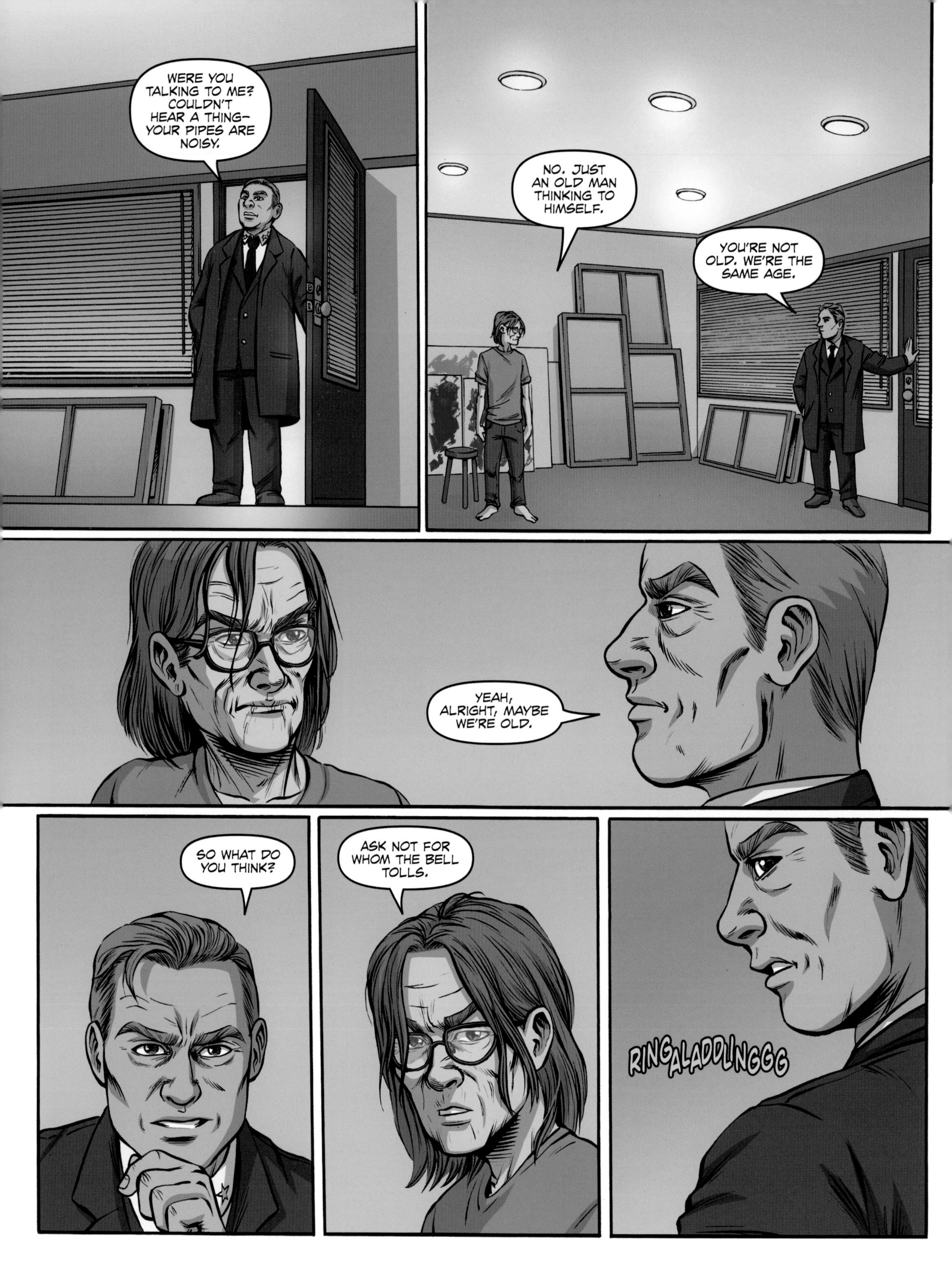
WERE YOU TALKING TO ME? COULDN'T HEAR A THING– YOUR PIPES ARE NOISY.
NO. JUST AN OLD MAN THINKING TO HIMSELF.
YOU'RE NOT OLD. WE'RE THE SAME AGE.
YEAH, ALRIGHT, MAYBE WE'RE OLD.
SO WHAT DO YOU THINK?
ASK NOT FOR WHOM THE BELL TOLLS.
RINGALADDLINGGG

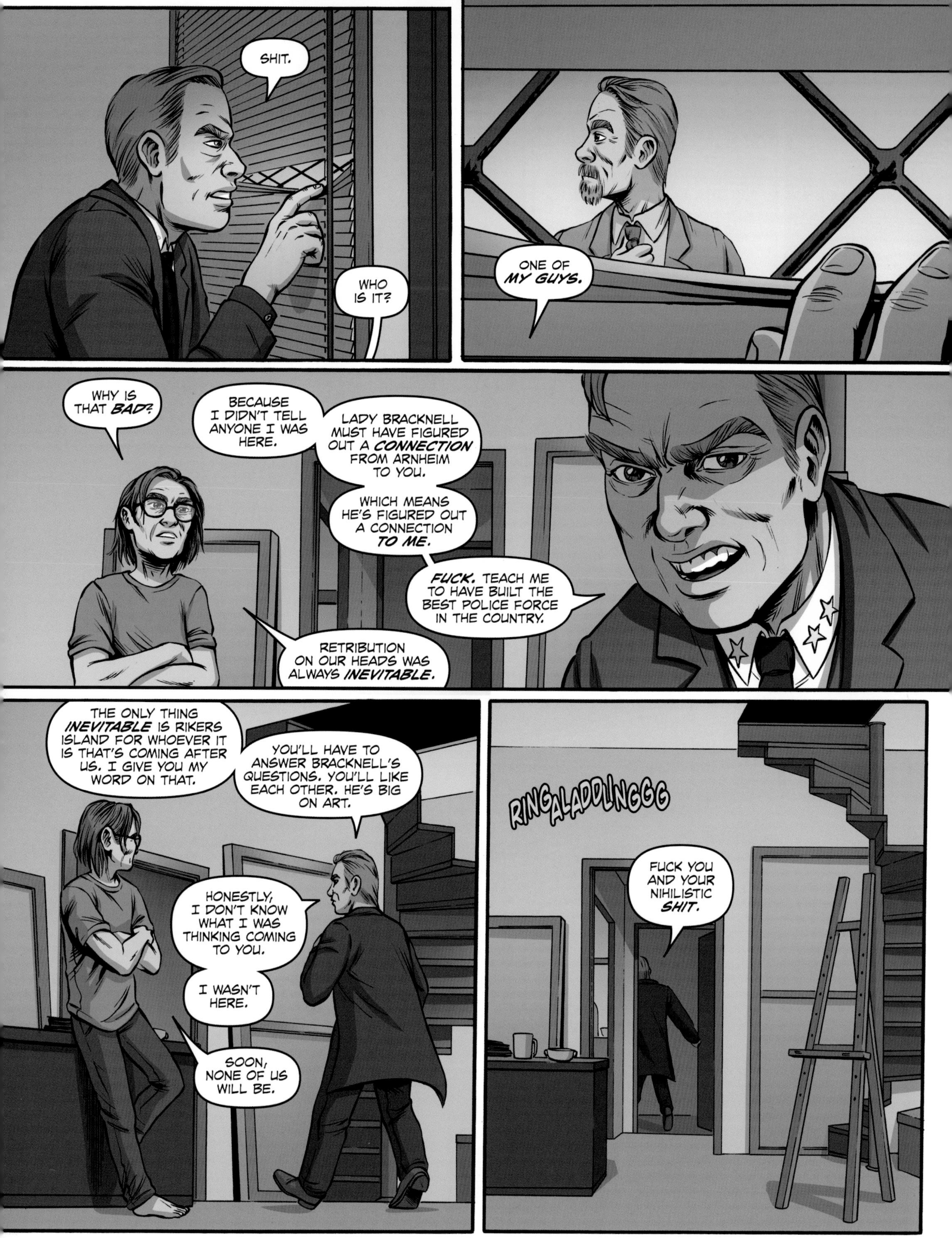
SHIT.
WHO IS IT?
ONE OF MY GUYS.
WHY IS THAT BAD?
BECAUSE I DIDN'T TELL ANYONE I WAS HERE.
LADY BRACKNELL MUST HAVE FIGURED OUT A CONNECTION FROM ARNHEIM TO YOU.
WHICH MEANS HE'S FIGURED OUT A CONNECTION TO ME.
FUCK. TEACH ME TO HAVE BUILT THE BEST POLICE FORCE IN THE COUNTRY.
RETRIBUTION ON OUR HEADS WAS ALWAYS INEVITABLE.
THE ONLY THING INEVITABLE IS RIKERS ISLAND FOR WHOEVER IT IS THAT'S COMING AFTER US. I GIVE YOU MY WORD ON THAT.
YOU'LL HAVE TO ANSWER BRACKNELL'S QUESTIONS. YOU'LL LIKE EACH OTHER. HE'S BIG ON ART.
HONESTLY, I DON'T KNOW WHAT I WAS THINKING COMING TO YOU.
I WASN'T HERE.
SOON, NONE OF US WILL BE.
RINGALADDLINGGG
FUCK YOU AND YOUR NIHILISTIC SHIT.

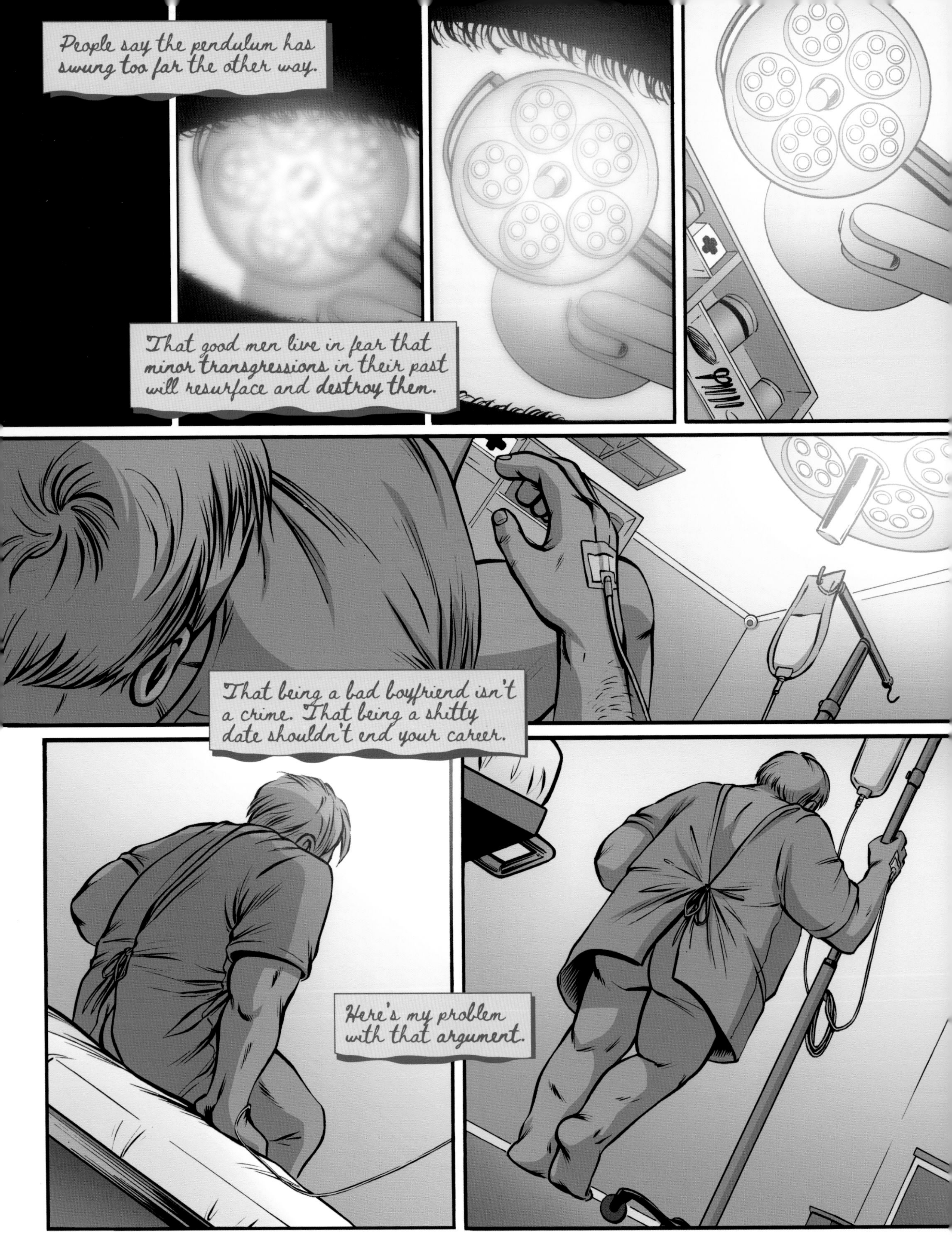
People say the pendulum has swung too far the other way.
That good men live in fear that minor transgressions in their past will resurface and destroy them.
That being a bad boyfriend isn't a crime. That being a shitty date shouldn't end your career.
Here's my problem with that argument.

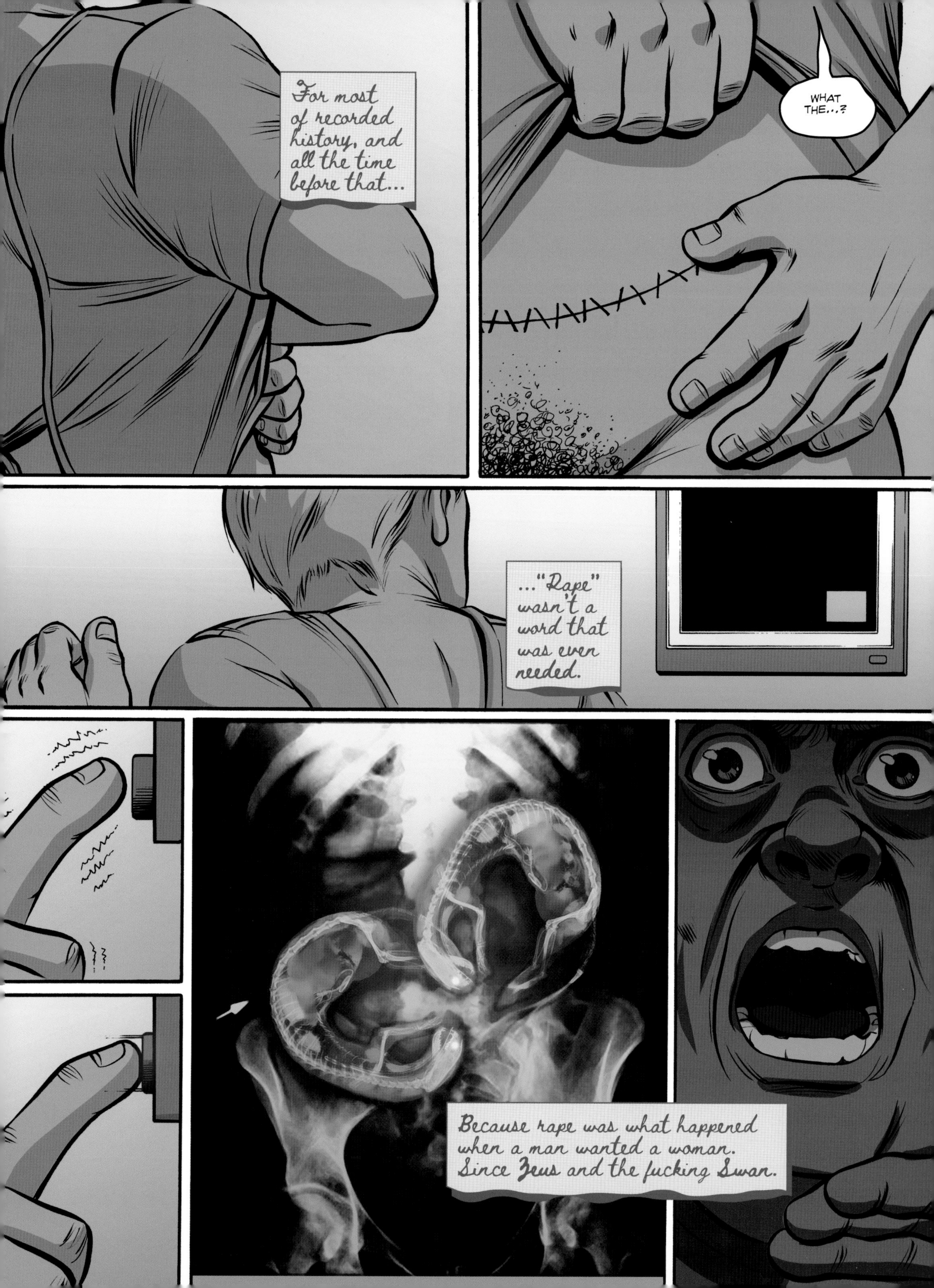
For most of recorded history, and all the time before that...
WHAT THE...?
..."Rape" wasn't a word that was even needed.
Because rape was what happened when a man wanted a woman. Since Zeus and the fucking Swan.

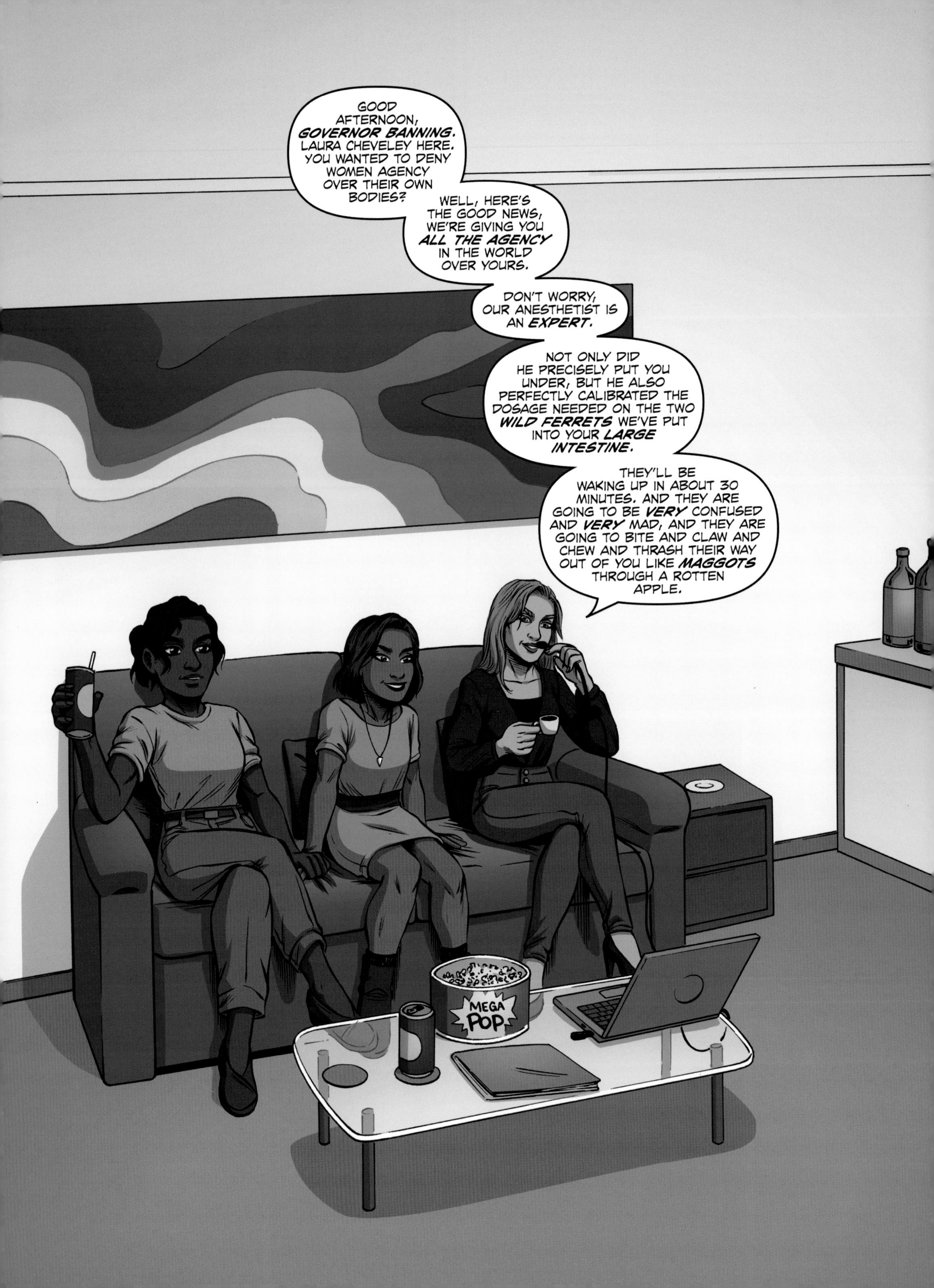
GOOD AFTERNOON, GOVERNOR BANNING. LAURA CHEVELEY HERE. YOU WANTED TO DENY WOMEN AGENCY OVER THEIR OWN BODIES?
WELL, HERE'S THE GOOD NEWS, WE'RE GIVING YOU ALL THE AGENCY IN THE WORLD OVER YOURS.
DON'T WORRY, OUR ANESTHETIST IS AN EXPERT.
NOT ONLY DID HE PRECISELY PUT YOU UNDER, BUT HE ALSO PERFECTLY CALIBRATED THE DOSAGE NEEDED ON THE TWO WILD FERRETS WE'VE PUT INTO YOUR LARGE INTESTINE.
THEY'LL BE WAKING UP IN ABOUT 30 MINUTES. AND THEY ARE GOING TO BE VERY CONFUSED AND VERY MAD, AND THEY ARE GOING TO BITE AND CLAW AND CHEW AND THRASH THEIR WAY OUT OF YOU LIKE MAGGOTS THROUGH A ROTTEN APPLE.
MEGA POP

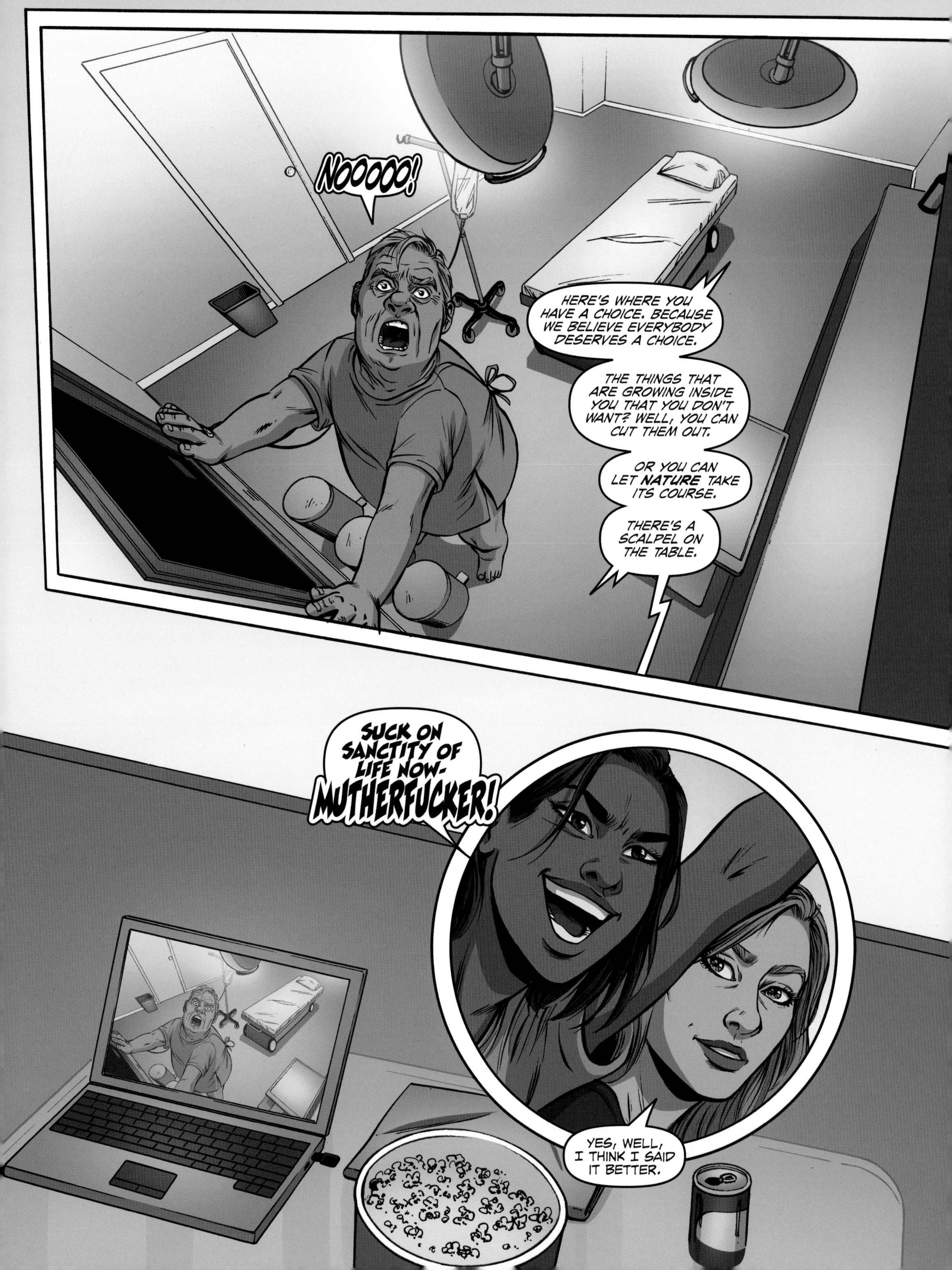
NOOOOO!
HERE'S WHERE YOU HAVE A CHOICE. BECAUSE WE BELIEVE EVERYBODY DESERVES A CHOICE.
THE THINGS THAT ARE GROWING INSIDE YOU THAT YOU DON'T WANT? WELL, YOU CAN CUT THEM OUT.
OR YOU CAN LET NATURE TAKE ITS COURSE.
THERE'S A SCALPEL ON THE TABLE.
SUCK ON SANCTITY OF LIFE NOW- MUTHERFUCKER!
YES, WELL, I THINK I SAID IT BETTER.

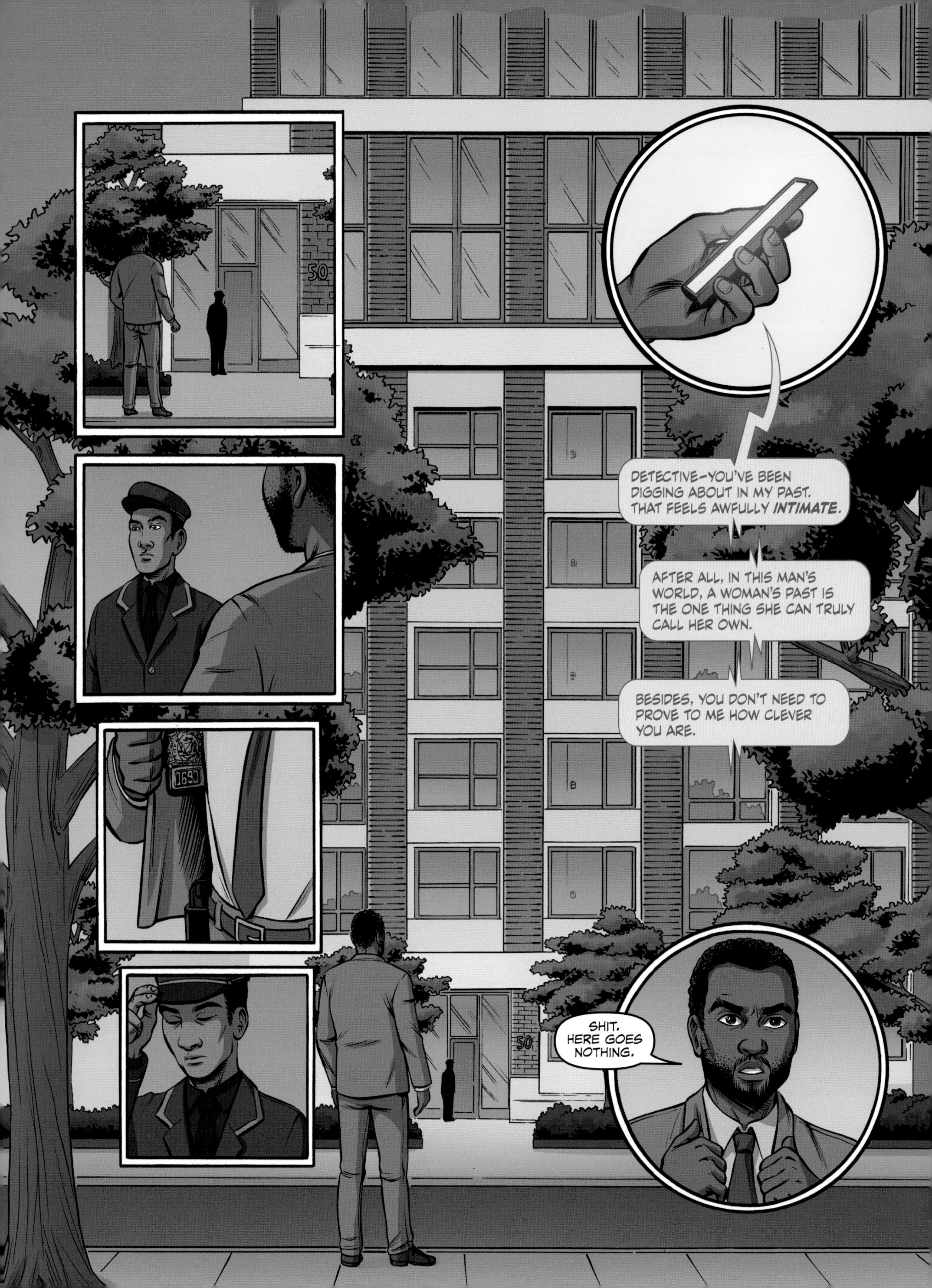
50
1690
DETECTIVE–YOU'VE BEEN DIGGING ABOUT IN MY PAST. THAT FEELS AWFULLY INTIMATE.
AFTER ALL, IN THIS MAN'S WORLD, A WOMAN'S PAST IS THE ONE THING SHE CAN TRULY CALL HER OWN.
BESIDES, YOU DON'T NEED TO PROVE TO ME HOW CLEVER YOU ARE.
50
SHIT. HERE GOES NOTHING.

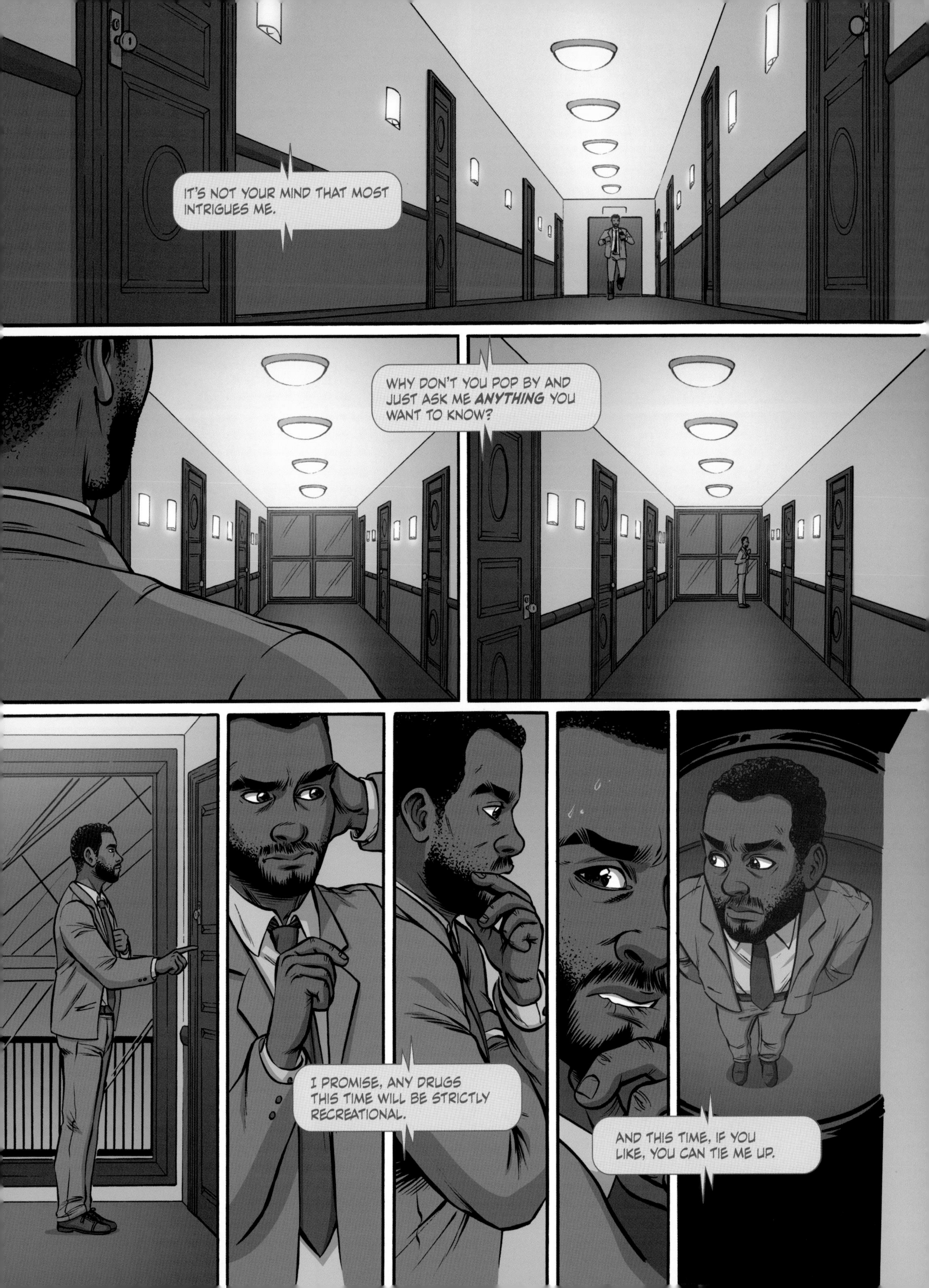
IT'S NOT YOUR MIND THAT MOST INTRIGUES ME.
WHY DON'T YOU POP BY AND JUST ASK ME *ANYTHING* YOU WANT TO KNOW?
I PROMISE, ANY DRUGS THIS TIME WILL BE STRICTLY RECREATIONAL.
AND THIS TIME, IF YOU LIKE, YOU CAN TIE ME UP.

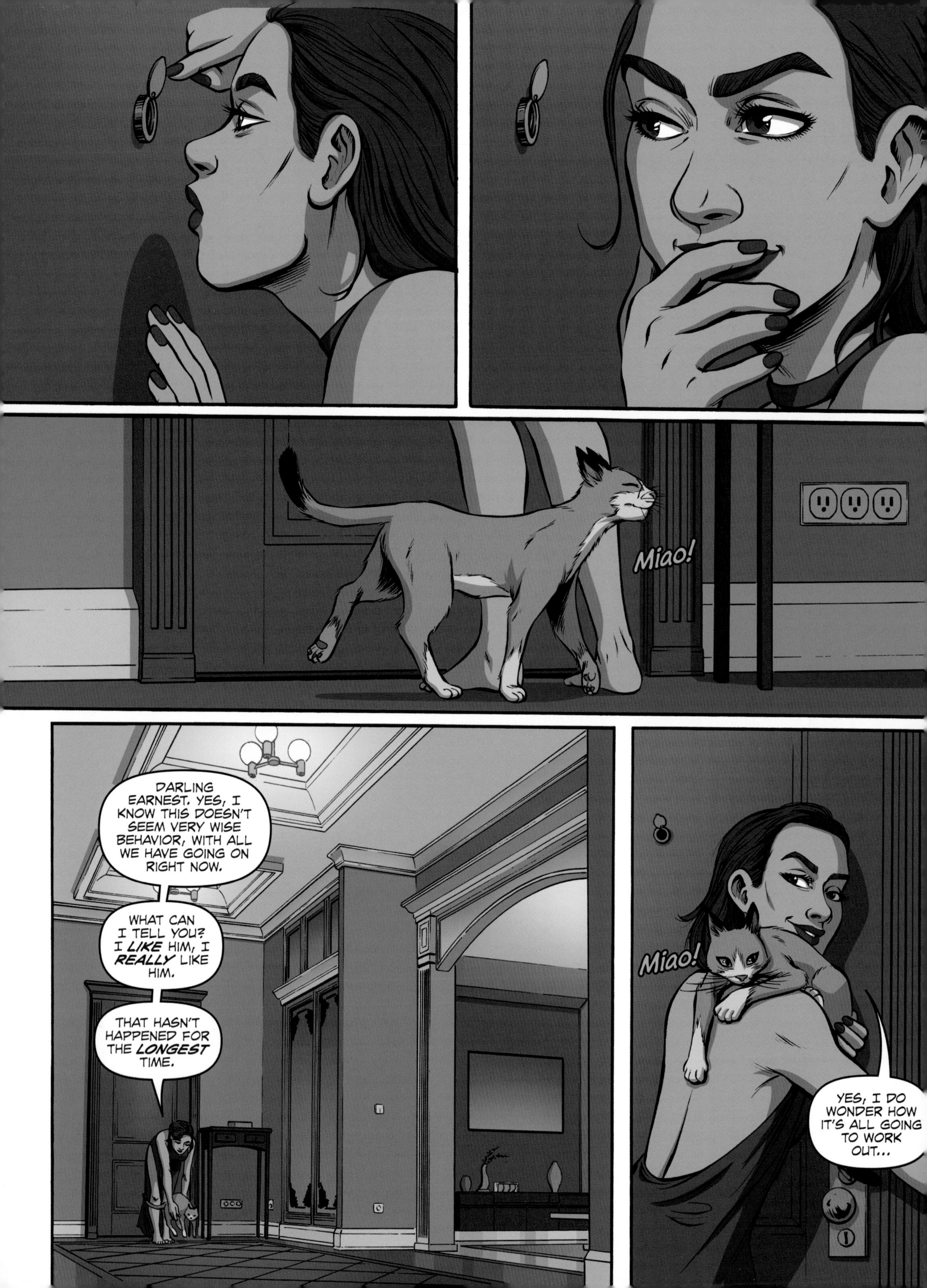
Miao!
DARLING EARNEST. YES, I KNOW THIS DOESN'T SEEM VERY WISE BEHAVIOR, WITH ALL WE HAVE GOING ON RIGHT NOW.
WHAT CAN I TELL YOU? I *LIKE* HIM, I *REALLY* LIKE HIM.
THAT HASN'T HAPPENED FOR THE *LONGEST* TIME.
Miao!
YES, I DO WONDER HOW IT'S ALL GOING TO WORK OUT...

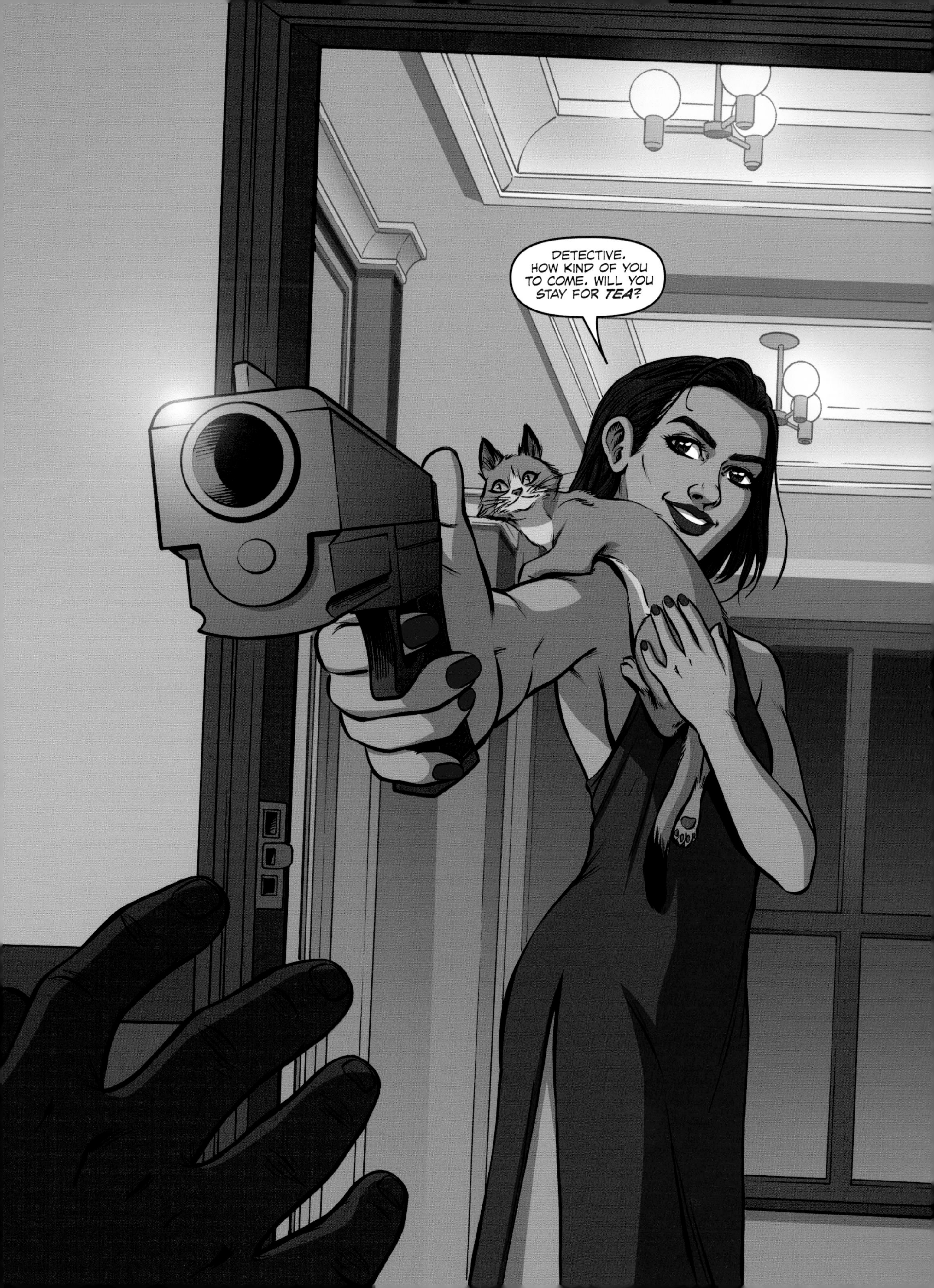
DETECTIVE. HOW KIND OF YOU TO COME. WILL YOU STAY FOR *TEA*?

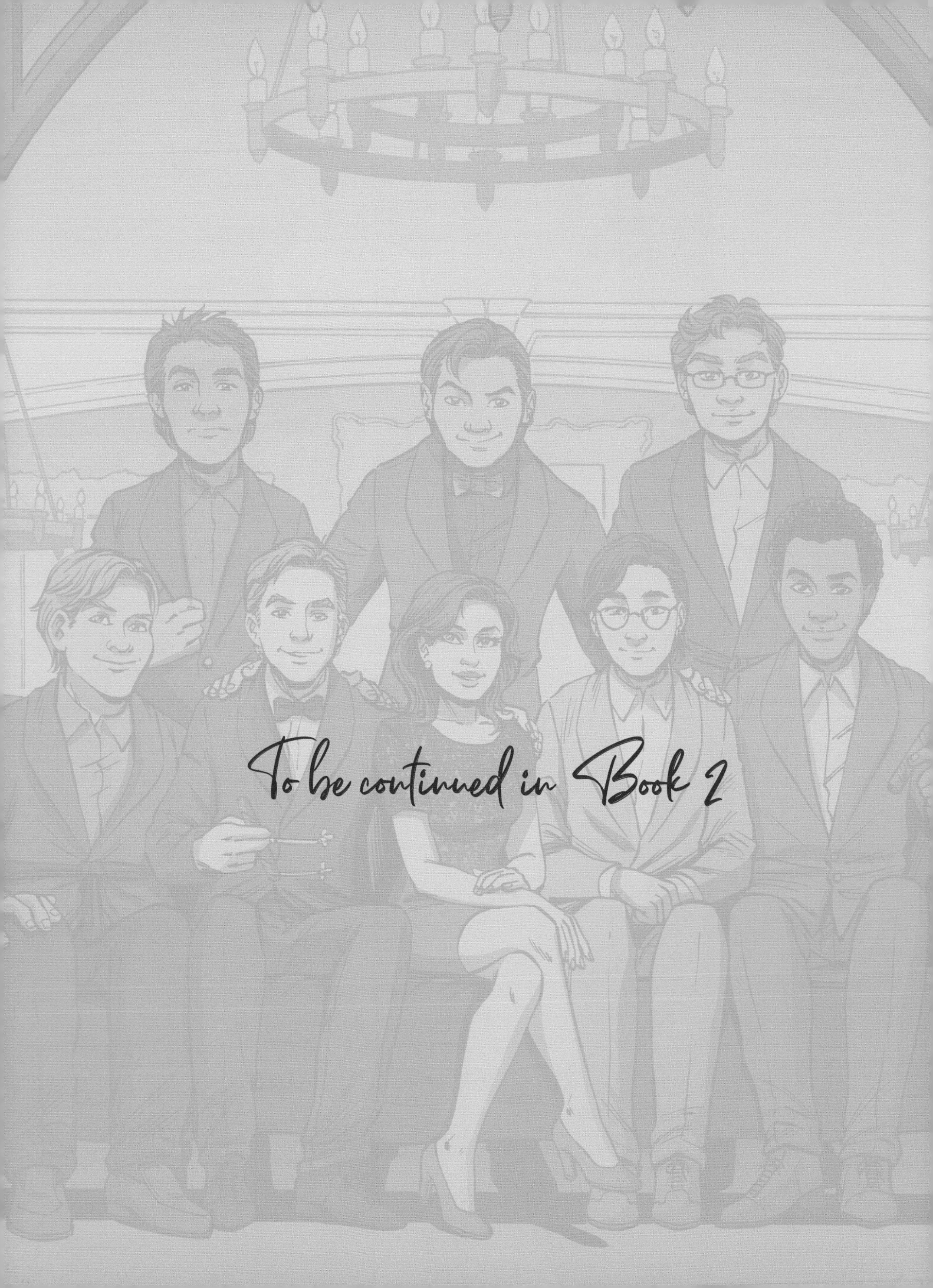

To be continued in Book 2

IF YOU OR A LOVED ONE HAVE EXPERIENCED SEXUAL VIOLENCE, THE NATIONAL SEXUAL ASSAULT HOTLINE IS AVAILABLE 24/7 WITH FREE, CONFIDENTIAL SUPPORT AT 800-656-HOPE (4673) OR ONLINE.RAINN.ORG

About the Author

Arvind Ethan David is a writer and producer of film, television, theatre, audio dramas, and comics.

In comics, David was Stoker-Nominated for his and Mike Carey's *Darkness Visible* graphic novel, which they are currently adapting for television for Intrepid Pictures. He wrote the critically acclaimed *Dirk Gently* comic for three years.

In audio, David wrote the Audible original, *The Neil Gaiman at the End of the Universe* starring Neil Gaiman and Jewel Staite. Which debuted at #4 on the Audible most listened chart.

In theatre, David is a lead producer on Broadway's fifteen-time Tony-Nominated and Grammy-Winning *Jagged Little Pill* musical, based on the seminal Alanis Morissette album.

In television, David was an Executive Producer of *Dirk Gently's Holistic Detective Agency* for Netflix and BBC America, based on the cult Douglas Adams novel. David has produced eight feature films, including the British hit comedy *The Infidel* and the Asian Academy Award-Winning *The Garden Of Evening Mists.*

David's career began in high school, when he adapted the Douglas Adams novel *Dirk Gently's Holistic Detective Agency* as a school play—and the legendary author came to see the production and endorsed it as the official adaptation. David's adaptation has been published by Samuel French and has been performed consistently worldwide for the last twenty years.

David is the Principal of Prodigal, Inc., a production company with a first-look deal with Warner Media and JJ Abrams' Bad Robot. He lives in California with his wife Janine N'jie David and their daughter Odetta.